GRE
写作高频题目
及考点精析

颜余真 王耕伟 陈琦 / 编著

浙江教育出版社·杭州

图书在版编目(CIP)数据

GRE写作高频题目及考点精析/陈琦主编. -- 杭州：
浙江教育出版社，2017.4（2018.7重印）
ISBN 978-7-5536-5536-9

Ⅰ．①G… Ⅱ．①陈… Ⅲ．①GRE—词汇—自学参考资
料 Ⅳ．①H315

中国版本图书馆CIP数据核字（2017）第056253号

GRE写作高频题目及考点精析
GRE XIEZUO GAOPIN TIMU JI KAODIAN JINGXI
陈 琦 主编

责任编辑	罗 曼
文字编辑	张 茜
美术编辑	韩 波
封面设计	大愚设计
责任校对	刘文芳
责任印务	时小娟
出版发行	浙江教育出版社
	地址：杭州市天目山路40号
	邮编：310013
	电话：（0571）85170300－80928
	邮箱：dywh@xdf.cn
	网址：www.zjeph.com
印 刷	廊坊十环印刷有限公司
开 本	787mm×1092mm 1/16
成品尺寸	185mm×260mm
印 张	13.25
字 数	277 000
版 次	2017年4月第1版
印 次	2018年7月第4次印刷
标准书号	ISBN 978-7-5536-5536-9
定 价	35.00元

很多事物在被征服后就会褪色，GRE是个例外。

远行前的栖居

开始备考 GRE 作文是在日本北海道的冬日。当时的备考资料很简陋，只有一本《北美 GRE 范文精讲》，但这本书却被我视若瑰宝。我醉心于其地道的语言，向往其精辟的思路，更钦佩作者能坚持写完数百篇范文的毅力。这本书被我用各色记号笔勾画得五彩斑斓，也算是皑皑白雪中的一抹亮色。

当这本书已不堪彩笔的重负，我终于开始向题目发起了进攻。花了一个月浸润这本 GRE 作文备考界的翘楚之作，我信心满满，以为厚积薄发的时刻终于到来。但官方给出的题目和《北美 GRE 范文精讲》中题目的巨大差异却让我手足无措——原来，号称囊括官方题目的《北美 GRE 范文精讲》收录的都是老 GRE 题目，而新 GRE 在其基础上删除了百来道题目，还给剩下的每一道题目增添了新的写作要求。

三月的北海道已然迎来春日，但却丝毫没有冰消雪融的意思。而新 G 写作的 329 个题目也如巨冰厚雪般压在我的心头。

沮丧之下，极少去自习的我每天窝在了北海道大学的图书馆里。三个小时背单词，两个小时看作文。这时一个志同道合的 G 友也加入了作文的备考队伍，这于我是不小的鼓励。我们每天各自在图书馆列出 20 道题目的提纲，晚饭的时候在食堂里交换心得，共享思路。校园食堂的菜品虽然常年不换，但饭桌上的讨论却时有新意，也算是相映成趣。

四月初，我赴东京考 GRE。作文一般，Verbal 惨败。四月的东京在樱花缤纷的落英中如新海诚的动漫一般温润、浪漫，但我的心境却如北海道将化未化的积雪一般湿冷。

回到北海道后，我又花了一个月时间备考。这次的重点是 Verbal，也顺带着练了十多篇作文，提高打字速度。一个月后我再赴东京，这回 Verbal 成绩还算看得过去，作文也给了我意外之喜：从 4 分提高到了 4.5。虽然不算很高，但申请我的意向院校却足够了。

前前后后三个月，我走过了备考申请路上最辛苦的一段。此时的北海道已然苏醒，准备迎接一年中最美的季节。

2014 年秋季，我来到了纽约的哥伦比亚大学，就读于以严谨治学闻名的东亚语言与文化系。本以为写作水平不错的我在这里频受打击。面对真正的学术写作，我才知道我之前的 GRE 写作备考都是以应试为导向，并没有帮我培养出足以应付高难度、高强度的研究生院写作的能力。

于是，我一方面通过每周上百页的学术 reading 积累学术写作的输入，一方面选修了跟学术写作相关的专业课程进行写作的输出训练。东亚系的资源丰厚，哥大的 Writing Center 也是藏龙卧虎。通过一年的努力，我切实感受到了自己学术写作能力的提升。

毕业前夕，很多哥大的研究生同学已经开始博士的申请。经过再三考虑，我决定回国。教授 GRE 写作也顺理成章地成了我的用武之地。犹记得纽约的最后一个夏季，我早早地写完了毕业论文，之后的三个月全身心地投入到了 GRE 写作的备课中。我一方面总结了市面上所有 GRE 老师的网络课及其著作的思路；另一方面将我在哥大学习的所有学术写作教材和《GRE 考试官方指南》（The Official Guide to the GRE Test）对比参看，进行提炼和归纳；最后将一套结合了学术写作和 GRE 写作备考的方法论运用到了数百道题目的分析中。三个月的备课暂告一个段落之后，我通过实战检验了自己的方法：5.5 分，一个还算让自己满意的成绩。而这套方法，也构成了本书的灵魂。

来到微臣已经一年半。这一年半中接触到了上千名线上线下的 GRE 考生。尤其通过和线下 325 班同学的接触让我明白了中国同学备考 GRE 作文的两大软肋：1. 题目太多不想看；2. 道理都明白，但缺少示例范文，所以下不了笔。也因此，我们希望学生通过研读高频题目的范文，既了解方法论，还能从语言和内容上做好积累，高效地完成 GRE 写作备考。并且，我们希望本书能够让国内的同学初步感受到学术写作的风格，并在 GRE 写作的备考中为以后的研究生院写作蓄力。

这本书的写作能够启动并且最终成书，必须感谢琦叔的鼓励和肯定。感谢琦叔对我的信任，能够让我把自己学生阶段所学和教学时期所感以书籍的方式和广大考生共享。还要感谢微臣的各位同事，是他们的帮助以及努力拼搏的身影激励我不断前行。

我还发自肺腑地感谢这本书的另一位作者，此刻正在普林斯顿的博士生院发光发热的颜余真老师。和他的频繁交流和讨论极大地启发了我的教学和写作。颜老师思维严谨，论证清晰，其文章也闪烁着理工科学神的光芒，希望我和颜老师的文章能从不同侧面为大家带来对 GRE 写作的多样感受。

另外，我要感谢母校清华的外教 Cassandra Woloschuk，是她帮本书的 40 篇文章一一校稿，对语言的细微之处修改润色，使其更加地道。同样感谢参与校稿的同学们，是你们的细致和认真帮我们避免了很多细小的错误。

最后，我想向《北美 GRE 范文精讲》的作者 Mark Alan Stewart 致以遥远的感谢和敬意。这本书是我 GRE 写作备考路上的启蒙教材，虽然它主要针对老 GRE，但其精妙的语言和雄辩的论证至今让我心向往之，也正是这本书启发我指导学生运用范文进行备考。大师在前，高山仰止。

曾经有学生以一句流行歌词形容 GRE 写作的备考："生活不止眼前的苟且，还有诗和远方。"其实，写作本是享受，应试写作也可以是一件美差。更何况 GRE 写作确实能够带领我们走向世界名校的美好远方。

若心中有远方，那眼前的苟且也就不是苟且，而是诗意的栖居了。

王耕伟

更遥远的征途

时钟拨到 2015 年 2 月 12 日，情人节前两天，美国东部时间早上 6 点。我早早起床，战战兢兢地打开了 YY 语音，进入了 "GRE 作文体验课" 的教室。作为第一次主讲作文的我，两个小时的课程感觉如临深渊，如履薄冰。令我释怀的是，课后同学们给予了我极大的肯定和支持。于是，备受鼓励的我作为 GRE 作文老师，开始了在微臣的授课生涯。

时至今日，我在线上开设了 16 次课程，听课人数超过 1000 人，批改了超过 700 篇线上课学生的作文。如果算上 15 年之前自己和朋友合办的作文批改小组的业务，零零总总经手的文章超过了 1000 篇。在这个过程当中，我可以深深体会到同学们在准备 GRE 作文过程中感到的痛苦。看到同学们作文中前后矛盾的逻辑、干涩单一的语言、似是而非的回答，我每次上课都希望能尽我所学所知解决这些问题，一节两小时的作文课常常要超出 15、20 分钟才能讲完。可惜的是，每每有同学在课上、课后问到 "能否推荐新 G 作文的书籍课后自学" 时，我只能回答：真正切合新 G 要求的书还没有。我可以想象到屏幕对面同学们渴望的目光，我也一直在问自己：为什么市场上针对新 G 作文的书籍不尽如人意呢？

正当我还苦于这个问题之时，琦叔降临了。

琦叔是一个在我生命中很重要的人物，我与琦叔的渊源可以追溯到老 G 时代的 GRE 圣坛——水清 501 的大教室，而琦叔就是圣坛上谈笑间类反题灰飞烟灭的教主。后来因为一次北大讲座和加入小牛人俱乐部的原因，算是正式结识了琦叔，并有幸进入了《GRE 核心词汇考法精析》"再要你命 3000" 新版的编辑队伍之中，再后来又成为《GRE 高分必备短语搭配》的编者之一。最近又承蒙琦叔赏识，成为了微臣留学团队的一员——当然，这是后话。

与我 "为什么不存在针对新 G 的作文书" 的科研思维不同，琦叔的工程师思维一针见血地提出："既然现在没有好的书籍，为什么我们不能写一本？" 是的，既然脚下没有路，那不如我们自己走出一条路。琦叔这一句话惊醒了我——为什么还没有针对新 G 的作文书？因为我们还没有写！

在琦叔的鼓励下我开始构思。但无奈作为 PhD 所肩负的科研压力，我无法长时间投入到书籍的编写过程中，这本书也就一拖再拖。特别是 2015 年 11 月，我踏上了为期两个月的南极之旅。正当我以为作文书的编写不得不暂时束之高阁之际，本书的另一位作者，目前也在微臣主讲作文的王耕伟老师出现了。

我是一个幸运的人。第一次碰到琦叔降临，这一次遇到王耕伟老师现身。王老师是一个极有热情而且极富责任心的人，是工作路上不可多得的伙伴。我们彼此发现对于新 GRE 的理解以及市面上书籍的匮乏有着高度一致的认识，也同样深刻感受到当下备战 GRE 学子的诉求。于是我们一拍即合，共同着手编写这本书，最终就有了现在大家手中的这个作品。

　　当然，这本书不可能一蹴而就。我们要对一个抽象的概念和框架不断填充扩展，然后不断雕琢、润色。琦叔、王老师和我都是对细节特别重视的人，这更增加了这本书的耗时程度。举个简单的例子，在"考生常见错误"中提到了一点叫"Issue 中的例证不具有说服力"。为了确保能找到同学们犯的真实的、典型的错误，我把邮箱中 300 多篇 Issue 重新阅读了一遍，挑选出针对一道 Issue 题最有代表性的四篇习作。正是有了这些真正出自同学们之手的文字，我们才能写出这本极具针对性的作文书。所以，在此我要感谢所有参加过线上作文课的同学，没有你们就不可能有这本书。

　　本书的成稿还离不开很多人的贡献，包括（但不限于）为我们把关语言的外教 Cassandra Woloschuk 老师，从她的批改中我学习到了很多；为我们做后期校对的同学们，他们细致的工作确保了本书的品质；微臣的同事们，感谢他们在工作中的支持；还有之前线上课的助教们，他们的辛勤付出保证了课程的顺利进行。当然，还要郑重感谢琦叔和王耕伟老师，没有你们，这本书就只能是微信聊天记录中的一个话题。

　　在经历了许多个日夜的工作之后，这本书终于呈现在了读者们的面前。但 GRE 不是大家旅程的终点，正如同这本书不会成为我们停止不前的理由一样。GRE 帮助你打开了一扇门，但这扇门之后，其实是更加遥远的征途。王老师从 GRE 走来，在日本、在纽约留下了他的足迹；我从 GRE 走来，从北京走向了普林斯顿，走向了南极；无数的考生从 GRE 走来，从故土走向了世界各个角落。时至今日我们仍然在路上，向着远方。

　　最后，我们的征途是星辰大海，谨希望这本书能在漫漫征途之中祝大家一臂之力。

颜余真

在美国教育考试服务中心（ETS，即 GRE 的官方出题机构）公布的 GRE 写作题库中，Issue 部分有 152 道题目，Argument 部分有 177 道题目。与老 GRE 相比，新 GRE 写作部分的题目数量虽然大为减少，但仍然是一个惊人的数字。而如何从 Issue 和 Argument 的上百道题目中各选出 20 道并给出相应的范文，则是一个应该深思熟虑的问题。是按照 Issue 题目所涉及的不同领域，将题目划分为艺术、政治、科技等类别？又或是按照 Argument 题目中不同的"逻辑错误"来挑选题目？亦或是应该按照其他标准？

最终，我们选择按照 Issue 和 Argument 的具体性指令（Direction）来分类、挑选题目。Issue 部分共有 6 种具体性指令，Argument 共有 8 种（可分为 4 大类）具体性指令，我们从每一种具体性指令所对应的题目中各挑选了 3~5 道题目，构成了本书最核心的部分。

这种挑选原则其实是源于广大考生在 GRE 写作备考之时极易忽略的盲区——自 2011 年 8 月 GRE 改革以来，写作部分加入了"Direction（写作指导，或称具体性指令）"。随之改变的是写作部分的评分标准。ETS 给出的官方评分标准明确说明：**如果考生对某一道题的 Direction 照应得不充分或者模糊不清，那么考生的整篇文章得分不会超过 3 分**。在我们所批改的七百余篇学生习作中，能够注意到 Direction 的考生比例不超过 5%。一些论点深刻、结构精巧、语言功底很不错的 Issue 作文因为完全偏离了 Direction 的写作要求而未能幸免 3 分；还有一些考生明显已经进行了长达数月的备考，看了参考书，也听了课，他们在 Argument 的写作中熟练地运用到了大量针对"逻辑错误"的表达和模板，但纵观其全文，却完全避开了 Direction 希望我们涉及的部分。对于这样的考生及其文章，我们为其扼腕叹息；但对于大多数还没有开始准备的考生，我们则希望大家在一开始就建立起"按照 Direction 来写文章"这一意识，从此避开"3 分雷区"。

虽然我们的文章是按照不同的 Direction 挑选出来的，但我们希望考生学到的不止于 Direction。我们在 Issue 部分的范文中，力争做到观点深刻，并嵌入了很多为观点服务的，并可以为考生所用的素材和例证；对相同意思的英文表达，我们也力求在每一篇 Issue 文章中都有所不同，从而让考生在语言多样性方面也能有所得。在 Argument 部分的范文里，每一篇文章中都可以见到"经典逻辑错误"的身影，但这种"逻辑错误"经过我们基于 Direction 要求的改写，比大家之前掌握的模板更加贴合新 GRE 的要求；另外我们提供的 Argument 的逻辑推理图，也将更好地帮助考生掌握全文的论证结构和框架。

GRE 写作的备考一定是"输入"与"输出"的结合，但考生往往耽于输入，怠于输出，在辅导教材的阅读上花费了太多时间。因此，本书没有连篇累牍的关于写作方法论的讲解，只是在每一个章节的开始部分，以及每一篇范文之后有精简的写作原理的点拨。希望考生将范文和原理点拨结合起来，通过这 40 篇范文的研读，完成"输入"部分的学习，为之后"输出"部分的篇章练习奠定良好的基础。

相较于市面上的同类参考书，本书具有如下的特点：

1. 以 40 道经典题目范文为全书主体，为考生提供语言、立场、例证等全方位参考素材。

2. 史无前例地以具体性指令为核心，透彻讲解 GRE 中最易失分点，并结合学术写作要求，让 GRE 写作与研究生院写作接轨。

3. 深入讲解官方评分标准，首次将"要求"转化为"方法论"，指导学生写出符合 ETS 要求的 GRE 作文。

4. 总结七百余篇学生习作，细致梳理考生常犯错误。

本书的使用方法：

1. **备考初期**：主要研读本书的方法论部分。包括第四章对评分标准的解析、第五章中对 Direction 的解析。

2. **备考中期**：将方法论和范文做结合，深入理解范文对方法论的照应；同时借助范文进行语言素材和内容素材的积累。

3. **备考后期**：进入全文练习阶段。考生既可从本书的 40 道高频题中选择题目进行练习；也可从第二章中给出的题目中挑选题目练习。建议考生至少进行十篇全文练习（Issue 六篇、Argument 四篇；每一种 Direction 对应一篇）。

另外，我们在每一篇英文范文之后还添加了中文翻译。为了最大程度上方便大家理解句子意思，我们在翻译的时候没有太大地改动英文句子的结构，这一点请大家注意。

希望这本书能让大家在 GRE 作文的备考之路上走得更好且更远。

目 录
Contents

第一章　常见问题集锦 1

第二章　GRE 写作题库分类 5

第三章　考生常犯错误 9

　　第一节　内容方面 9

　　第二节　形式方面 20

第四章　GRE 写作官方评分标准精析 29

　　第一节　Issue 评分标准分析 30

　　第二节　Argument 评分标准分析 39

第五章　具体性指令与范文精讲 47

　　第一节　Issue 具体性指令与范文精讲 48

　　　　1. "是非判断类" Direction 48

　　　　2. "因果类" Direction 65

　　　　3. "两种看法类" Direction 75

　　　　4. "敌方看法类" Direction 85

　　　　5. "建议类" Direction（一） 97

　　　　6. "建议类" Direction（二） 111

　　第二节　Argument 具体性指令与范文精讲 118

　　　　1. "Assumption 类" Direction 120

　　　　2. "Evidence 类" Direction 138

　　　　3. "Explanation 类" Direction 155

　　　　4. "Question 类" Direction 172

附录　　所有 Argument 3s 版本及专业词汇 194

第一章　常见问题集锦

Q1：GRE 改革之后，作文部分发生变化了吗？

2011 年 GRE 改革之后，作文部分发生了两个重要的变化：

1. 总题目数量由 486 道减少为 329 道，这减轻了大家的备考负担。

2. Issue 和 Argument 当中都加入了 Direction，这应该是最重大的改变。随之改变的是评分标准：如果没有按照 Direction 来写，分数不会高过 3 分。因此，Direction 应该是大家备考 GRE 作文中的重中之重。

Q2：GRE 写作分成几部分？

GRE 写作分为 Analyze an Issue Task 与 Analyze an Argument Task。前者考查大家围绕一个话题发表自己的看法并对该看法做出论证的能力；后者考查大家对某一段推理过程进行分析评价的能力。

Q3：GRE 写作的考试时间多长？

GRE 写作会在语文和数学部分之前进行测试，时长一小时。Analyze an Issue Task 与 Analyze an Argument Task 各 30 分钟，中间没有休息。写作之后会是语文部分的测试。写作与语文部分的测试之间也没有休息时间。

Q4：作文会被几位阅卷人批阅？

一篇作文会先由一位自然人评委批阅并给出分数，之后会由机器（E-rater）批阅并给出分数。如果两个分数相差在 1 分以内则取平均数并以此作为考生最终得分；如果相差在 1 分以上则引入另一位自然人评委的评审，最终分数为两位自然人评委的分数取平所得。

Q5：考完试后能立即知道分数吗？

GRE 的语文和数学部分会在考完后立即出分，但写作部分的分数会在考完试后的 10~15 天内公布。

Q6：GRE 写作有多少道题目？

GRE 写作的题目均已在 ETS 官网上公布，其中 Issue 部分有 152 道题目，Argument 部分有 177 道题目。考生在考场上抽到的两道题目均来自已公布的题库，不会做任何修改。

Q7：需要在上考场之前把 GRE 的写作题目都列提纲吗？

如果时间充足（备考时间在一个月以上），建议大家把题库中的所有题目的提纲都列一次。就算没有时间列提纲，也建议大家把所有题目都思考一遍，这样起码能够保证在考场上不会遇到陌生的题目。

Q8：GRE 作文要写多少字？

ETS 并没有对 GRE 写作的字数做任何硬性要求。在 ETS 给出的 6 分范文中，既有接近 700 字的文章，也有的文章不足 500 字。真正重要的不是字数，而是如何用有限的字数把道理说清楚、说好。

但是，由于 GRE 写作是机考，而很多考生使用键盘打字的速度都有进步空间，因此提高打字速度是考生们的必要任务。

Q9：GRE 作文要写多少段？

和字数相同，ETS 对 GRE 写作的段落数也没有固定的要求。但一般来说，Issue 部分写五段（开头段、结尾段和三个中间段），Argument 部分写五到六段，这是比较符合实际写作时间、也便于操作的段落数。

Q10：Issue 部分需要背很多名人名例吗？

首先，例子永远是为论证服务的。因此，只有在事理说明已经透彻的情况下才应该用例证来补充说明，而不是整篇文章都靠事例来堆积。

其次，好的例子是无所谓雅俗与真假的，真正重要的是如何使用例子。关于如何使用例子，大家可以参考对 Issue 的 6 分评分标准的解析。

Q11：听说 GRE（包括 GRE 作文）不考查语言是真的吗？

GRE 考试是以语言为载体的考试，ETS 默认考生的语言水平已经过关了。但对于中国考生来说，语言仍然是一个老大难。

Q12：GRE 作文里需要用很多高级复杂的语言表达吗？

这个问题和上一个问题形成了极端的对立，但都是大家常问的问题。GRE 作文考查的是大家用基本标准、正确的英语去说理、分析的能力。大家在语言层面首先需要追求正确、准确，而不需要刻意追求复杂、高级或标新立异的表达。

Q13：Argument 有几类常见的逻辑错误？

这样问的考生想必都是把 Argument 的备考重点放在了所谓的"逻辑错误"（如臆造因果、错误类比等）的判断和分析上。这是针对老 GRE 的准备方法。面对新 GRE 的 Argument，如果只关注"逻辑错误"，最终的得分不会高过 3 分。因此，准备重心应该放在 Direction 上。大家可以参见范文之前对各类 Direction 的讲解。

Q14：上考场之前需要进行全篇练习吗？

这个一定是需要的。但建议大家把全篇练习放在临考前十天左右。Issue 和 Argument 都可以按照 Direction 来挑选题目进行全篇练习。练习数量在 20 篇（Issue 和 Argument 各 10 篇）或以上为佳。

但一定注意，写完一篇文章之后一定要对其进行修改。建议大家至少对自己的文章进行两次修改。第一次是修改基本的语法错误；第二次是修改语法上正确，但不够准确、地道的表达。第二次修改可能对于考生自身来说有一定困难，这时大家可以和同伴结成小组进行互批互改，或请比自己有经验的师兄师姐或是老师帮忙修改。

Q15：GRE 写作和托福写作有什么关系？

托福写作的考查对象是语言；而 GRE 写作是以语言为载体考查考生的批判性思维和分析能力。因此对于英语为非母语的中国考生来说，GRE 写作既考查我们的语言，又考查我们的思维。就难度而言，GRE 写作和托福写作在语言层面并没有太大的差别，都要求考生运用正规的书面英语进行写作；但在内容层面，GRE 写作题目比托福写作题目更复杂，也要求考生对题目的认识更透彻，分析更全面深刻。

因此，考完 GRE 并在作文方面取得不错成绩的考生如果参加托福考试，不会在写作部分出现太大的问题。不过考生应该加强听力的训练，因为托福写作的综合写作有相当部分依赖于大家的听力能力。

而刚取得不错的托福写作成绩的考生如果要备考 GRE，则需要把重点放在 GRE 题目本身的分析上，力争把每一道题目都分析得全面、透彻。

Q16：GRE 写作和未来的学术写作有什么关系？

GRE 写作是研究生院在录取研究生和博士生时参考的重要元素。GRE 写作所看重的批判性思维（Critical Thinking）和分析性写作（Analytical Writing）能力同样也是大家未来在进行学术写作时必不可少的能力。

因此，GRE 的准备应该以大的学术写作的要求为导向；而学术写作能力的初步形成也应该是在 GRE 写作的备考阶段。故而此书将 GRE 写作的诸多要求和考生即将接受的专业学术写作训练的要领相结合，指导考生以研究生写作为导向进行备考。让 GRE 写作的备考利在当下，功在长远。

第二章　GRE 写作题库分类

Issue 题库分类

"是非判断类" Direction（54 道）

1; 2; 9; 11; 17; 18; 21; 24; 26; 27; 28; 33; 34; 38; 41; 42; 43; 45; 53; 55; 56; 57; 58; 62; 63; 64; 66; 71; 74; 75; 76; 77; 78; 91; 93; 101; 103; 106; 107; 108; 112; 114; 115; 116; 117; 118; 119; 124; 137; 141; 143; 144; 146; 147

"因果类" Direction（19 道）

5; 8; 22; 40; 44; 49; 70; 79; 87; 88; 89; 105; 113; 120; 131; 133; 134; 139; 142

"两种看法类" Direction（18 道）

7; 16; 20; 67; 68; 69; 85; 86; 109; 121; 125; 128; 130; 132; 138; 140; 150; 151

"敌方看法类" Direction（25 道）

3; 4; 13; 15; 29; 30; 32; 65; 84; 94; 95; 96; 97; 99; 104; 110; 111; 122; 123; 126; 127; 136; 145; 148; 152

"建议类" Direction（一）（24 道）

6; 19; 23; 25; 36; 37; 39; 46; 47; 48; 50; 51; 52; 54; 59; 60; 61; 80; 81; 82; 83; 90; 92; 129

"建议类" Direction（二）（12 道）

10; 12; 14; 31; 35; 72; 73; 98; 100; 102; 135; 149

Issue 六大 Direction 破题要点总结

Direction 分类	破题要点
"两种看法类" Direction Write a response in which you discuss which view more closely aligns with your own position and explain your reasoning for the position you take. In developing and supporting your position, you should address **both of the views presented**.	题目中的两种观点都要讨论
"敌方看法类" Direction Write a response in which you discuss the extent to which you agree or disagree with the claim. In developing and supporting your position, be sure to address the most compelling reasons and/or examples that could be used to **challenge your position**.	不仅要阐述考生自己的立场，一定还要阐述敌方观点以及敌方观点背后的原因和例子
"因果类" Direction Write a response in which you discuss the extent to which you agree or disagree with the claim and the reason on which that claim is based.	既要提到题目的原因（Reason），又要提到结论（Claim）
"是非判断类" Direction Write a response in which you discuss the extent to which you agree or disagree with the statement and explain your reasoning for the position you take. In developing and supporting your position, you should consider **ways** in which the statement might or might not hold true and explain how these considerations shape your position.	对行文并无特别要求
"建议类" Direction（一） Write a response in which you discuss the extent to which you agree or disagree with the recommendation and explain your reasoning for the position you take. In developing and supporting your position, describe specific **circumstances** in which adopting the **recommendation** would or would not be advantageous and explain how these examples shape your position.	讨论建议所发生的条件
"建议类" Direction（二） Write a response in which you discuss your views on the policy and explain your reasoning for the position you take. In developing and supporting your position, you should consider the possible **consequences** of implementing the **policy** and explain how these consequences shape your position.	讨论政策可能带来的结果

Argument 题库分类

Argument 题库分类

"Assumption 类" Direction （50 道）

4; 9; 14; 16; 18; 23; 28; 32; 33; 34; 41; 44; 46; 49; 54; 55; 56; 59; 60; 62; 63; 65; 68; 73; 77; 87; 89; 90; 95; 98; 100; 101; 107; 109; 111; 115; 117; 121; 129; 130; 132; 137; 142; 143; 144; 148; 153; 157; 161; 173

"Evidence 类" Direction （52 道）

1; 6; 8; 12; 13; 17; 20; 21; 25; 26; 27; 30; 31; 36; 37; 38; 39; 40; 42; 43; 47; 48; 50; 53; 57; 58; 70; 71; 72; 78; 83; 85; 86; 88; 91; 99; 105; 108; 124; 125; 126; 128; 133; 134; 135; 138; 141; 146; 147; 155; 158; 172

"Explanation 类" Direction （11 道）

2; 15; 84; 92; 103; 104; 116; 119; 122; 165; 176

"Question 类" Direction （64 道）

3; 5; 7; 10; 11; 19; 22; 24; 29; 35; 45; 51; 52; 61; 64; 66; 67; 69; 74; 75; 76; 79; 80; 81; 82; 93; 94; 96; 97; 102; 106; 110; 112; 113; 114; 118; 120; 123; 127; 131; 136; 139; 140; 145; 149; 150; 151; 152; 154; 156; 159; 160; 162; 163; 164; 166; 167; 168; 169; 170; 171; 174; 175; 177

Argument 四大 Direction 破题步骤汇总

Direction 分类	单段写法	段落连接
Question 类 Direction Write a response in which you discuss what questions would need to be answered in order to decide whether the recommendation is likely to have the predicted result. Be sure to explain how the answers to these questions would help to evaluate the recommendation.	① 指出现在还无法评价原 Argument 中的某一论断 ② 说明为了更好地评价这一建议，还需要问什么样的问题 ③ 给出问题的答案 ④ 用答案来评价题目中的建议（既可以正面评价，也可以负面评价）	根据逻辑图，作者做了几次结论推导，就写几个中间段
Evidence 类 Direction Write a response in which you discuss what specific evidence is needed to evaluate the argument and explain how the evidence would weaken or strengthen the argument.	① 指出现在还无法评价作者的某一个论断 ② 说明为了更好地评价这一论断，还需要什么样的新证据 ③ 用新证据削弱或者增强作者的这一论断	
Assumption 类 Direction Write a response in which you examine the stated and/or unstated assumptions of the argument. Be sure to explain how the argument depends on these assumptions and what the implications are for the argument if the assumptions prove unwarranted.	① 找出原文中各论断或结论所依赖的 Assumption ② 指出这些 Assumption 在什么情况下不成立 ③ 阐明这些 Assumption 一旦不成立，作者的结论就会被削弱	
Explanation 类 Direction Write a response in which you discuss one or more alternative explanations that could rival the proposed explanation and explain how your explanation(s) can plausibly account for the facts presented in the argument.	① 指出还有其他解释 ② 说明其他解释如何解释得清楚原 Argument 中的现象	

第三章 考生常犯错误

把常犯错误单独成章并放在所有方法论和范文之前，是源于我们所坚信的"不破不立"的想法。只有让大家先把一些错误的观念排除，学习方法论才更有效。

因此，我们总结了迄今为止批改过的七百余篇学生的 GRE 作文习作，并征得作者的同意，将其写作中所犯错误提炼归纳、分门别类地总结如下。我们将错误类型分为内容和形式两大部分，内容包括文章的立意、主旨、组织等；形式即语言层面，包括用词、句式、语法等。

希望大家用心研读这一章，对于所罗列的错误，有则改之，无则加勉。

第一节 内容方面

常犯错误一 没有按照 Direction 来写

自 2011 年 GRE 改革之后，Issue 和 Argument 部分都加入了 Direction。Direction 可以翻译为具体性指令或写作指导。它本意是指导考生从具体的角度分析题目，但考生往往因为忽视 Direction 的要求而得低分（**ETS 明确表示如果不按照 Direction 来写不会高过 3 分**）。Issue 部分有 6 类 Direction，Argument 部分有 8 种（四大类）Direction。对于每一种 Direction 的处理方法请详见第五章的讲解。下面我们就从 Issue 和 Argument 的学生习作中各举一例，展示什么情况下文章会偏离 Direction 的要求。

> **Issue:**
>
> Governments should offer a free university education to any student who has been admitted to a university but who cannot afford the tuition.
>
> Write a response in which you discuss your views on the policy and explain your reasoning for the position you take. In developing and supporting your position, you should consider the possible consequences of implementing the policy and explain how these consequences shape your position.

"政府是否需要为每一个被大学录取但无力承担费用的学生提供全额补助？"很明显，这是一道关于"政府责任"的题目。下面是同学们给出的两种提纲。

提 纲 一

> **总立场**：同意题目观点
> **分论点 1**：政府需要这么做，因为政府有引导、保证高等教育顺利进行的责任。
> **分论点 2**：政府有能力这么做，因为政府的号召力和影响力大，财力也比企业和个人雄厚。

提 纲 二

> **总立场**：有保留地同意题目观点
> **分论点 1**（同意题目观点）： 题中的建议具有一定的必要性（necessity）。政府需要这么做，因为政府有引导、保证高等教育顺利进行的责任。
> **分论点 2**（同意题目观点）：题中的建议具有可行性（feasibility）。政府有能力这么做，因为政府的号召力和影响力大，财力也比企业和个人雄厚。
> **分论点 3** （反对题目观点）：但是，题目建议的必要性并不高，因为有一些替代策略（alternative options），如为学生提供半工半读的机会；让有财力的校友捐钱等等。
> **总结**：题目的问题具有复杂性，我们不能对其一概而论，而应该充分考虑到题目政策的必要性、可行性和替代观点。

提纲二看上去似乎在提纲一的基础上做了不少提升，如：

1. 增加了一个观点，阐明题目中的政策并非解决问题的唯一办法。
2. 在三个观点之中都运用了比较概括抽象的概念（necessity, feasibility, alternative options），使表意更加凝练。
3. 对全文有一个总结，说明题目的复杂性，不能对其一概而论。

纵观修改之后的论点，比原论点更全面、辩证，表意也更凝练，扩展成全文之后字数上也似乎更有保障。**但是，不论是哪一篇文章，都不会高过 3 分。因为它们都没有按照 Direction 来写。**

这道题的 Direction 中最核心的字眼是"consequence"，即要求我们讨论采取题目中政策可能出现的或好或坏的结果。所以，**只要没有从结果层面对题目进行论证，就可以判为偏题。**

所以，针对新 GRE 的要求，我们应该结合 Direction 列出类似以下的观点：

> **总立场**：同意题目观点
> **分论点 1**：题中的建议具有一定的必要性（necessity）。政府需要这么做，因为政府有引导、保证高等教育顺利进行的责任。**政府如果不这么做，会引起人才流失，导致社会发展停滞不前。**
> **分论点 2**：题中的建议具有可行性（feasibility）。政府有能力这么做，因为政府的号召

力和影响力大，财力也比企业和个人雄厚。**因此，由政府出资，可以减轻企业和个人的负担，并且引起广泛的、正面的社会反响。**

分论点 3：但是，题目中建议的必要性并不高，因为有一些替代策略（alternative options），如为学生提供半工半读的机会；让有财力的校友捐钱等等。**这些策略可以激励学生奋发向上，同时也在一定程度上减轻政府财政压力。**

总结：我们不能对题目的观点一概而论，**而应充分考虑到题目政策所带来的后果。**

这样修改之后，原本的观点并没有发生很大的变化，但却从"政策的结果"这一层面很好地照应了 Direction 的要求，也就在文章内容上突破了 3 分的瓶颈。

Argument:

The vice president for human resources at Climpson Industries sent the following recommendation to the company's president.

"In an effort to improve our employees' productivity, we should implement electronic monitoring of employees' Internet use from their workstations. Employees who use the Internet inappropriately from their workstations need to be identified and punished if we are to reduce the number of work hours spent on personal or recreational activities, such as shopping or playing games. Installing software on company computers to detect employees' Internet use is the best way to prevent employees from wasting time on the job. It will foster a better work ethic at Climpson and improve our overall profits."

Write a response in which you discuss what specific evidence is needed to evaluate the argument and explain how the evidence would weaken or strengthen the argument.

下面是一位同学针对这道题草拟的提纲：

总立场：作者的结论看上去有理，其实错误很多。具体错误如下：

分论点 1：作者无端假设现在确实有需要安装这个软件，因为很有可能员工根本没有滥用网络进行娱乐活动。

分论点 2：作者在软件安装和员工效率提升之间臆造了因果联系，此联系很可能不成立。

分论点 3：作者称安装软件是防止员工浪费时间的最好办法，显然作者没有考虑其他替代措施。

总结：综上，作者的结论漏洞百出，除非解决以上问题，否则他的结论不可信。

列好提纲，就可以开始写文章了。这时，大家的一个普遍想法是：自己文章的分数是取决于自己的语言表达，即把提纲中的中文转化为什么档次的英文。例如：

"无端假设"：一些同学会用"The author thinks in a wrong way"，而另一些同学可能会用"The author falsely assumes that..."

"在 AB 间臆造因果联系"：一些同学可能会说"A did not cause B"，另一些同学可能会说"The presumed causal relationship between A and B is open to doubt."

不可否认，上面这两个例子中，第二种表达比第一种看上去更加正式、准确。然而，在新 GRE 写作中，这样表达的两种文章的最后得分可能相差不大，并且一定都不会超过 3 分。**究其原因，还是没有按照 Direction 的要求来写**。

Write a response in which you discuss what specific evidence is needed to evaluate the argument and explain how the evidence would weaken or strengthen the argument.

从这个 Direction 中，我们至少可以读出两点信息：
1. **我们现在还不能评价原 Argument；**
2. **但是在提出了新证据之后，我们就可以评价了。**

所以，应对这种 Direction 的做法应该是：
1. 给出新证据；
2. 用新证据评价原 Argument。

并且，针对这种 Direction 写出来的文章里面出现的最高频的词，就应该是该 Direction 的几个核心词：**evidence; evaluate; weaken; strengthen**。

可以参考的提纲如下：

总立场：现在证据不足，我们无法评价原 Argument。所以我们需要新证据。
分论点 1：我们需要新证据表明是否需要安装此软件（**主题句**）。新证据可能包括员工使用电脑的实际状况（**给新证据**）。如果新证据表明员工确实花费大量时间在个人娱乐上，那么作者的结论被增强；反之则被削弱（**用新证据评价**）。
分论点 2：我们需要新证据证实软件安装和员工效率提升之间是否存在因果联系。（**主题句**）（之后的展开同上段）
分论点 3：我们需要新证据去验证安装软件是否是最好方法。（**主题句**）（之后的展开同上段）
总结：当我们给出如上的一系列新证据后，我们就可以评价作者的观点了。

常犯错误二 Issue 立意不高

一篇 Issue 文章的好坏，很大程度上取决于**论证是否深刻**。而论证的深刻与否很大程度上又取决于对于主题的把握，或者称之为文章的立意。优秀的文章能够准确把握 Issue 问题的核心、探索题目背后的假设、给出明确的定义。相反，普通的文章立意往往不高，受限于题目的表象，没能挖掘题目背后更为深刻的内涵。

举一个数学上的例子作为类比："三角形的内角和是 180 度。"假设这是一道 Issue 题，该如何下笔？立意高的文章能敏锐地抓住这句看似是数学公理背后的假设：**这是一个平面空间**；换句话说，这句话在欧式几何的框架内是成立的。当我们跳出平面空间这个限制，开始考虑曲面空间时，一个更为广阔的世界出现了：三角形的内角和既可以大于 180 度，也可以小于 180 度。我们不妨把地球表面想象成一个曲面空间，赤道上任何两点和极点都可以构成一个曲面三角形，但这个三角形的内角和不等于 180 度。相反，立意不够深刻的文章就会把目光聚焦在"如何证明三角形内角和是 180 度"上。诚然这样的论证本身是没有错的，但由于全文的立意只停留在问题表面，很难写出精彩的文章。

这里我们举一篇比较有挑战的 Issue 文章作为范例：

> As we acquire more knowledge, things do not become more comprehensible, but more complex and mysterious.
>
> Write a response in which you discuss the extent to which you agree or disagree with the statement and explain your reasoning for the position you take. In developing and supporting your position, you should consider ways in which the statement might or might not hold true and explain how these considerations shape your position.

如果我们仅限于题目既定的框架，很容易陷入"什么时候变得更容易理解"、"什么时候变得更加复杂和神秘"的分类讨论中。有一位同学的提纲就是这样的：

> **总立场**：支持
> **分论点 1**：过多的信息和知识会让我们难以理解世界，因为我们会更为紧张，认知能力会下降——有研究表明接触过量信息导致的 IQ 下降比吸食大麻更加明显（例证）。
> **分论点 2**：过多的信息使得分析某件事情时要考虑更多因素，这时问题的更多面就会显露出来，从而变得更加复杂。例如我们从小学习物理，会发现随着物理知识的增多，世界就会变得越来越复杂（例证）。
> **分论点 3**：知道得越多并不代表知道得越好和越深刻。
> **总结**：随着人们获取越来越多的信息，世界并非变得更加容易理解，而是变得更复杂和更神秘。

这样的文章立论中规中矩，如果语言上没有什么大问题的话，**4 分**的水平是可以达到的。读者可能会问：为什么这个论证不能冲击更高的分数呢？原因就在于它只看到了题目的表象，没有深入挖掘"more comprehensible"和"more complex and more mysterious"之间的关系，以及这关系背后的意义。首先我们不妨仔细看一下这三个关键词各自的解释："comprehensible"译作"可被理解的"，"complex"译作"复杂的"，"mysterious"译作"神秘的"。

讲到这里其实第一层立意突破就浮现了出来：一个东西能否被理解与它是否复杂有关系吗？换言之，comprehensible 和 complex 是反义词吗？显然不是的，一个复杂机器的背后是可以被理解的工程原理，但一个构造简单的混沌摆的背后却是困扰了人类数百年的三体问题。可见一个对象复杂与否与它能否被理解并没有直接关联。如果把 complex 和神秘分开来讨论，我们不禁要问：世界是否复杂？答案是显而易见的，因此我们获取更多的知识，其实只是更多看到了世界的原本的复杂面目。换言之，世界并没有变复杂，而是我们对于世界的认知复杂化了。

第二层立意突破来自于 comprehensible 和 mysterious 这对反义词，虽然看起来它们是矛盾的，但如果我们进一步挖掘就会发现它们的对象发生了变化：更容易理解的是现有的问题，而神秘是源自通过知识发现的新问题。从这个层面上我们可以继续挖掘，如果知识产生了新的问题，这些新的问题以后可以被解决吗？从不同时间来看是可以的，于是 comprehensible 和 mysterious 的矛盾有可能得到解决：知识的获取可能带来新问题，从而让世界显得更加神秘，但运用更新的知识便能在未来解决这些问题。

敏感的同学看到这里，也许已经开始思考：新的知识带来新的问题，这些问题可以被更新的知识所解答，但更新的问题又出现了……我们如果在时间维度上不断迭代下去，对于最后人们的认知究竟该持悲观态度（因为总有不断的新问题出现）还是乐观态度（因为新知识总能解决问题）呢？这就是立意第三层突破口，世界究竟是不是可知的。这个问题有两派哲学观点，不可知论（agnosticism）认为诸如上帝是否存在、宇宙的起源一类的哲学问题是不可被知晓（unknowable）的，而对立的观点则认为宇宙万物的原理总是可以穷尽的，我们人类目前只是没有足够的认知能力和工具罢了。其实这道题归根结底就是在帮你寻找你自己的世界观。

由此，我们给出一篇立意深刻的 Issue 提纲供大家参考，意在说明：其实 Issue 的立论本身没有太大的限制，下文的提纲认为世界终究是可知的，但把文章的基调定位为"世界总有一部分是不可知的"也未尝不可，只要能自圆其说就好。

总立场：complex 部分支持，mysterious 部分反对

分论点 1：把 complex 单独拿出来分析，指明复杂和神秘是两个概念，复杂也并非是神秘的原因，而是世界本来就是如此。故而更多的知识改变了人们的认知，让人们意识到世界比之前想象得要复杂，但客观来看世界本身并没有变。

分论点 2：承认新知识解决了问题，从而让世界 comprehensible；另一方面承认新知识也带来了新问题，从而让世界更加 mysterious。

分论点 3：针对 2 之中的矛盾进行解析，第一，comprehensible 和 mysterious 所针对的对象是不一样的——comprehensible 是过去的世界，mysterious 是新的世界。第二，两者在时间维度上是不一样的，comprehensible 是针对过去的事物，mysterious 是面向未来的事物。

分论点4：3 当中的讨论其实涉及世界究竟是不是 agnostic，我们认为不是，也即世界的知识是有限的，未知的东西终究可以穷尽。从这个角度来看，随着新知识解决了老问题，世界总体是 more comprehensible 的。

总结：更多的知识把世界的 complexity 揭露了出来，与此同时也暴露了新的未知。但随着知识越来越多，加上我们认为世界是可知的，世界总体而言是 more comprehensible。

常犯错误三 Issue 中的例证不具说服力

在英文写作当中"举例子"是最常见的论证方法，它一方面能帮助支撑论点，使文章更加让人信服；另一方面，好的例子能让文章生动活泼，不再是干巴巴的说教，从读者的角度来看是能提高文章可读性的。

在 ETS 官方的 Issue 评分标准中就明确指出了例子的重要性：6 分文章往往"develops the position fully with compelling reasons and/or persuasive examples"，5 分文章往往"develops the position with logically sound reasons and/or well-chosen examples"。当然，在 GRE 考试中，举例还有一个实用功能是显著提升文章长度。由此可见，举例在 Issue 写作中非常重要，但例子要怎么举才能恰当、有效呢？我们通过一道 Issue 的真题，配合同学们的真实习作来进行讲解。

To be an effective leader, a public official must maintain the highest ethical and moral standards.

Write a response in which you discuss the extent to which you agree or disagree with the claim. In developing and supporting your position, be sure to address the most compelling reasons and/or examples that could be used to challenge your position.

以下是四篇未经我们任何修改的学生文章，我们截取其中例证的部分进行点评，分析大家在举例过程当中常见的问题：

习作一

Finally I want to introduce the achievement of the First Emperor of Qin. He unified China in 221 BC and built the Great Wall as well as Terra Cotta Warriors and many other great things. And he died when he was 49. It is obvious that he is an effective leader but he never maintain high ethical and moral standards in any sense, he even buried Confucian scholars alive.

I think the effectiveness of a public official springs from many aspects of his or her personality, maybe one of them is maintaining high ethical and moral standards. But it is hard to believe that one must maintain highest standards to become an effective leader.

点评：

1. 冗余信息太多，例如秦始皇 49 岁去世有什么意义？

2. 有用的信息没有论证到点子上，为什么统一全国、建造长城和兵马俑体现出他是有效的领导人？我们不能把一切都认为理所应当（"It is obvious that he is an effective leader..."），这样的例证是没有说服力的。

3. 例子缺乏总结，仅仅是平铺直叙说完了故事之后就匆忙结尾，与结尾段的衔接显得生硬。

习 作 二

> although people may have different opinions on what is an effective leader, to me the defining character of an effective leader is that who makes as more as possible substantial benefit for the public. in 1776, the xxx as an effective leader put the right to life before every other right for defending the right for public. when he writing the law, he maintaining the ethical and moral standards, but we can't sure whether the highest ethical and moral standards. the change must hurt some interest of some people.

点评：

1. 首先，在文章开头给出 effective leader 定义的尝试值得肯定，但为什么这种定义是合理的？原文缺乏论证，使得这个观点不够令人信服。

2. 例证环节细节太少，而且文中的"xxx"给人一种捏造的感觉。

3. 中间属于循环论证，没有说服力：xxx 是一个有效的领导人，他认为 the right to life 是最重要的。这就说明要成为有效的领导人就必须尽可能为人民的利益服务吗？

4. 最后两句表意混乱，特别是"but we can't sure whether the highest ethical and moral standards"一句表意不完整，而且后半部分的反驳与中心句"the defining character of an effective leader is that who makes as more as possible substantial benefit for the public"没有直接联系。

5. 每句话第一个词的第一个字母请大写。

习 作 三

> Being effective need the leader do the things by the rules. First we have to know that the effectiveness is. Effectiveness demand the leader use the limited time to make decisions which requires much to a person. If there is no standers to follow, it hardly make the correct conclusion in a short time in such a short time. Only by maintaining the highest standard moral and ethical standards, can he/she think of the problems more objective having the rules to follow. For example, the prime of England, when he help the queen to mange the country, it is just that he have the highest standard on moral and ethical that make him waked and clever.

点评：

1. 前面一部分的逻辑演绎有可圈可点之处，但从"遵守规则"到"必须得拥有最高的道德准则"之间欠缺足够的论证。

2. 后半部分说英国首相时，"it is just that he have the highest standard on moral and ethical that make him waked and clever" 这个 claim 本身缺乏必要的论证支持，很难给本段的观点进行有力支撑。

3. 为什么是英国首相？美国总统不行吗？中国国家主席不行吗？这个例子中强调英国首相的意义何在？

习作 四

Secondly, the claim have an underlying statement that harboring the highst ethic and moral principles is a necessary condition for being an effective, which remains an open debate that if a leader lack of standards of highest level could be an excellent leader. I think the story of the 32nd president of United States, Franklin D. Roosevelt could give me an answer. With his achivments in economy and politics during the Great Depression, he dragged America out of the financial crisis and turmoil society environment. For this reason, he was titled with one of the most great presidents in United States，and others granted with this glory were America's founding fathers. It is undoubtable that he is an absolutely effective leader and an excellent public official. But the fact always omitted by citizens is that he had affairs with his secretary for a very long time until his death. Generally speaking, adultery is definatily violation to basic moral principles, needless to say the highest moral standards. But no one would deny his effective accomplishment and contribution to USA only because he did not maintain the basic morality. Consequently, the statement would not hold true taking account into such circumstances. And this phenomenon is not rare among those great effective political figures. William Jefferson Clinton's sexual scandal and Obama's drug addiction when he was young, all of these give me a lesson that even the greatest celebrities may have ethical or moral flaws which could not veil their effective doings in their field.

点评：

1. 例子中的细节很充分，这一点做得不错。

2. 论证都落实到了点子上（With his achivments in economy and politics during the Great Depression, he dragged America out of the financial crisis and turmoil society environment. For this reason, he was titled with one of the most great presidents in United States, and others granted with this glory were America's founding fathers.），这都是切实的逻辑演绎，而不像第一篇习作的"It is obvious..."。

3. 缺点：稍微冗长了一些，有一些细节可以合并简化，其实大家看 Clinton 和 Obama 的例子就很好，一两句话把问题讲清楚，然后说明白例子折射出来的道理就 ok 了。

总结一下，举例时需要注意的三点：

第一，例子本身要可信。我们不建议捏造例子的行为，这样一方面是有违诚信的原则，另一方面捏造的例子写出来很假。如果大家真的想不到例子，不妨假想一个情况——例如这道题我们可以假想，当一个国家的领导人因为道德原则而使得国家利益受损时，他不是一个有效的领导人。虽然这样的故事你不一定在考场上想出来，但它是符合逻辑，可以被人接受的。在这里，大家要区分好"假设性的例子"和"造假"的例子，前者可以被接受，但后者不被提倡。

第二，so what？用中文来解释就是问，**你所举的例子究竟说明了什么道理？这些例子是怎么支撑你的观点的？**有时作为举例的人会心存侥幸，以为读者一眼就能看明白例子的用意。但注意，GRE 归根到底是一场考试，作为考生的你需要向考官展示你自己清晰的逻辑，关键的地方宁愿多说一点也一定不能含糊。

第三，浓缩才是精华。举例固然能够帮助增加文章的长度，但太长的例子有喧宾夺主之嫌（思考：Issue 作文中的"主"应该是什么？）。真正的好例子应该是起到画龙点睛的作用，毕竟最精彩的论证不需要例子——你见过多少优美的数学定理是用穷举法证明的？大家备考 Issue 的过程中还是应该加强锻炼自己的批判性思维，然后用例证锦上添花。

常犯错误四 Argument 组织不当

面对一篇 Argument，要写几段，每一段包括哪些内容，这两个问题至关重要。这两个问题如果处理得好，就能有序地组织文章，也就能达到 6 分评分标准中所说的"有逻辑地组织观点（organize ideas logically）"；如果处理得不好，就可能陷入 3 分评分标准中所说的"观点的发展和组织不够有逻辑（limited in the logical development and organization of ideas）"。下面的一个例子就在组织上略有欠缺。

原题：

The following was written as a part of an application for a small-business loan by a group of developers in the city of Monroe.

"A jazz music club in Monroe would be a tremendously profitable enterprise. Currently, the nearest jazz club is 65 miles away; thus, the proposed new jazz club in Monroe, the C-Note, would have the local market all to itself. Plus, jazz is extremely popular in Monroe: over 100,000 people attended Monroe's annual jazz festival last summer; several well-known jazz musicians live in Monroe; and the highest-rated radio program in Monroe is 'Jazz Nightly,' which airs every weeknight at 7 P.M. Finally, a nationwide study indicates that the typical jazz fan spends close to $1,000 per year on jazz entertainment."

Write a response in which you discuss what specific evidence is needed to evaluate the argument and explain how the evidence would weaken or strengthen the argument.

某同学对此给出的提纲如下：

> **总立场：** 我们还需要一些具体的证据才能评价作者提出的"在 M 新建 jazz club 会盈利"这一结论。
>
> **分论点 1：** 作者给出了"最近的 jazz 在 65 英里之外"这一证据，并以此认为新 jazz club 会拥有所有本地市场，但我们还需要一些新证据才能判断这一结论是否正确。
>
> **分论点 2：** 作者告诉我们去年有 10 万人参加了 M 的年度音乐节，但我们不知道这 10 万人是否愿意花钱在 jazz club 上。因此还需要新证据来帮助判断这一点。
>
> **分论点 3：** 有几个 jazz 音乐人住在 M，并不代表他们会去新开的 jazz club。我们需要相应的新证据来帮助判断这点。
>
> （注： 分论点 4 和分论点 5 只出现在了该同学的提纲中，因为写作时间所限，正文段中并没有出现这两点）
>
> **分论点 4：** 虽然广播音乐节目很受欢迎，但也不代表人们会去新开的 jazz club。我们需要相应的新证据来帮助判断这点。
>
> **分论点 5：** 全国的调查不一定适用于本地，我们需要新证据帮助判断本地是否也有典型的 jazz fan。

最后我们给这篇文章的参考分数是 3。究其原因，并非因为其没有按照 Direction 的要求来写（提纲中反复出现了"证据"一词，说明文章基本符合 Direction 的要求），也不是语言不合格，而是因为全文的组织不当。

我们可以对原 Argument 的结构通过以下的逻辑图来表示：

通过这个逻辑推理图我们可以清晰地看出，文章中给出的证据（①②③④⑤）并非直接推出总结论⑨的。而是由证据①推出小结论⑥，由证据②③④推出小结论⑦，由证据⑤推出小结论⑧，然后再由小结论⑥⑦⑧推出最终结论的⑨。每一次由证据推到结论的过程都是有问题的，而原文一共推了四次结论（前三次是由证据推到小结论，最后一次是由小结论推到最终结论），所以有四处推理过程都有问题。因此，理论上讲，我们应该写出四个中间段来分别评价这四次推理。具体内容应该如下：

中间段 1：评价由证据①推出小结论⑥的推理过程。

中间段 2：评价由证据②③④推出小结论⑦的推理过程。

中间段 3：评价由证据⑤推出小结论⑧的推理过程。

中间段 4：评价由小结论⑥⑦⑧推出最终结论⑨的推理过程。

如上所示，"需要写几段"、"每一段应该包括哪些内容"这两个问题的答案非常明显。按这种方式组织出来的段落才最贴近原 Argument 的推理过程，才能满足 6 分评分标准中所说的"有逻辑地组织观点（organize ideas logically）"。

组织好了每一段，接下来就是从 Direction 要求的角度组织每一段的文字。大家可以参考第五章给出的这一道题目的范文。

第二节　形式方面

常犯错误一　句子连接

错误句子 1：Imagination is significant, we should make good use of it.

错误句子 2：Imagination is significant, therefore we should make good use of it.

错误原因：逗号"，"不能连接具有完整主谓宾的两个句子。有同学认为此时加上一个表示因果关系的词"therefore"就可以连接两个句子了，但是 therefore 是副词，同样不能连接两个完整句子（与 therefore 类似，thereby, hence, thus, consequently 等都是副词，都不能连接两个完整句子）。

改正后的句子：

改法 1: Imagination is significant; we should make good use of it.

改法 2: Imagination is significant. We should make good use of it.

（分号和句号前后可以连接两个完整的句子。但原句想要表达的因果关系并没有被凸显，因此不如下面两种改法）

改法 3: Imagination is significant, **so** we should make good use of it.

改法 4: **Since/Because** imagination is significant, we should make good use of it.

（so, since, because 都是连词，都可以连接两个完整的句子，而且也凸显了原文的因果关系，比较妥帖）

常犯错误二　代词使用

错误句子 1：Great leaders should be tough. That is to say, he can stick to his own principles.

错误原因：前一句的 leaders 是复数形式，而后一句却用第三人称单数形式的 he 和 his 对其进行指代，前后单复数不统一。

改正后的句子：Great leaders should be tough. That is to say, they can stick to their own principles.

错误句子 2：Novelists create a considerable number of brilliant novels. They contribute greatly to the society.

错误原因：前一句出现了 novelists 和 novels 两个复数形式的单词，因而我们不清楚后一句中的 they 到底指代哪一个单词。

改正后的句子：Novelists create a considerable number of brilliant novels. Those novelists/Their novels/Those novels contribute greatly to the society.

错误句子 3：It is unacceptable.

错误原因：代词无所指代。按理说，根据代词的指代，是可以回归到上文或下文中的某个词或某个概念。而同学在写作文的时候常常使用在上下文中都找不到指代的代词。（这位同学的这句话中的 it 确实在其上下文中都找不到指代，这里因为篇幅所限，无法详尽展示其上下文）

改正方法：取消代词 it 的使用，或者在上下文中明确出 it 的指代对象。

常犯错误三 名词单复数

错误句子 1：We need several evidences to demonstrate the validity of this argument.

错误原因：这句话在 argument 中经常用到。但 evidence 通常用作不可数名词。要表示"一条证据"，用 a piece of evidence；要表示很多证据，可以用 abundant, plentiful, ample 等词，也可以用 a body of, a mass of 等短语。

改正后的句子：We need several **evidence** to demonstrate the validity of this argument.

错误句子 2：Book enlightens us.

错误原因："书本启迪我们"，这里的 book 应该是泛指意义上的书。所以要用表示泛指意义的"books"或"a book"。

改正后的句子：**Books** enlighten us./**A book** enlightens us.

常犯错误四 冠词误用

错误句子 1：The disagreement promotes innovation.

错误原因："分歧促进创新"，这里的"分歧（disagreement）"应该表泛指，所以不需要定冠词"the"。

改正后的句子：**Disagreement** promotes innovation.

错 误 句 子 2：Disagreement of these two artists' opinions on this artwork encouraged them to delve into more thorough research.

错误原因："这两个艺术家关于这幅艺术品的看法的分歧激励他们进行更全面的研究"，这里的"分歧（disagreement）"应该是特指这两个人对于某个艺术品的看法的分歧，所以需要用定冠词"the"。

改正后的句子：**The** Disagreement of these two artists' opinions on this artwork encouraged them to delve into more thorough research.

常犯错误五 混淆主动被动

错误句子 1： Comparing to the first opinion, the second one makes more sense.

错误原因： 非谓语动词 "compare" 的逻辑主语应该和主句主语 "the second one（opinion）" 一致。而 "opinion" 只能是 "被比较" 而不能主动发出 "比较" 这个动作。

改正后的句子：**Compared** to the first opinion, the second one makes more sense.

错误句子 2： The "field" in this issue is consisted of three parts: science, literature and art.

错误原因： "consist of" 意为 "由…组成"，英文释义为 "to be formed from/by"，已然含有被动语义。通常以 "A consist of B" 这样的主动形式表示 "A 由 B 组成"。（要表示 B 组成 A，我们可以用 B constitute/make up A）

改正后的句子：The "field" in this issue **consists of** three parts: science, literature and art.

常犯错误六 从句误用

错误句子 1： This is apparently the best solution which can change the situation.

错误原因： 定语从句修饰的先行词 solution 被形容词最高级 the best 修饰，所以定语从句应该用 that 引导而非 which。

改正后的句子：This is apparently the best solution **that** can change the situation.

错误句子 2： This argument is unconvincing due to several questionable assumptions lack support.

错误原因： "几个缺少支持的有问题的假设让这篇 argument 不可信"。当先行词在定语从句中充当主语时，定语从句的引导词不能省略。

改法 1： This argument is unconvincing due to several questionable assumptions **that/which** lack support.（补全定语从句的引导词）

改法 2： This argument is unconvincing due to several questionable assumptions **lacking** support.（将 lack 变为非谓语动词，做后置定语修饰 assumption）

错误句子 3： Educators should prevent students from choosing fields which are unlikely to succeed.

错误原因： which 引导的定语从句修饰先行词 field，翻译成中文是 "不太可能成功的领域"，我们虽然能够明白其中文句意，但放在英文中却说不通。因为 succeed 这个动作的发出者应该是人（people）而不是领域（field）。

改正后的句子：Educators should prevent students from choosing fields **in which students** are unlikely to succeed.（**注意：有同学把 students 换成 they，这就犯了 "指代不明" 的错误，因为句子中有 educators 和 students 两个复数概念。**）

错误句子 4：The author claims this recommendation will work well and this company will make more money.

错误原因：在正规书面语中，宾语从句的 that 一般不省略。而且此句中 claim 后面有两个宾语从句，同学们经常忘记第二个宾语从句的引导词 that。

改正后的句子：The author claims **that** this recommendation will work well and **that** this company will make more money.

错误句子 5：The reason why leaders should listen to the public is because leaders are selected by the public.

错误原因："the reason is because"，搭配错误。当 reason 作主语时，表语从句的引导词是 that 而不是 because。

改正后的句子：The reason why leaders should listen to the public is **that** leaders are selected by the public.

错误句子 6：No matter who has the courage to break the old rules is likely to succeed.

错误原因：no matter who 只能引导让步状语从句。而 whoever 既可以引导让步状语从句也可以引导名词性从句（whatever/however/wherever 等同理）。这句话中，has the courage 前缺少主语，因此我们需要主语从句的引导词 whoever。

改正后的句子：**Whoever** has the courage to break the old rules is likely to succeed.

错误句子 7：We should always doubt that whether the authority is right.

错误原因："doubt"后可以跟宾语从句，但宾语从句的引导词只需要一个。因此该句子中 that 是多余的。

改正后的句子：We should always doubt **whether** the authority is right.

错误句子 8：Despite the author provides several evidence, this argument is questionable.

错误原因："despite"后面只能跟名词性成分而不能跟句子（与之类似的还有 in spite of）。

改法 1：**Although** the author provides several evidence, this argument is questionable.

（although 是连词，后面可以跟完整句子充当让步状语从句）

改法 2：**Despite** the evidence the author provides, this argument is questionable.

（将原句中 despite 之后的句子改成名词性成分）

错误句子 9：Plausible as appears this argument, it is unconvincing.

错误原因："as"作"虽然"讲时可以引导倒装的让步状语从句，但同学们往往搞不清楚句子中主谓宾的顺序。正确的顺序应该是"adj / adv / 分词 / 名词（要省略冠词）+ as + 主语 + 谓语动词"。

改正后的句子：**Plausible as this argument appears**, it is unconvincing.

错误句子 10：The government should give financial support to big cities where are the major places for culture development.

错误原因：定语从句修饰的先行词 cities 在定语从句中作主语，因此定语从句的引导词应该用关系代词 that 或者 which。（而如果先行词在定语从句中作状语，则应该用关系副词 where，when 等引导定语从句，如改法 2 的句子）。

改法 1：The government should give financial support to big cities 「that」 are the major places for culture development.

改法 2：The government should give financial support to big cities 「where」 culture develops/flourishes.

错误句子 11：It is in small cities where artists can do whatever they want.

错误原因：这句话的错误比较难以发现。很多同学认为 where 引导定语从句修饰 small cities，但如果按照这种思路，我们会发现 small cities 前面的 It is in 的意思无从解释。其实，这句话是混淆了定语从句和 It 引导的强调句型。作者真正想表达的意思是"艺术家**只有在大城市**才能够做他们想做的事情"（强调"大城市"）。

改正后的句子：It is in small cities 「that」 artists can do whatever they want.

错误句子 12：One may ask: is this quality that an effective leader should have?

错误原因：这句话的错误比较难看出来。很多同学都认为 that 引导的定语从句修饰先行词 quality，但如果我们按照这种思路把原句换成陈述句的语序，则错误就显而易见了：this quality that an effective leader should have is。我们可以发现，is 后面缺少表语，句子不完整。因此我们需要添加表语使得句子完整。

改正后的句子：One may ask: is this quality 「the one」 that an effective leader should have?

常犯错误七 误用"大词"

由于花了大工夫在 GRE 单词的背诵上，因此会有同学存在一种不把它们用出来就不甘心的冲动。于是，就有了以下一些错误：

错误句子 1：This argument is unconvincing due to its numerous logic flaws.

错误原因：numerous 意为"极其多的，数不胜数的"，程度非常深。而 argument 当中所谓的"逻辑错误"虽然不少，但离"数不胜数"还有相当的距离。故 numerous 用在这里不妥。

改正后的句子：This argument is unconvincing due to 「several」 logic flaws.

错误句子 2：In this way the conclusion of this argument is vandalized.

错误原因：虽然我们在背单词的时候可能会简单地把 vandalize 记作"破坏"，但在真实使用中，vandalize 常指"对公物的蓄意破坏"，用在这里显然不合适。

改正后的句子：In this way the conclusion of this argument is 「undermined」.

错误句子 3：Therefore the author's conclusion is preposterous.

错误原因：我们可能在背诵 GRE 词汇的时候，出于便利将 preposterous 记成"错误的"。但这个词的程度很深，而且极具负面的感情色彩，可以翻译成"荒谬绝伦的"，或"岂有此理的"，用在这里太过偏激。

改正后的句子：Therefore the author's conclusion is **unconvincing/questionable**.

错误句子 4：To draw a conclusion, while this policy might bring about some benefits, I have to argue that it is abysmal.

错误原因：abysmal 的意思类似于 terrible，程度极深，甚至可以夸张地翻译为"无底洞般地差劲"。而原句明明一定程度上肯定了 this policy，所以用 abysmal 就显得很不妥。

改正后的句子：To draw a conclusion, while this policy might bring about some benefits, I have to argue that in most cases it is **harmful**.（harmful 的程度不如 abysmal 深，再加上一个 in most cases 使得原句逻辑更加严谨）

错误句子 5：Clearly, she gets a sanguine opinion so she can ignore so many difficulties.

错误原因：作者本身希望表达的意思可能是"很明显，是她的乐观让她能够克服这许多的困难"。但是，sanguine 这个词是非常正式的书面语，用在这句话中和作者的 get, ignore 等不太准确的表达显得格格不入。

改法 1：Clearly, she has been very optimistic, so she could overcome so many difficulties.

（舍弃 sanguine，让整句话更加平实但不失准确）

改法 2：Clearly, it is her sanguine attitude that enabled her to surmount all the difficulties.

（保留 sanguine，但同时也对句式和表达做一些改写，让句子更加凝练且重点突出。这句话可能会比改法 1 更为正式、书面，或者"高大上"，但不是说我们就应该追求改法 2 这样的句子。在 GRE 中，我们追求的永远只有"准确"。）

错误句子 6：Though there are so many attractions, we should be **ascetic** to have a healthy value of life.

错误原因：大家对 ascetic 这个词应该很熟悉，因为它出现在单词书的 A 打头的那一章。事实上，这个词很少用在一般的作文中。因为它往往指西方宗教里所倡导的为达到精神救赎而对诸般欲望的禁锢，"六根清净"这个词也许能比较好地传达其意思。

改正后的句子：Though there are so many attractions, to form a healthy value of life, we should better **abstain/refrain/keep away from** some of them.

综上所述，GRE 单词还真不是我们想用就能用的。就现阶段来看，盲目使用 GRE 词汇至少可能会存在以下问题：

1. 拼不对。GRE 词汇大多不短，考场上不一定能打对。

2. 意思用错。GRE 词汇的意思往往很窄，很容易用错。

3. 很多 GRE 词汇非常学术化，这就有可能和大家作文中的一些比较口语化的表达冲突，从而让文章的整体风格显得比较别扭。

附：清华外教致中国英语考生的一些话

在本书的 40 篇文章全部完成之后，我们有幸请到了清华大学外文系负责学术英语教学和商务英语教学的外教 Cassandra Woloschuk 女士为这 40 篇文章修改润色。当聊到彼此所见到的中国考生的写作短板时，我们不谋而合地提到了"乱用大词"、"语义不明"等问题。在下面的几段话中，Cassandra 总结了中国考生在写作时的几个典型问题，这和本章"考生常犯错误"各自从宏观和微观两个层面为大家提供了修改自己文章的指导性建议。

另外，我们还附上了外教对我们文章修改的范例。"好文章是改出来的"，在经过自我修改、同事老师互改、学生阅读反馈等环节之后，本书的 40 篇文章依然需要更加专业权威的人士进行批评指教，Cassandra 在这方面给予了我们很大的帮助。当大家进入研究生院进行正式的学术写作并需要发表论文时，十数遍乃至几十遍的修改是在所难免的。希望大家从现在起就养成改文章的好习惯，真正为自己的笔头文字负责。

外教寄语：

It has been a pleasure reading and editing these responses. Their succinctness and simplicity should be the goal of any Chinese student hoping to write like a foreigner.

Teaching in China has given me new insight about how Chinese students approach the mechanics of writing. Because the immediate task facing you is to improve writing skills, I want to highlight a couple of problematic tendencies among Chinese writing in English.

Many students deliberately write long, complicated passages because they believe this makes their writing more sophisticated. Unfortunately, this practice erodes writing quality. The best writing is clear and concise. Using three words when one will do often obscures meaning. It does not matter how good an idea is if the author does not explain it clearly. Instead of sacrificing clarity, enhance your writing by focusing on coherence and cohesion, lexical resource, and grammatical range and accuracy.

Passive writing is another tendency among Chinese students—as well as in English translations throughout China. I have seen many signs that are longer than they need to be due to this passive voice preference. Writing in the passive voice may be clear but it contains redundancies that the active voice eliminates. The ability to write in the active voice is essential in academia. Writing in the passive voice damages the authoritative tone academic writing requires.

Writing is an art. Never fall into the trap of believing your first draft cannot be improved upon. Editing is a crucial process so write your first draft with your heart and your second draft with your head. By this I mean that you should first write what you feel is important then clean up the writing in the second draft. If you become attached to a particular phrase or sentence you will have difficulty editing it if necessary in a subsequent draft.

I hope that you will find the essays in this volume helpful as you strive to improve your own writing.

Cassandra Woloschuk

外教修改样例：

36. The following report appeared in the newsletter of the West Meria Public Health Council.

"An innovative treatment has come to our attention that promises to significantly reduce absenteeism in our schools and workplaces. A study reports that in nearby East Meria, where fish consumption is very high, people visit the doctor only once or twice per year for the treatment of colds. Clearly, eating a substantial amount of fish can prevent colds. Since colds represent the most frequently given reason for absences from school and work, we recommend the daily use of Ichthaid—a nutritional supplement derived from fish oil—as a good way to prevent colds and lower absenteeism."

Write a response in which you discuss what specific evidence is needed to evaluate the argument and explain how the evidence would weaken or strengthen the argument.

In this report, the author alleges the efficiency of Ichthaid—a nutritional supplement derives from fish oil—in preventing colds and further asserts the capability of Ichthaid to lower absenteeism in local schools and workplaces. To buttress his recommendation, the author cites a study showing high fish consumption and low doctor-visiting frequency in Meria. We are also informed that colds are the most frequently given reason for absences from school and work. However, close scrutiny of this argument reveals a lack of critical evidence and we are therefore unable to evaluate the conclusion. As a result, further information is needed to form a better evaluation of the author's recommendation.

To start with, while the author provides information concerning the high fish consumption and less frequent medical visits for the treatment of colds in Meria, we need more evidence to demonstrate the casual relationship between the former and the latter. For example, we need to know whether high fish consumption in Meria means that people eat a large amount of fish; in addition, detailed proof will be of great significance to determine whether people visit doctors infrequently ~~due to an authentically low frequency of~~ because of a lower incidence of catching colds ~~but not~~ as opposed to other reasons, such as excessively high hospital fees. If new evidence shows that people do eat a massive amount of fish and catch colds less often, then fish's efficiency in preventing colds can be confirmed and the author's recommendation is thereby more convincing.

In addition, although the writer claims that the most frequently given reason for absences from local school and work is colds, he needs to provide more evidence to validate the assertion. Since ~~asking for absence by claiming to be sick~~ absence due to illness is widely accepted ~~usually gains greater acceptance~~ in both schools and workplaces, using colds as an excuse not to study or work is naturally a reasonable possibility. Therefore, we need additional evidence indicating whether people asking for absence have lied about the reasons ~~for leaving schools or work~~. If new evidence shows that colds do play a crucial role in absenteeism, then we are disposed to believe that the author's conclusion is advisable. On the contrary, if the evidence shows us ~~the other way around~~ the contrary, then we remain doubtful of the recommendation given in the argument.

Even if new evidence is provided that demonstrates both fish's efficiency in preventing colds as well as the contribution colds make towards local absenteeism, we need more information to show that Ichthaid is as effective, if not more, as fish in the prevention of colds. Specifically, we need to know whether fish's ability to prevent colds originates in its oil and not in other parts such as the bones. Moreover, it would be of great help to know whether elements in fish remain functional after a series of artificial processes. In addition, the author would benefit from clarifying the relationship between the usage of Ichthaid and its efficiency in preventing colds. If it is fishbone instead of fish oil that prevents colds, or artificially processes medicine lags in efficiency, or overuse of Ichthaid ~~turns out to be~~ is found to be counterproductive, then the author's conclusion is weakened and the recommendation should therefore be rejected. Otherwise, it should be encouraged.

To sum up, the current ~~available~~ information available in this argument dose not sufficiently substantiate that the proposed usage of Ichthaid will preclude colds in schools and workplaces and further lower local absenteeism. As a result, we need more evidence to better evaluate the writer's recommendation.

第四章 GRE 写作官方评分标准精析

对 GRE 写作官方评分标准的解析是本书的一大亮点。

我们选择对 Issue 和 Argument 的评分标准做解析，从根本上说是因为这是我们**唯一可以参照的、由官方给出**的 GRE 作文判分依据。当我们向作文得高分的师兄师姐讨教 GRE 写作的经验，或是求助于诸多辅导书的"高分秘籍"时，得到的答案都是经过个人主观加工的信息，是没有经过官方认可的。

例如，最常被问到的一个问题是："要写多少字？"可能有师兄师姐说："我第一次写了 500 字，得了 4 分；第二次写了 600 字，得了 4.5。"对此，我们可能就会在分数和字数之间建立起正向的因果联系，甚至觉得要得 5 分及其以上需要至少 700 字。但是，ETS 就给出过一篇 500 字不到的 6 分范文，这充分说明了字数和分数之间的关系并不如大家想得那么紧密。

虽然字数和分数是有关系的，但并非直接相关。这是因为如果我们想得到高分，就必须把观点讲清楚，而要做到这一点，对于大多数考生来说往往需要相对较多的字数。所以，**高分文章虽然可能有"字数多"这一特征，但这一特征下的本质却应该是"把观点讲清楚的能力"**。如果不了解这一点，我们很可能就会把"写多"当作第一要务，而不顾内容和语言质量，这一做法必然导致南辕北辙，最后得分也可能不尽如人意。

因此，评分标准为我们提供了明确的、也是唯一的努力方向。对评分标准的解析也自然变得非常重要。

但是，评分标准中的语言非常抽象，让考生读完之后只能明白一个大致的方向，却不知道具体应该怎样做。比如 6 分的评分标准要求文章的观点做到"insightful（有洞察力的）"，那么什么叫"有洞察力"？考生还是不知所云。而对于评分标准的处理，市面上的参考书也基本停留在翻译和同义复述的层面，如：一些参考书告诉我们：为了做到"insightful"，需要深刻地而不是肤浅地看问题。那何又为"深刻"？何又为"肤浅"？我们仍然一无所知。

因此，我们对评分标准的解析方式是：通过对 ETS 给出的范文分析，以及将评分标准和学术写作的诸多要领相结合，最后**将"评分标准"变为"如何取得高分的方法论，即怎么做"**。因为相比于"是什么"，"怎么做"对我们来说更有指导意义。所以，我们会把评分标准中的每一个关键词都变成一个具体的、具有动词意义的词语，以此来指导考生进行写作。

更重要的是，考生们一定都能在我们的每一篇范文中找到它对评分标准的照应。解析评分标准就如同告诉大家如何生产一个符合 ETS 要求的产品，而 40 篇范文就是 40 个这样的产品。这 40 篇范文不论是在整体还是在局部上都符合对评分标准的解析，**希望考生在阅读范文之时能够结合评分标准以及范文之后的评语**，对其反复揣摩，用心体会。

第一节　Issue 评分标准分析

Issue 部分的评分标准主要围绕以下三点：

1. 是否按照 **Direction**（具体性指令）来写

2. 立意和观点发展如何

3. 语言如何

请看不同分数段对我们的要求。

【**Score 6**】

In addressing the **specific task directions**, a 6 paper presents a **cogent, well-articulated** analysis of the issue and **conveys meaning skillfully**.

A typical paper in this category exhibits the following characteristics:

1. It articulates a **clear** and **insightful** position on the issue in accordance with the assigned task.
2. It develops the position fully, with **compelling reasons** and/or **persuasive examples**.
3. It sustains a **well-focused**, **well-organized** analysis, **connecting ideas logically**.
4. It conveys ideas fluently and precisely, using **effective vocabulary** and **sentence variety**.
5. It demonstrates facility with the conventions of **standard written English** (i.e., grammar, usage, and mechanics) but may have **minor errors**.

⌘ 中文翻译

在照应具体性指令的基础上，6 分的文章对原 Issue 题目进行了**具有说服力的、清楚的**分析，且**运用（多种）技巧传词达意**。

典型的 6 分文章具有如下特征：

1. 根据题目要求，对原 Issue 题目给出**清楚而有洞察力**的立场。
2. 在完整地展开立场时，运用了**严密的推理**和/或具有说服力的事例。
3. 全文**焦点明确，组织清晰**，观点和观点之间的衔接符合逻辑。
4. 运用**有效的词汇**和**多样的句式**，流畅、准确地传达观点意思。
5. 熟练掌握**标准书面英语**的写作习惯（语法、用法、技法等），但仍存在一些细小错误。

解 析

6 分的评分标准是我们最应该详细琢磨的评分标准，因为它代表着我们努力的方向。在之后的分数段的讲解中不难发现，5 分和 4 分的评分标准其实就是 6 分的弱化版，其大方向是一致的，只不过是程度上的差异。因此，请认真研读下面对 6 分标准中关键词的解析：

specific task direction：**照应具体性指令是得 6 分的最基本的要求，这也是 5 分和 4 分标准的要求**。对具体性指令的照应方法详见第五章。

convey meaning skillfully: 这是 6 分标准区别于 5 分和 4 分的一大亮点。6 分标准要求我们运用**多种技巧**阐述论证我们的观点。因此，常见的道理论证和事例论证自不必说，其他的论证方法，如比喻论证、反证法等都可以酌情使用。

clear position: 立场和论点要清楚。这里的 clear（清楚）应当包括两层意思。

1. 首先是**位置的清楚**。即要把总论点和分论点放在最显眼、清楚的位置（总论点放首段；分论点放每一段的段首）。

2. 其次是**语义的清楚**。要清楚地传达意思，需要大家对每一种表达、句式都能够信手拈来并且准确运用。但现实情况是，考生倾向于用一些"高级"的表达和复杂的句式（比如：定语从句），却没有足够的语言能力去驾驭这些表达和句式，结果只能是观点表意不清。**所以，如果对自己的语言不太自信，可以在中心句的表达时尽量采用简短、清楚的词汇、短语和句式。**

insightful position: 有洞察力的立场和观点。这一要求是和 GRE 写作中要求的 Critical Thinking（批判性思维）紧密结合的。但不论是前者还是后者，都让我们感到很大、很空，不知道具体如何操作。对此，我们把 insightful（有洞察力的）这个词具象为"**全面而深刻**"。

1. 全面。面对一道 Issue 题目，我们要对其做全面的分析。这种全面可以包括但不局限于以下几方面：

①正反兼备地看问题。对题目的观点，可以既赞同，又反对。

②抓住题目中含义丰富或具有复杂性的词语，对其进行不同维度的分析。如：在题目 "In order for any work of art—for example, a film, a novel, a poem, or a song—to have merit, it must be understandable to most people" 中，我们可以全面分析 "merit（价值）" 这一词。艺术品的价值可能包括审美价值、收藏价值、市场价值等等，但并不是每一种价值的实现都要依赖于艺术品的通俗性。我们可以按照这样的思维展开我们的中间段三段。

2. 深刻。一道 Issue 题目所讨论的问题往往不是如它表面看上去的那么简单，这时就需要我们**透过现象看本质**，抓住题目的核心问题。需要注意的是，这里的"核心问题"只是一个相对概念，且不唯一，不同的考生对于相同题目的核心问题可能有着不同的理解，但只要这些理解都相对深入即可。如，对于 Issue13 题所探讨的，大学是否应该让学生选修很多本专业之外的课程，表面上是在讨论要不要选专业外的课程这一问题，但有考生可能会认为这道题本质上是在探讨"专才（specialist）"和"通才（generalist）"；而另一些考生可能会认为"同一性（conformity）"和"多样性（diversity）"才是本题的核心问题；甚至会有考生认为本题应该落脚在"知识（knowledge）"和"方法论（methodology）"的对立统一之上。这些观点都比较深入，但很难判断孰是孰非，孰优孰劣。所以，大家可以选择自己认为好写的观点对其进行论证。

compelling reason：严密的推理。这里的 reason 虽然是名词（"理由"），但我们把它动词化，翻译成"推理"，这样更便于理解。"严密的推理"其实照应的就是议论文中常见的"道理论证"。但是，大家在以往的写作中对某一观点进行道理论证时，往往是在对这一观点进行同义重复，或隔靴搔痒般的浅显解释，这在 GRE 写作中是不够的。**我们需要做的，是再现推理的过程**。即：在论证观点 A 时，我们需要给出得到观点 A 的思考过程，即从 A1 到 A2 再到 A3（A4，A5...）最后到 A 的推理步骤。其中的 A1，A2 和 A3 等称为"桥梁概念"，是辅助读者理清作者的推理思路的重要概念。桥梁概念的数量并非越多越好，但却是 GRE 写作中展现我们逻辑脉络的关键要素。例如，如果我们的某个论点是"不通俗易懂的艺术作品也可以有价值"，为了论证这个论点，我们需要再现推理过程。如："艺术作品的价值主要体现在创作者的技艺和其个人世界的展现中（A1）。其技艺有时高超晦涩，其个人世界的展现往往又极具个性（A2），因此不具备相关知识的外行人，或是没有和创作者类似经历的人，往往不能理解作品的手法或内容（A3）。因此这些人也无法理解该艺术品的价值（A4）。但这并不妨碍这些作品成为有价值的作品（A）。"如上所示，从 A1 到 A 的推理过程就比较饱满，也使得论点更具有说服力。

persuasive example：具有说服力的事例。即事例论证。"举例子要有说服力"，这几乎是一句在各大英语写作考试中都耳熟能详的套话。但如何具有说服力？这却似乎是大家一直没有弄明白的问题。对此，我们给出一个总的原则和几个具体的建议，帮助大家构建具有说服力的例子。**总的原则是：照应推理过程**。具体建议如下：

1. 找同义概念。**即找推理过程中关键信息的同义或者近义概念**。如：在推理过程中出现了"assume an important role"这一表达，那么在举例子的时候可以换用"play a significant part"。要注意的是，推理过程中出现的表示逻辑连接的词语（如 therefore, however 等），更需要在举例子时同义重复（如 hence, nevertheless 等）。

2. 找下义概念。**即找推理过程中出现的比较宽泛的概念的具体体现**。如：在推理过程中出现了 law，那么在举例子的时候可以举出更加具体的、法律的下义词：tax law。

3. 如果是对自己驾驭语言的能力缺少信心的考生，甚至可以比较机械地尝试这种做法：**在事理推理过程中写了几句话，在举例子时就参照其句式进行更加具体的仿写，依旧写出同样数量的句子**。这虽然有一点死板，但至少能保证关键信息的一一照应，也不失为构建具有说服力例证的一种方法。

well-focused：焦点明确。要做到焦点明确，只需要做到以下两点：

1. 不偏题。尤其不要偏离具体性指令的要求。
2. 文章的分论点围绕总论点展开。

well-organized：组织清晰。要做到组织清楚，需做到以下两点：

1. 各分论点之间层次清楚，且和总论点的关系紧密。
2. 多用、用准逻辑连接词。

connecting ideas logically：有逻辑地组织观点。要做到这一点，可以参照以下两条对策：

1. 在保证逻辑本身没有问题的基础上，**多用、用准逻辑连接词**。

2. 前文的相同概念在后文再次提及时，在不影响意思传达的基础上，可以尝试**同义改写或者用指示代词（this, that 等）对其进行指代**。另外，如 previous, former, aforementioned, latter, following 等词虽然不属于指示代词，但同样具有指示的作用，大家也可以多多使用，以体现前后文的联系。

effective vocabulary：使用有效词汇。"有效的"词汇**首先要做到准确，在此基础上尽可能地追求生动形象**。以下两条策略可以帮助大家选择那些准确、生动的词汇：

1. 词语意思越具体、越实在，就越准确，这一点在动词上体现尤为明显。大家经常用到的 get, let, make 等词，往往意思太宽，在表意上不够精准。如：与其说 "get a clear understanding（得到清楚的认知）"，不如把 "get" 换成 "acquire"，"form" 等，意思更具体，表意更准确。

2. 具有画面感的词语比较生动，也因此更加有效。这样的词语有很多，但需要平日的积累。如：表达 "A 不那么重要" 时，与其说 "A is not that important"，不如说 "A pales/dims in significance"，"pale" 有 "变得苍白" 的意思，"dim" 有 "变得昏暗" 的意思，在这里和 significance 连用，极具画面感，就比单纯用 be 动词显得更加生动形象。

sentence variety：一提到句式多样性，大家可能直接会将其等同于花哨多样的句式，即语言层面的多变。但语言终究是为思想服务的。只有当我们的思维多样时，我们才会启用相应多样的语言。如：只有当我们在想要表达具有层级关系的意思时，我们才会使用从句以突出主句的地位。因此，**在追求句式多样性之前，我们首先应该追求传词达意的准确，在此基础上再求变**。在能够做到用相应句式准确表达意思时，可以适当考虑以下几点策略：

1. 倒装。我们广泛接触到的 "not only...but also..."，"as/though"，"nor"，"only"，"nor" 等词都可以引起倒装，大家可以酌情使用。但一定注意，只有当想要强调倒装部分时，才用倒装句式。

2. 省略。前后两句话中出现相同成分时，我们完全可以将部分成分省略，这样既显得简洁，又可以使前后的句子长短不同，错落有致。如 "Such a policy is not an elixir, but (it is) just a pain-killer（这个政策并非万灵药，而只是止痛药）"。

3. 换主语。在表意清楚的前提上，我们可以多换主语。动词不定式、人、事、物、句子、it 等都可以做主语。如，在想要表达 "我们需要关注 sth" 的时候，可以有以下几种表达：

a. We need to pay attention to sth.

b. It is necessary to pay attention to sth.

c. What we need to pay attention to is sth.

d. Sth requires our attention.

e. To pay attention to sth is of great necessity.

standard written English：GRE 写作要求我们运用标准的书面语。这一点看上去比较有难度，但实则却是大家掌握得最好的。因为从小学开始到大学的四六级考试，又到托福考试，大家所学习的英语都可以算是标准的书面英语。广大中国留学生真正薄弱的环节应该是口语（这里的口语不单指"说的能力"，也是指和比较正式的"书面表达"相对立的"口语表达"）。因此，只要大家注意**不要在 GRE 写作中过度使用俗语、俚语或粗俗的表达**，就基本符合书面英语的写作要求了。

minor errors：这里的"minor"包含两层意思，其一是"**程度较轻**"，其二是"**数量较少**"。所谓"程度较轻"的错误，**是指这个错误既不影响阅读，也不会反映出作者在语法层面的能力缺陷**，如某个单词的某两个字母错位了，某个单词忘了变复数等，这些都是可以接受的错误类型；而所谓的"数量较少"，则是希望大家尽量把全篇文章的错误数量控制在 **5 个以内**。

综上，本书将 6 分评分标准中的每一个关键词语都做了详细的讲解，并将其转化为具体的方法论，指导大家写作。需要注意的是，6 分的评分标准（包括 5 分和 4 分的评分标准）说道：**要满足标准中的所有要求**，文章才能达到相应的分数。因此，大家需要结合上述解析，从每一个方向努力。

【 **Score 5** 】

In addressing the **specific task directions**, a 5 paper presents a **generally thoughtful**, **well-developed** analysis of the issue and conveys meaning **clearly**.

A typical paper in this category exhibits the following characteristics:

1. It presents a **clear** and **well-considered** position on the issue in accordance with the assigned task.

2. It develops the position with **logically sound reasons** and/or **well-chosen** examples.

3. It is **focused** and **generally well organized**, **connecting ideas appropriately**.

4. It conveys ideas clearly and well, using **appropriate vocabulary** and **sentence variety**.

5. It demonstrates facility with the conventions of **standard written English** but may have **minor errors**.

🖉 **中文翻译**

在照应具体性指令的基础上，5分的文章对原Issue题目进行了**比较缜密的、发展充分的**分析，且**清楚地传词达意**。

典型的 5 分文章具有如下特征：

1. 根据题目要求，对原 Issue 题目给出**清楚而考虑充分**的立场。

2. 在完整地展开立场时，运用了**逻辑正确的推理**和**精心挑选的事例**。

3. **全文有焦点**，**组织比较清晰**，观点和观点之间的衔接恰当。

4. 运用**合适的词汇**和**多样的句式**，清楚地传达观点意思。

5. **熟练掌握标准书面英语**的写作习惯，但仍存在一些**细小错误**。

解 析

5 分的评分标准不论从哪一个角度讲其实都是 6 分的弱化版，所以大家只需要以 6 分的要求为目标努力就行了。所谓"求上得中，求中得下"，只有把目标定得高一些，才更有动力。

值得注意的是，**得到 5 分的一个前提是，要按照具体性指令来写**。这一点和 6 分相同。

【Score 4 】

In addressing the **specific task directions**, a 4 paper presents a **competent** analysis of the issue and conveys meaning with **acceptable clarity**.

A typical paper in this category exhibits the following characteristics:

1. It presents a **clear** position on the issue in accordance with the assigned task.

2. It develops the position with **relevant reasons** and/or **examples**.

3. It is **adequately focused** and **organized**.

4. It demonstrates sufficient control of language to express ideas with **reasonable clarity**.

5. It **generally** demonstrates control of the conventions of **standard written English** but may have **some errors**.

中文翻译

在照应具体性指令的基础上，4 分的文章对原 Issue 题目进行了**足够的**分析，且比较清楚地传词达意。

典型的 4 分文章具有如下特征：

1. 根据题目要求，对原 Issue 题目给出**清楚**的立场。

2. 在展开立场时，运用了**相关的推理**和/或**事例**。

3. **全文有焦点**，**组织基本清晰**。

4. 能**比较清晰**地传达观点意思，展示出对语言足够的驾驭能力。

5. 能够**基本**掌握标准书面英语的写作习惯，但仍存在**一些错误**。

解　析

4 分的评分标准其实是 5 分的进一步弱化版。如：4 分标准已经不要求大家的观点深刻，而只是观点清楚即可；推理与事例也不再需要严谨并具有说服力，而只需要相关。所以，Issue 取得 4 分并非遥不可及之事。

同样值得注意的是，**得到 4 分的一个前提是，要按照具体性指令来写**。

【 Score 3 】

A 3 paper demonstrates **some competence in addressing the specific task directions**, in analyzing the issue, and in conveying meaning but is **obviously flawed**.

A typical paper in this category exhibits **ONE OR MORE** of the following characteristics:

1. It is **vague** or **limited** in addressing the specific task directions and in presenting or developing a position on the issue.
2. It is **weak** in the use of relevant reasons or examples, or relies largely on **unsupported claims**.
3. It is **poorly focused** and/or **poorly organized**.
4. It has problems in language and sentence structure that result in **a lack of clarity**.
5. It contains **occasional major errors** or **frequent minor errors** in grammar, usage, or mechanics that can **interfere with meaning**.

中文翻译

3 分文章**对具体性指令有一定的照应**，对原 Issue 题目也有一定的分析，并且能够在一定程度上传词达意，但是文章**存在明显的缺陷**。

典型的 3 分文章具有以下的**一个或者多个**特征：

1. 文章对具体性指令的照应，以及在传达和发展立场时显得**不够且比较模糊**。
2. 文章中**几乎没有**相关的推理或例证，或是**观点几乎没有支持**。
3. 全文**焦点不明**并且/或者**组织不清**。
4. 文章在语言和句式上存在问题，以至于**语意不明**。
5. 文章存在语法、用法和技法方面的**一些重大错误**或**大量细小错误**，以至于**表意不明**。

解　析

3 分评分标准的评分维度其实和之前的评分标准类似，但有两点需要注意：其一，所有维度的特征都转向负向评价；其二，**这些特征中只要满足一个，考生的文章就会被判为 3 分**。这一点尤其需要大家引起注意，不要在任何一个方面粗心大意，让自己的文章被判 3 分。

另外，**3 分及其以下分数的一个共同特征是：都没有很好地照应具体性指令的要求**。具体性指令一直是考生的一个盲点，从评分标准可以看出，文章很容易就踏进了 3 分的泥沼。但换句话说，如果考生的英语基础不错，再稍微注意一下具体性指令的要求，就很容易突破 3 分、冲向 4 分甚至更高的分数。

需要额外提醒一下，虽然很多同学（特别是理工科的同学）只求 3 分，事实上很多同学凭借 3 分的写作分数也去了国外。然而，这样的分数虽然可能不会成为大家踏进美国大学的致命的绊脚石，但却清楚表明大家在写作上存在着很大的缺陷。熟悉 GRE 写作分数的同学就会知道，3 分的分数表示该考生只打败了全球范围内 10% 左右的对手，这样的写作水平是远远不能满足研究生院的正常写作要求（包括日常作业、科研报告以及毕业论文等）的。因此，**强烈建议大家在去国外之前努力提升学术英语的写作能力**，才能更好地适应美国大学高强度的学术生活。

【Score 2】

A 2 paper **largely disregards the specific task directions** and/or demonstrates serious weaknesses in analytical writing.

A typical paper in this category exhibits **ONE OR MORE** of the following characteristics:

1. It is **unclear** or **seriously limited** in addressing the specific task directions and in presenting or developing a position on the issue.
2. It provides **few**, if any, relevant reasons or examples in support of its claims.
3. It is **unfocused** and/or **disorganized**.
4. It has serious problems in language and sentence structure that **frequently interfere with meaning**.
5. It contains serious errors in grammar, usage, or mechanics that **frequently obscure meaning**.

中文翻译

2 分文章对具体性指令基本没有任何照应，并且 / 或者在分析性写作方面存在重大问题。

典型的 2 分文章具有以下的**一个或者多个**特征：

1. 文章对具体性指令的照应，以及在传达和发展立场时显得**模糊不清**或**严重不足**。
2. 文章中**几乎没有任何**相关的推理或例证以证明其观点。
3. 全文**无焦点**并且/或者**无组织**。
4. 文章在语言和句式上存在重大问题，**严重影响意思传达**。
5. 文章存在语法、用法和技法方面的**重大错误**，使**表意严重不清**。

解　析

　　2 分文章在诸多维度上呈现出比 3 分文章更加不足的能力。2 分文章的基本特征是：没有照应具体性指令来写，并且观点肤浅，论证无力，有大量语言错误。

【 Score 1 】

A 1 paper demonstrates **fundamental deficiencies** in analytical writing.

A typical paper in this category exhibits **ONE OR MORE** of the following characteristics:

1. It provides **little or no evidence of understanding** the issue.
2. It provides **little or no evidence of the ability to develop an organized response**.
3. It has severe problems in language and sentence structure that **persistently interfere with meaning**.
4. It contains **pervasive errors** in grammar, usage, or mechanics that **result in incoherence**.

中文翻译

　　1 分文章在分析性写作方面存在**根本性不足**。

　　典型的 1 分文章具有以下的**一个或者多个**特征：

1. 文章**几乎没有理解**原 Issue 题目。
2. 文章中**几乎没有表现出任何组织语言的能力**。
3. 文章在语言和句式上存在重大问题，**持续影响意思传达**。
4. 文章存在**大量语法、用法和技法方面的错误**，严重影响文章连贯性。

解　析

　　诙谐一点说，1 分的文章同 6 分的文章一样难以企及。可以说只要具备了正常的写作能力的同学（通过了国内大学的四六级英语考试），都不会得 1 分。

【 Score 0 】

A 0 paper is off topic (i.e., provides no evidence of an attempt to respond to the assigned topic), written in a foreign language, merely copies the topic, consists of only keystroke characters, or is illegible or nonverbal.

中文翻译

0 分文章完全偏离题目（或没有表现出任何答题意愿）；用非英语写作；单纯照抄题目；文章为胡乱敲击键盘所得；文章不可读或非语言。

解　析

考生之所以得 0 分，并非其语言水平不足，而是态度不端。0 分文章的特征是：不写或乱写。

第二节　Argument 评分标准分析

Argument 部分的评分标准主要围绕以下三点：

1. 是否按照 Direction 来写

2. 文章组织是否有逻辑

3. 语言如何

和 Issue 相比，Argument 部分也同样注重对 Direction 的照应。同时，Argument 还要求考生文章组织具有逻辑性，这就需要注意到**题目本身的**推理过程和行文逻辑，并在文章中对其加以照应。

下面是具体分数标准的解析：

【Score 6】

In addressing the specific task directions, a 6 response presents a **cogent, well-articulated** examination of the argument and **conveys meaning skillfully**.

A typical response in this category exhibits the following characteristics:

1. It **clearly identifies aspects** of the argument **relevant to the assigned task** and examines them **insightfully**.
2. It **develops ideas cogently**, **organizes them logically**, and connects them with **clear transitions**.
3. It provides **compelling and thorough support** for its main points.
4. It conveys ideas fluently and precisely, using **effective vocabulary** and **sentence variety**.
5. It demonstrates facility with the conventions of **standard written English** (i.e., grammar, usage, and mechanics) but may have **minor errors**.

中文翻译

在照应具体性指令的基础上，6 分的文章对原 Argument 题目进行了**具有说服力的、清楚的分析，且运用（多种）技巧传词达意**。

典型的 6 分文章具有如下特征：

1. **根据题目要求，清楚地识别出了原 Argument 题目的各方面**，并对其进行了**具有洞察力**的分析。
2. **对观点的发展清晰有力，对观点的组织富有逻辑**，并且用**清晰的逻辑连接词**连接各观点。
3. 各主要观点都有**透彻而有力的支撑**。
4. 运用**有效的词汇和多样的句式**，流畅、准确地传达观点意思。
5. **熟练掌握标准书面英语**的写作习惯（语法、用法、技法等），但仍存在一些细小错误。

解　析

和 Issue 部分一样，Argument 部分的 6 分评分标准也应该是我们详细研读并且力争达到的。有一句英文谚语说："Jump for the Sun, at least you land on the Moon"，大家不妨用这句话激励自己，向 6 分发起冲击。

下面我们来看一下对评分标准中关键概念的解析：

specific task direction：**照应具体性指令是得 6 分的最基本的要求，这也是 5 分和 4 分标准的要求。且与 Issue 相比，Argument 中 Direction 对大家行文的影响更大。对 Direction 的具体照应方法详见第五章。**

convey meaning skillfully：与 Issue 相比，Argument 并不要求我们的论证方法丰富多变，**而是要求我们给出紧贴 Direction 的论证。**

clearly identify aspects of the argument：清楚地识别原 Argument 的各方面。这里的 aspect（方面）指的是原 Argument 的推理过程当中的一些重要元素，如**结论（conclusion）、支持结论的事实（fact）或证据（evidence，证据本身也是事实的一种）、对事实的解释（explanation）以及作者的推理过程所依赖的假设（assumption）。**

relevant to the assigned task：这一点和上面一点一脉相承，也至关重要。这两点告诉我们：不仅要识别出原 Argument 当中的各方面（aspect），还应该识别出和这道题（the assigned task）相关的方面。

一道题目是由题干和 Direction 组成的，也就是说，**我们还要识别出那些和 Direction 相关的方面**。结合第五章的 Direction 的讲解大家就会明白，如果原 Direction 是让我们从证据（evidence）角度切入，那我们就应该重点识别出原 Argument 的证据；而如果 Direction 要求我们着重讨论原 Argument 的假设（assumption），那我们的文章就不应该再围绕证据，而应该围绕假设来展开。**因此，识别出原 Argument 的各要素只是第一步，之后我们还应该根据 Direction 的侧重来筛选这些要素，只留下和 Direction 相关的要素并对其进行审视和讨论。**

（examine them）insightfully：在完成了以上两步，即从原 Argument 中挑选出符合 Direction 的元素之后，就需要进行对其进行审视和讨论（examine）了。这种审视和讨论要做到 insightful，**不仅要求正确认识这些元素本身，还需要认识到这些元素之间的关系**。这就需要结合逻辑图对原 Argument 进行分析。对逻辑图的使用大家可以参照第五章。

develop ideas cogently, organize them logically：清晰有力地发展观点，有逻辑地组织观点。大多数考生对待 Argument 的策略是：找到一个逻辑漏洞之后，用一段话去写这个错误；找到下一个逻辑漏洞之后，另开一个新的段落。如果整个文章中有五个漏洞，而考生的时间又不够，这时考生可能就会选择其中的三个进行分析。这样的文章最后得分普遍不高。而考生对此的反省可能是：如果我把五个漏洞分析完全，可能分数就上去了。然而事实并非如此。**究其原因，是因为大家还是在寻找 Argument 中零碎的逻辑漏洞，而没有把它看作一个完整的推理过程。大家所找出来的错误都是各自孤立的，彼此之间没有任何呼应，更没有形成一个封闭的体系。**对此，我们提倡的应对方法是：**画出逻辑推理图**。大家可以随意参见后面的任何一篇 Argument 范文，在文章之后都附有一个逻辑推理图。而文章就是在这个逻辑推理图的基础之上构建起来的。这样才能让文章的发展脉络完全对应原 Argument 的脉络。这样的分析才是有力（cogent）、富有逻辑（logical）的分析。

clear transitions：Argument 的写作对逻辑连接是异常重视的。**保证句内句间的逻辑本身没有问题之后，大家可以尽量使用正确的逻辑连接词来展现逻辑关系。**下面总结了常见的逻辑连接表达。

因果关系：therefore; thereby; hence; thus; accordingly; consequently
注意：以上的词都是副词，因此都不能连接两个完整的句子。

并列关系：moreover; in addition; furthermore; likewise; similarly; also; besides; namely; firstly; secondly; thirdly
注意：以上的词都是副词，因此都不能连接两个完整的句子。

转折关系：but; yet; however; nevertheless; nonetheless; conversely
注意：but 和 yet 表示转折时可以做连词，可以连接两个完整的句子；而 however 做连词时表示的是"不论…"的意思，如"However hard it is, I will try"，但它在表示转折的"然而"时，是副词，不能连接两个完整的句子；其余的词都是副词，都不能连接两个完整的句子。

compelling and thorough support：所谓透彻而有力的支持，无非包括事理支持和事例支持，但不论是哪一种支持，**都要紧密贴合 Direction 的要求**。因此，请详细解读第五章对 Direction 的讲解即可。

effective vocabulary：这一点和 Issue 部分的讲解相同。

sentence variety：这一点和 Issue 部分的讲解相同。

standard written English：这一点和 Issue 部分的讲解相同。

minor errors：这一点和 Issue 部分的讲解相同。

【Score 5】

In addressing the **specific task directions**, a 5 response presents a **generally thoughtful**, **well-developed** examination of the argument and **conveys meaning clearly**.

A typical response in this category exhibits the following characteristics:

1. It **clearly identifies aspects** of the argument **relevant to the assigned task** and examines them in a **generally perceptive** way.
2. It **develops ideas clearly**, **organizes them logically**, and connects them with **appropriate transitions**.
3. It offers **generally thoughtful and thorough support** for its main points.
4. It conveys ideas clearly and well, using **appropriate vocabulary** and **sentence variety**.
5. It demonstrates facility with the conventions of **standard written English** but may have **minor errors**.

📝 中文翻译

在照应具体性指令的基础上，5 分的文章对原 Argument 题目进行了**比较缜密的、发展充分的分析**，且**清楚地传词达意**。

典型的 5 分文章具有如下特征：

1. **根据题目要求，清楚地识别出了原 Argument 题目的各方面**，并对其进行了**比较具有洞察力**的分析。
2. **对观点的发展清晰，对观点的组织富有逻辑**，并且用**合适的逻辑连接词**连接各观点。
3. 各主要观点都有**比较缜密而透彻**的支撑。
4. 运用**合适的词汇和多样的句式**，清楚地传达观点意思。
5. 熟练掌握**标准书面英语**的写作习惯，但仍存在一些**细小错误**。

📝 解　析

和 Issue 部分一样，Argument 的 5 分评分标准也是 6 分的弱化版。大家可以直接以 6 分为奋斗目标。但要注意，**5 分的评分标准仍然要求我们紧密贴合 Direction 的要求来写**。

【Score 4】

In addressing the **specific task directions**, a 4 response presents a **competent** examination of the argument and **conveys meaning with acceptable clarity**.

A typical response in this category exhibits the following characteristics:

1. It **identifies and examines aspects** of the argument **relevant to the assigned task** but may also discuss some **extraneous points**.

2. It **develops and organizes ideas satisfactorily** but **may not connect them with transitions**.

3. It **supports its main points adequately** but may be **uneven in its support**.

4. It demonstrates sufficient control of language to convey ideas with **reasonable clarity**.

5. It **generally** demonstrates control of the conventions of **standard written English** but may have **some errors**.

中文翻译

在照应具体性指令的基础上，4 分的文章对原 Argument 题目进行了**足够的**分析，且**比较清楚地传词达意**。

典型的 4 分文章具有如下特征：

1. **根据题目要求，识别并分析了原 Argument 题目的各方面**，但同时可能有一些**无关的讨论**。
2. **对观点的发展和组织比较好**，但**没有用逻辑连接词衔接各观点**。
3. **主要观点有一定的支撑，**但部分地方尚显不足。
4. 文章体现出作者对英语的足够的把控能力，**能够比较清楚地**传达观点意思。
5. **基本**掌握标准书面英语的写作习惯，但仍存在一些错误。

解 析

4 分的评分标准实则是 5 分的弱化版，但其中有两点需要引起我们的注意：

1. 4 分文章的一个典型特征是：对具体性指令有一定照应，**但同时文章的部分内容已经偏离了要求**。如 Direction 要求从 evidence 的角度切入，但考生的文章却有一部分是在探讨 assumption。
2. 为了避免得 4 分，**大家一定要加强逻辑连接词的使用**。

【Score 3】

A 3 response demonstrates **some competence in addressing the specific task directions**, in examining the argument, and in conveying meaning but is **obviously flawed**.

A typical response in this category exhibits **ONE OR MORE** of the following characteristics:

1. It **does not identify or examine most of the aspects** of the argument **relevant to the assigned task**, although **some relevant examination of the argument is present**.

2. It mainly discusses **tangential or irrelevant matters**, or **reasons poorly**.

3. It is **limited** in the logical development and organization of ideas.

4. It offers **support of little relevance and value** for its main points.
5. It has problems in language and sentence structure that result in **a lack of clarity**.
6. It contains **occasional major errors** or **frequent minor errors** in grammar, usage, or mechanics that can **interfere with meaning**.

中文翻译

3 分文章**对具体性指令有一定的照应**，对原 Issue 题目也有一定的分析，并且能够在一定程度上传词达意，但是文章**存在明显的缺陷**。

典型的 3 分文章具有以下的**一个或者多个**特征：
1. 虽然对原 Argument 题目有**一些相关的分析**，但并未根据题目要求识别并分析原 Argument 题目的**绝大多数方面**。
2. 文章主要在讨论**和题目不相关的话题**，或是**推理不足**。
3. 观点的发展和组织**不够有逻辑**。
4. 主要观点**缺少相关的或有价值的支撑**。
5. 文章在语言和句式上存在问题，以致**语意不明**。
6. 文章存在语法、用法和技法方面的**一些重大错误**或**大量细小错误**，以致于**表意不明**。

解 析

虽然 Argument 文章得三分的原因通常有很多，但很大程度上可以归结为没有照应 Direction 的写作要求，具体体现如下：
1. 没有识别出原 Argument 当中的诸要素，如 evidence, conclusion, explanation, assumption 等。
2. 虽然识别出了原 Argument 当中的诸要素，但没有根据 Direction 的要求对其进行筛选。
3. 完全没有按 Direction 的要求，而是按照老 GRE 的思路展开文章。即：找出逻辑错误（"臆造因果"、"错误类比"、"问题数据"等），批判逻辑错误。

因此，为了避免得 3 分，考生虽然要在语言、文章的组织上下功夫，**但最关键的一点还是不能偏离 Direction 的要求**。

【Score 2】

A 2 response **largely disregards the specific task directions** and/or demonstrates serious weaknesses in analytical writing.

A typical response in this category exhibits **ONE OR MORE** of the following characteristics:
1. It does not present an examination based on logical analysis but may instead **present the writer's own views** on the subject.
2. It **does not follow the directions** for the assigned task.

3. It **does not develop ideas**, or **is poorly organized** and **illogical**.

4. It provides **little**, if any, relevant or reasonable **support** for its main points.

5. It has serious problems in language and sentence structure that **frequently interfere with meaning**.

6. It contains serious errors in grammar, usage, or mechanics that **frequently obscure meaning**.

中文翻译

2 分文章**对具体性指令基本没有任何照应**，并且 / 或者在分析性写作方面存在重大问题。

典型的 2 分文章具有以下的**一个或者多个特征**：

1. 文章缺少逻辑性分析，而是在**陈述作者自身对于这个话题的看法**。

2. **没有照应具体性指令的要求**。

3. **对观点没有任何发展**，或是**组织混乱**。

4. 主要观点（几乎）**没有任何相关的或合理的支撑**。

5. 文章在语言和句式上存在重大问题，**严重影响意思传达**。

6. 文章存在语法、用法和技法方面的**重大错误**，使**表意严重不清**。

解 析

对 Argument 本质没有了解的考生最容易犯 2 分禁忌中的一个错误，**即没有分析原 Argument 的论证过程，而是对 Argument 中的话题发表自己的看法**。如：原 Argument 的论点是某大学要采用网络授课的形式，作者为了支持这一论点进行了一系列论证。而有的考生可能并没有分析这些论证是否合理或完善，而是发表自己对网络授课的诸多见解，如"网络授课能促进教育资源共享"、"网络授课能节约资源"等。这样的写法是 Issue 的写法，而不满足 Argument 的要求，请一定切记勿犯此类错误。

【 Score 1 】

A 1 response demonstrates **fundamental deficiencies** in analytical writing.

A typical response in this category exhibits **ONE OR MORE** of the following characteristics:

1. It provides **little or no evidence of understanding** the argument.

2. It is **extremely brief and/or disorganized**, providing little evidence of an organized response.

3. It has severe problems in language and sentence structure that **persistently interfere with meaning**.

4. It contains **pervasive errors** in grammar, usage, or mechanics that **result in incoherence**.

中文翻译

1 分文章在分析性写作方面存在**根本性不足**。

典型的 1 分文章具有以下的**一个或者多个**特征：

1. 文章**几乎没有理解**原 Argument 题目。
2. 文章中几乎没有表现出任何组织语言的能力，文章**非常简短并且/或者无组织结构**。
3. 文章在语言和句式上存在重大问题，**持续影响意思传达**。
4. 文章存在**大量**语法、用法和技法方面的**错误，严重影响文章连贯性**。

解　　析

这里的讲解同 Issue 部分。

【Score 0】

A 0 paper is off topic, written in a foreign language, merely copies the topic, consists of only keystroke characters, is illegible, or is nonverbal.

中文翻译

0 分文章完全偏离题目；用非英语写作；单纯照抄题目；文章为胡乱敲击键盘所得；文章不可读或非语言。

解　　析

这里的讲解同 Issue 部分。

第五章　具体性指令与范文精讲

- **GRE 作文改革之后加入了 14 种具体性指令。**
- **每种具体性指令都有特殊的照应方法。**
- **不按具体性指令写最多只有 3 分。**
- **具体性指令会影响整篇文章的布局和行文。**

以上所有要点，都将在本章中一一呈现。

老 GRE 写作样题：

题干：

A nation should require all its students to study the same national curriculum until they enter college rather than allow schools in different parts of the nation to determine which academic courses to offer.

新 GRE 写作样题：

题干：

A nation should require all of its students to study the same national curriculum until they enter college.

具体性指令：

Write a response in which you discuss the extent to which you agree or disagree with the claim. In developing and supporting your position, be sure to address the most compelling reasons and/or examples that could be used to challenge your position.

对比可见，新 GRE 中加入了具体性指令。

但广大考生往往忽略了具体性指令的要求，这也导致最终分数不超过 3 分。

但很多同学仍然对此没有察觉，即使有所察觉也可能苦于找不到应对之策，因此这一章我们会用详尽的篇幅来精讲这些具体性指令。

自 2011 年 8 月 GRE 考试进行改革之后，作文部分中的一个显著变化是 Direction（具体性指令，即题目下方的几行对写作要求的说明性文字）的加入。Issue 部分加入了 6 种 Direction，Argument 部分加入了 8 种 Direction。

Direction 可以翻译为"具体性指令"或"写作指导"。随着 Direction 的加入，评分标准也相应改变。在前一章中我们已经提到，**如果对 Direction 照应得不够，文章的最终得分不会超过 3 分**。因此，虽然 ETS 在 GRE 写作部分中加入 Direction 的本意是帮助考生在学术写作方面拓展思路，指导考生从比较具体的角度破题，但现实情况是考生因为对 Direction 没有引起足够的重视或者完全忽视其存在，导致最后的得分不尽如人意。因此，在这一章中，我们会详细解析每一种 Direction，并且在讲解之后附上范文，让考生对其有更深入的理解。

第一节　Issue 具体性指令与范文精讲

1 "是非判断类" Direction

Write a response in which you discuss **the extent** to which you agree or disagree with the statement and explain your reasoning for the position you take. In developing and supporting your position, you should consider ways in which the statement **might or might not hold true** and explain how these considerations shape your position.

中文翻译

写一篇文章，在这篇文章中讨论你在**多大程度**上同意或者不同意题目中的陈述，解释你所采取的立场的理由。在发展和支持你的立场的过程中，你应该考虑这个陈述**成立或者不成立**的情况，并且解释这些情况如何影响你的立场。

讲　解

这类 Direction 所对应题目的语气通常是"作判断"或者"下定义"，是在讨论某一件事情的"是"与"非"，而 Direction 则是要求我们表明：我们在多大程度上同意这种"判断"或者"定义"，并且说明我们什么时候同意、什么时候反对。**这种 Direction 对我们在行文的内容和立场上并没有本质上的影响，我们可以把它视为"最安全"的一种 Direction。**

另外，从"extent"这个词可以看出，我们可以 100% 同意题目观点，也可以 50% 同意题目观点。亦即：**ETS 对我们所采取的立场并不看重。这一点适用于 Issue 部分的所有 Direction。**

讲解浓缩版

"最安全"的 Direction，对我们写作并无特别要求。

学术写作拓展

在学术写作里，对某一问题的"是非曲直"做出自己的判断并且用比较规范的书面语言表达出自己的立场是最基本的要求。这种 Direction 就是对应这样一种要求。

例如，大家以后将要写到的每一篇论文其实都是在讨论一个问题的是非曲直，《日本前卫书法家与传统的决裂比中国书法家更明显》，《储氢材料的开发会推动电动汽车的发展》，诸如此类。对这样一些命题采取何种态度，理由是什么，如何阐述，大家可以通过这一种 Direction 略作感受。

例题举证

As we acquire more knowledge, things do not become more comprehensible, but more complex and mysterious.

Write a response in which you discuss the extent to which you agree or disagree with the statement and explain your reasoning for the position you take. In developing and supporting your position, you should consider ways in which the statement might or might not hold true and explain how these considerations shape your position.

比如这道题，我们可以列出如下的提纲：

> **总立场**：有保留地反对题目。
>
> **分论点 1**（同意题目）：宇宙万物往往比我们想象得要更为复杂。我们也的确遇到了很多靠现在的知识无法解决的问题。
>
> **分论点 2**（反对题目）：以前被我们认为很简单的事物现在变得更加复杂，这刚好证明了我们在认识事物的道路上又前进了一步。所以不是事物变复杂，而是我们的认知在完善。
>
> **分论点 3**（反对题目）：就理论上来讲，我们终将穷尽宇宙的奥秘。而题目的观点极易让我们陷入不可知论的泥沼之中。

如提纲所示，我们表达了我们在多大程度上同意或反对题目的观点（有保留地反对），并且以三个分论段分别说明了我们同意或者反对的具体情况。所以这个提纲是符合 Direction 要求的。

题库范文

（注：范文题目前的序号与第二章"GRE 写作题库分类"中的序号一一对应。ETS 官网给出的题目本无序号，为了方便读者查阅题目，所以本书为题目标明了序号。）

55 In order for any work of art—for example, a film, a novel, a poem, or a song—to have merit, it must be understandable to most people.

Write a response in which you discuss the extent to which you agree or disagree with the statement and explain your reasoning for the position you take. In developing and supporting your position, you should consider ways in which the statement might or might not hold true and explain how these considerations shape your position.

Puzzled by perplexing paintings, we are nevertheless enamored by a painter's impressive strokes. And while the meaning of a poem may elude us, its emotional expression does not pale. Such ambiguity in comprehensibility and complexity of art constantly occurs in various art works. While the author declares art's intelligibility to be paramount, I appreciate obscure art works as well. The seeming obscureness actually mirrors the artists' dignity as well as the affluence of both the expression and representation of the artists' mental worlds. All of these characteristics contribute to the irreplaceable merits of art.

I have to admit, on the one hand, that lucidity abounds in a great amount of popular artwork, from a Hollywood action movie to a catchy street song. Thanks to the work's clarity in terms of content and expression, people come to know it, accept it and, finally, are inclined to spread it. This characteristic of being understandable enables artwork, which used to be exclusive to the noble and upper class, to flourish in public and thereby attain fresh significance in modern society.

Artists, however, do not always have to pander to the market, sometimes even at the cost of sacrificing art's integrity and uniqueness. Neither is it possible that every single individual would have an equal aesthetic appreciation of the works created by a great master with peerless skills and special personal experience.

While I cannot turn a blind eye to copious popular movies, songs and TV shows which emphasize the market over grace and elusiveness, I am hesitant to hastily generalize all kinds of art in the same way. Pandering to the public may gain handsome profits for a while, but the resulting artwork will soon lose its value due to the absence of enduring attraction. For supporting examples, let us turn to popular artwork: an album with a flamboyant cover, or a film lavishly decorated with advanced visual technology. Have they gained enviable popularity in the public? Possibly. Has their adulatory catering to the public taste earned them abiding merits? Hardly. The very fact that these music and film companies must conjure up various new productions one after another ironically reveals the producers' awareness of the evanescent value of their works and their trepidation of losing the market due to such fleeting value.

More importantly, the possession of merit does not necessarily require artwork to be intelligible. In fact, art's merit is primarily embodied in the artist's skill mastery, as well as by the representation of his/her inner world. Such skills frequently remain exclusive to the artist due to its opaqueness; likewise, the artist's unique personal experience also alienates him/her from those who do not share similar stories. The artwork, therefore, is not always understandable to most people, but under no circumstance does this complexity hinder the artwork from achieving its intrinsic worth. Picasso's "Guernica", one of many possible examples, sufficiently supports my claim. Prestigious for its adept expression of cubism and surrealism, as well as its vivid portrayal of the painter's mental agony and fury about violence, "Guernica" has achieved worldwide fame. However, the abstruseness of this work's expression precludes common appreciation; similarly, people with no experience under the devil's trample fail to sympathize with the painter. Nevertheless, few dispute "Guernica's" arcane expression and theme, but applaud it as a highly meritorious masterpiece.

To summarize, while we may feel a sense of closeness with the artists when previously elusive artwork becomes accessible, such a switch in most scenarios takes place at the expense of art's integrity. To gain a better understanding of art, we should better foster our aesthetic appreciation, rather than juvenilely demanding the convergence of elegance and mediocrity. (608 words)

中文翻译

尽管曾经为一些费解的画作感到困惑，但我们仍会爱上画家独到的笔触。尽管诗歌的意义有时让我们难以理解，但它的情绪影响力并不会因此而失色。这种艺术创作中"理解的模糊性"与"内涵的复杂性"在许多作品当中都有呈现。尽管作者称艺术创作中的"清晰易懂"最为重要，但与此同时，我也不得不强调"模糊朦胧"的艺术价值。事实上，这种表面上的"模糊性"恰好能够体现作品的脱俗品质以及作者对自我精神世界的丰富表达。

然而，从另一个角度来看，我必须承认"清晰易懂"这个优点存在于大量的流行作品当中——从好莱坞的动作电影到朗朗上口的街头歌谣。由于作品在内容和表达上存在"清晰易懂"的优势，人们很快能够理解、接受并乐意将其最终推广开来。这种便于理解的优势将那些曾经被贵族和上流社会所专享的艺术作品带入公众视野，它们在经历繁荣发展的同时并开始在现代社会中取得显著地位。

不过，艺术家们一般不大可能去迎合市场的口味，更不可能为此去牺牲作品中的艺术追求与独特性。同样不可能的还有，面对这些承载着超凡技艺和独特个人经历的伟大作品，不同的受众能具有相同的审美品味。

尽管我无法回避这样一个事实：那些信奉"市场重于高雅和模糊性"的流行电影、歌曲和电视剧正在不断获得更多的关注，但我很难认同这种试图"将所有艺术统归为一类"的做法。过度迎合市场需求在短时间内固然可以带来可观的收益，但放弃对创作风格的坚守将导致作者失去其一贯的吸引力，进而导致作品中核心价值的丧失。拿流行艺术品举例：一张有着花哨外观的唱片，或者一部充斥着先进视觉技术的华丽电影，它们可以获得可观的流行度吗？有可能。但是，它们对市场需求的一味迎合就能够帮助他们取得持续的优势吗？不太可能。讽刺的是，这些唱片和电影公司必须不断推出新产品的行为恰好反映了他们深知这些作品价值匮乏，以及对因此而被市场淘汰的担忧。

更为重要的是，想要获得艺术价值，并不意味着必须使作品简单易懂。事实上，作品的价值主要体现在艺术家的高超技艺及其内心世界的生动呈现。而由于其专业性，这些技巧很难被普通大众所理解；同样，作者特有的人生经历也疏远了那些缺乏类似经历的受众。因此，艺术作品并不总能被大部分人理解；但可以确定的是，这种复杂性并不会阻碍作品实现其内在价值。比如，毕加索的《格尔尼卡》就可以很好地佐证我的观点。由于对立体主义与超现实主义的娴熟运用，以及作者生动地呈现了面对暴力时的痛苦与愤怒，《格尔尼卡》在世界范围内赢得广泛美誉。但是，作品的复杂却让大众难以理解；未能亲历邪恶势力折磨的观众也难以切身体会作者的创作背景。然而，《格尔尼卡》并未因其"模糊朦胧"的表达方式与主题而受到诟病；相反，人们对此纷纷给予极高的赞许。

总的来说，如果将"模糊朦胧"的艺术作品转为"清晰易懂"，似乎能够让我们更加接近创作者；但是，这种转变往往会以牺牲艺术品的脱俗品质为代价。因此，为了能够更好地欣赏艺术，我们应该培养更好的审美品味，而非幼稚地要求"转雅为俗。"

文章解析与点评

在这篇文章中，我们希望带着大家一起分析：什么样的事例才是具有说服力的（persuasive）。请大家着重看第五段。

第五段一共有三层，第一层是第一句，也就是这一段的中心句；第二层是从 in fact 到 intrinsic worth 是对中心句的事理论证；接着是从 Picasso 到这段末尾，即对中心句的事例论证。其中，事例论证非常紧密地贴合了事理论证，让全段更有说服力。事例论证对事理论证的贴合主要体现在以下几方面：

1. 内容和推理的一致性。
事理论证说了四层意思：
① 艺术作品的价值主要体现在作品的技艺和作者内心世界的展现中。
② 作品的技艺通常高深难懂，普通人难以理解。
③ 作品所体现的作者的内心世界也往往让没有相似经历的人不知所云。
④ 这样的作品往往让普通人难以企及，但这并不阻碍该作品价值的实现。

相对应的，事例部分同样也说了四层意思：
① 毕加索的《格尔尼卡》以其高超的立体主义和超现实主义，以及画家面对暴力的痛苦而愤怒的内心世界的展现而闻名。

② 《格尔尼卡》技艺的晦涩让普通人难以理解。

③ 并且，没有经历过邪恶势力折磨的人也很难与作者有共鸣。

④ 但人们不但不责备《格尔尼卡》晦涩的手法和曲折的主题，反而把它奉为价值倾城的经典之作。

事例部分和事理部分的推理过程和主要内容完全一致，这就使事例最大程度地发挥了其辅佐事理进行论证的效果。

2. 语言上的照应。

这一点主要体现在用词上。在事理部分出现过的一系列关键概念，如"难懂（opaqueness）"，"理解（understand）"在事例说明中不断进行着同义改写，如"难懂（abstruseness, arcane）"，"理解（sympathize with, common appreciation）"等。

另外，事理说明中相当关键的逻辑连接词如"but"，"likewise"等也呼应着事例说明中的"however"，"similarly"。事例论证通过这样同义改写的方式对事理论证进行照应，一方面能让这二者在内容和逻辑上浑然一体，另一方面也可以增加语言表达的多样性。

综上，要举出具有说服力的例子，我们必须要做到：1. 使事例和事理在内容与逻辑上保持一致；2. 语言上进行同义改写。

11 People's behavior is largely determined by forces not of their own making.

Write a response in which you discuss the extent to which you agree or disagree with the statement and explain your reasoning for the position you take. In developing and supporting your position, you should consider ways in which the statement might or might not hold true and explain how these considerations shape your position.

Human behaviors are interesting in that they can either be spontaneous or driven by external forces. Opinions vary greatly regarding the importance of these factors. The statement suggests that our behaviors are largely determined by external forces rather than our own qualities. While it may be true that external forces can greatly shape our behavior, from my perspective, our own making also plays a role that cannot be overlooked. What is more, since external and internal forces have distinct natures and mechanisms to affect human behaviors, any attempt to claim one is more influential than the other is overly simplistic.

External forces can play a critical role in regulating human behavior, because human beings are social animals and respond to external stimuli. Therefore, social norms determine to a large extent what can be or cannot be done. The reason why humans are a social species can be traced back to ancient times, when individuals were vulnerable to nature's elements. When they acted collectively, however, humans became much stronger which substantially increased their chance of survival. Over time, being a part of a group or tribe became a survival advantage, with banishment often equaling demise. In this sense, one would face the risk of perishing alone if he or she defied social norms. Even though modern tools have drastically increased the odds of survival, we are still emotionally attached to society, the modern tribe we belong to, and yearn for social recognition. Some of our basic motivations, such as aspiring to become wealthy, beautiful, intelligent, or powerful, can be explained by this desire. This yearning also prevents us from behaving outside of socially acceptable norms.

That being said, I must point out that humans are mentally capable of making choices of their own will and are physically capable of executing these choices. This is particularly true when our choices involve little, if any, interaction with the external environment. In this case, our choices do not conflict with societal guidelines. If one wants to pick up a restaurant for dinner in the Midtown of New York City, for example, there are many choices at his or her disposal: French, Asian, American, and Mexican and so on. This choice is not determined by external factors, but rather depends on a person's own will. Examples like these suggest that when our behavior has little to do with our social environment, we can and will make choices that reflect our own volition.

From the discussion above, it is clear that both external and internal forces are capable of determining human behavior, and most of the time we cannot disregard either's influence. But neither can we compare their importance. In some cases, external forces determine what needs to be done but we ultimately decide how to behave while adhering to social norms. For instance, a scientist will be forced to secure funding if his or her laboratory faces financial hardship. Though this necessity is solely determined by external forces, how best to secure those funds is at the scientist's discretion: he or she can seek federal support or form a collaborative relationship with industry. Either way, his or her action is not influenced by external factors. How external and internal forces can jointly shape human behavior has been demonstrated from different perspectives in this response. External forces offer us challenges and stipulate rules which must be followed but solutions are based on internal factors. This makes it difficult to argue that external forces play a more significant role in determining people's behavior.

To sum up, I have demonstrated that both external and internal forces are capable of determining people's behavior. Given the different mechanisms through which external and internal forces shape how we behave, conclusions drawn from a hasty comparison would certainly be oversimplified.
(627 words)

📝 中文翻译

人类的行为是很有趣的，因为他们的行为可能是自发的、可能是由外力驱动的。人们对这些因素的重要性持有不同的看法。题干认为我们的行为很大程度上是由外力而不是我们自身的素质所决定的。虽然外力可以大大塑造我们的行为的观点可能是正确的，但在我看来，我们自身的内在作用也发挥着不可忽视的作用。更重要的是，因为外部和内部力量的本质以及它们影响人类行为的机制截然不同，任何试图宣称一种力量比另一种力量更有影响力的人都过度简化了问题。

外部力量在控制人类行为中可能发挥了关键作用，因为人类是社会性动物，会对外部刺激作出反应。因此，社会规范很大程度上决定了什么能做、什么不能做。人类是一种社会性物种的原因可以追溯到古代，那时个人很容易受到自然因素的影响。然而，当他们集体行动时，人类变得更为强大，这大大增加了他们的生存几率。随着时间的推移，加入一个群体或部落成为了生存优势，被放逐往往意味着死亡。在这个意义上，一个人如果违背社会规范，就会面临孤立的风险。即使现代工具已经大大增加了生存的几率，我们在感情上仍然依附于社会——我们所从属的现代部落——并渴望获得社会认可。这一渴望可以解释我们的一些基本动机，如渴望变得富有、美丽、聪明或强大。这种渴望也阻止了我们进行不被社会规范所接受的行为。

话虽如此，我必须指出人类在精神上有能力出于自己的意愿作出选择，在肉体上有能力执行这些选择。当我们的选择同外在环境几乎没有关系（或只有很少的关系）时，这一点尤其正确。在这种情况下，我们的选择并不会和社会准则产生冲突。例如，如果一个人想在纽约市中心地区找一家餐馆吃晚饭，会有多种选择任他/她挑选：法国菜、亚洲菜、美国菜、墨西哥菜等等。这种选择不是由外部因素决定的，而是取决于一个人的个人意志。这样的例子表明当我们的行为和社会环境无关时，我们可以并愿意做出能反映我们自身意愿的选择。

从上面的讨论可以清楚地看出，外部和内部力量都能决定人的行为，大多数时候我们不能忽视任何一方的影响力。但我们也无法比较它们的重要性。在某些情况下，外部力量决定了我们需要做什么，但在遵守社会规范的同时最终决定如何行事的人还是我们自己。例如，当一个科学家的实验室面临财务困难时，他/她会被迫寻求资金。虽然这种需求完全由外部力量决定，但如何最好地获取资金是由科学家自行决定的：他/她可以寻求联邦政府的支持，或和工业界建立合作关系。无论采取哪种方式，他/她的行为都不只受到外在因素的影响。本文从不同角度证明了外部和内部力量如何共同塑造人类的行为。外部力量提供了挑战、规定了必须遵守的规则，但解决方案是基于内部因素的。这使得我们很难认为外部力量在决定人类的行为中起着更为重要的作用。

总而言之，我已经证明外部力量和内部力量都能决定人类的行为。考虑到外部力量和内部力量塑造我们行为的机制是不同的，从仓促比较中得出的结论显然过度简化了问题。

文章解析与点评

这道题目涉及 AB 两个概念的比较。Issue 题库中有很多比较两个概念的题目，这两个概念通常看上去比较矛盾，如这道题中的 "force" 和 "one's own making"。又如第 123 题 "The best way for a society to prepare its young people for leadership in government, industry, or other fields is by instilling in them a sense of cooperation, not competition." 中的 "cooperation" 和 "competition"。应对这种涉及两种概念作比较的题目，一种简单又不失深刻的写法是：用一段同意 A 概念，另一段同意 B 概念，最后一段阐明 A 和 B 的关系（通常情况下，AB 并不矛盾）。

这篇文章就是采用这样的思路来辩证地讨论了题目所涉及的两个概念。一方面，人类行为必须要受外力束缚，这是由社会规范所决定的；另一方面，人们既可以在心智层面做决定，又可以身体力行地去践行这个决定。而人们最终的决定其实是由内因和外力一起决定的，因此偏废其一的做法无疑是草率的。

另外，这篇文章所提到的 "social norm（社会规范）" 一词是大家应该积累的。社会规范指的是人们社会行为的规矩和准则，是在社会活动和历史进展中逐渐衍生而来的。社会规范是诸多学科共同研究的对象，如心理学、社会科学、人类学、历史学、哲学等。正是因为它在诸多学科中都有着广泛的运用和引用，因此非常适合作为涉及范围广泛的 Issue 文章的理论支持。如与历史相关的 57 题、与法律相关的 21 题和 65 题、与社会心理学相关的 38 题等，在写作中大家都可以援引这一概念。但要注意，大家在查阅这个词语的意义的时候，千万不要图方便而生硬地套用如维基百科等平台上的英文释义，这极容易被判为 "plagiarism"（学术剽窃）。

33 As we acquire more knowledge, things do not become more comprehensible, but more complex and mysterious.

Write a response in which you discuss the extent to which you agree or disagree with the statement and explain your reasoning for the position you take. In developing and supporting your position, you should consider ways in which the statement might or might not hold true and explain how these considerations shape your position.

Since the first human gazed up at the night sky, human beings have never stopped acquiring knowledge and attempting to understand the surrounding world. However, there is a claim that as people gain more knowledge, things do not become more comprehensible but rather more complex and mysterious. I believe that knowledge does not make things more complex but rather reshapes our perception. However, in the process of acquiring knowledge, some things can become more comprehensible while new mystery emerges.

There is a difference between complexity and incomprehensibility. Although it is undeniably more challenging to understand a complicated object, being difficult to grasp does not necessarily mean that it is impossible to comprehend. Has the world become more complex as we come to know more of it? I doubt this is the case, because the world's complexity does not depend on our comprehension level. For example, rules governing the movements of stars have been always the same, from the time of the first stargazer, but our understanding of these laws has improved. Reductionists may argue that knowledge simplifies our understanding but this view does not always hold true because we have not discovered every piece of information about the physical world. That is, as people acquire more knowledge, new information emerges which makes things more complex to them.

As mentioned above, incomprehensibility does not arise from complexity. The question about whether the world becomes incomprehensible in light of new knowledge therefore requires additional discussion. Due to the disparate nature of different "things", it would be an oversimplification to claim that new knowledge makes things more mysterious. New knowledge endows us with powerful tools with which to examine the things around us. For instance, advancements in laser technology, benefiting from new optic knowledge, have given us new information about biological process in human body and shed light on the mechanism of chemical reactions on an unprecedented microscopic level. Thus, many biological and chemical processes that used to be mysteries are now comprehensible to us.

On the other hand, new knowledge often raises new questions which cannot be answered without further inquiry. Those questions may seem to be mysterious at first glance. Expanding on the example about optics, the nature of light is still an intriguing and unresolved topic which attracts scholarly debate. Our current understanding is that light is both in a form of waves and particles, but this counterintuitive explanation itself seems a mystery that no one at this moment can elucidate. Thus the understanding of light's true nature requires additional study. Similar logic can be applied to the study of climate change. It was not until Milankovitch's insolation theory that scientists could quantitatively explain and predict glacial-interglacial cycles. However, this knowledge raised new questions regarding mysterious events in Earth's climate history that have not yet been adequately explained.

The fact that new knowledge raises new questions does not suggest that we are unable to understand. On the contrary, those questions, coupled with our curiosity, drive our quest for knowledge. For example, there are many climate events that remain unaccountable by Milankovitch theory. In those cases, the Earth actually warmed despite very low energy flux from the Sun. Such mysteries actually led to a new subfield in climate science and to many new insights, which made the Earth's climate system more comprehensible to us. Mysteries are not permanent and are likely to be solved in the future.

As I have discussed, the world does not become more complex as a result of new knowledge but instead we gain a more comprehensive perception of it. New knowledge can indeed explain things we once found mysterious, but at the same time, it raises new, often puzzling questions. However, those questions are only mysterious until they are solved. (624 words)

🖉 中文翻译

自第一个凝视着夜空的人起，人类从未停止获取知识并尝试理解周遭世界。然而，有人声称，随着人们获得了更多的知识，事物变得更为复杂和神秘，而不是更易于理解了。我认为知识重塑了我们的观念，而不是让事物变得更为复杂。然而，在获取知识的过程中，一些事物可能会变得更容易理解，而与此同时新的谜题又出现了。

复杂性和不可理解性是不同的。虽然我们不能否认理解复杂的对象更具有挑战性，但难以理解并不一定意味着不能理解。因为我们了解更多，所以世界变得更加复杂了吗？我对这种说法存疑，因为世界的复杂性并不取决于我们的理解水平。例如，自第一位占星师所在的时代起，星球运动的规则始终如一，但我们对这些规律的理解却进步了。还原主义者可能会说知识简化了我们的理解，但这一观点并不总是正确的，因为我们并没有发现有关物理世界的每一条信息。也就是说，当人们获得了更多的知识，新的信息出现会让事物变得更加复杂。

如上所述，不可理解性并不来自于复杂性。因此，关于世界是否因为新知识而变得不可理解的问题需要进一步讨论。由于不同的"事物"具有截然不同的性质，宣称新知识会让事物更为神秘是一种过度简化。新知识为我们提供了强大的工具来考察我们周围的事物。例如，受益于新的光学知识而进步的激光技术让我们了解了人体中的生物过程，并在前所未有的微观水平上阐明了化学反应的机制。因此，我们现在可以理解许多一度难以理解的生物和化学过程。

另一方面，新知识常常引发新的问题，如果没有进一步探究我们就无法回答这些问题。这些问题乍一看似乎是难以理解的。让我们来扩充一下光学例子——光的本质仍然悬而未决，引发学术辩论。目前我们的理解是，光既具备波的形式又具备粒子的形式，但这种反直觉的解释本身似乎就是一个目前无人可解的谜题。因此对光的真正本质的理解还需要更多研究。同样的逻辑也可以应用于气候变化的研究。直到 Milankovitch 提出了日照理论，科学家才得以定量解释和预测冰期—间冰期循环。然而，这种知识就地球气候历史中尚未得到充分解释的神秘事件提出了新的问题。

新的知识提出了新的问题并不意味着我们无法理解。相反，这些问题，伴之以我们的好奇心，推动了我们对知识的求索。例如，Milankovitch 的理论无法解释很多气象事件。在这种情况下，尽管来自太阳的能量通量非常低，地球实际上变得更暖了。这些谜团开辟了气候科学中一个新的子领域并催生了许多新见解，使地球的气候系统变得更容易理解了。谜题并不永远是谜题，在未来我们很有可能解决它们。

正如我所讨论的，世界并不因新知识而变得更为复杂，相反，我们获得了对它更为全面的认识。新知识确实可以解释我们一度认为难以理解的事物，但同时，它也提出了新的、常常令人困惑的问题。然而，这些问题在被解决后就不再难以理解了。

文章解析与点评

这道题目是一道极具思辨色彩的题目。当我们积累的知识与日俱增，我们所研究的对象似乎变得更复杂并且难以捉摸。然而，果真是这样吗？

这篇文章首先厘清了两个概念："复杂"不等于"难懂"。"复杂"是事物的客观属性，而"难懂"是人们对待事物的主观感受。我们认为事物变得越来越难懂，这其实是我们在认识到事物的复杂性上又进了一步，而非事物变得越来越复杂。

另一方面，逐日增加的知识储备确实引发了一些新的、看起来扑朔迷离的（mysterious）问题，而很多这样的问题确实还没有得到完美的解答或解决。

除了思路，这篇文章在例证的使用层面也启发了我们。很多同学发愁自己的例证储备太少，但是，很多时候我们可以把一个例子从不同的侧面切入。比如这篇文章，运用一句"Expanding on the optical example"，自然引出了对于上一段已经讨论过的"optical example"的进一步分析。把一个例证从不同侧面进行分析，既减轻了我们的记忆负担，同时还显示出我们的思辨能力。

此外，在论证一个道理时，我们有时需要引用不止一个例子。在两个例子之间，我们需要加入一个过渡的句子。这篇文章的第四段就引用了两个例子，而两个例子之间用一句"Similar logic can be applied to XX"来连接就显得比较自然。

---

38 It is primarily through our identification with social groups that we define ourselves.

Write a response in which you discuss the extent to which you agree or disagree with the statement and explain your reasoning for the position you take. In developing and supporting your position, you should consider ways in which the statement might or might not hold true and explain how these considerations shape your position.

Self-definition is gained through association with social groups, but is not achieved through self-identification. By arguing this, the author puts forth an interesting puzzle concerning the morphology of the root "self". Admittedly, being gregarious and pursuing self-definition through contact with outside groups distinguishes us from other animals. We attend schools, we join parties, we engage in a variety of volunteer activities—it is through such social activities that we gain individual value and correctly locate ourselves. However, I argue that in many, even most, circumstances social groups play a disappointing role in helping us to define ourselves. In extreme circumstances, we may even be tossed about aimlessly in the turbulent ocean of society, deprived of appropriate self-definition.

To begin with, the author turns a blind eye to the great number of cases in which we fail to define ourselves through interaction with other social groups. To exemplify this, we can consider a failed marriage, an unsuccessful job experience, or a discouraging defeat in a contest. Not only do such interactions with others fail to contribute to satisfactory self-definition, but more importantly, they could possibly strip us of the confidence needed in life and hinder our ability to positively self-identify.

Moreover, the author overlooks the vital role played by space in helping us to define ourselves. While it might be significant to maintain contact with others, it is equally important to reserve privacy for our spirit. Private space is especially vital in current society which is marked by the hustle-and-bustle pace of life. Shopping malls, bars, parks, these are all paradise for those in need of animated communication with others; however, a secluded study room, a quiet house in the countryside, or even the lonely street corner in New York city might benefit us considerably in terms of introspection. Through such introspection we are able to liberate ourselves from the outside world's distracting forces and further attain some semblance of peace. This peace occupies an irreplaceable space in our city dwellers' hearts.

Last but not least, as we go through different phases in life, we are bound to attempt different ways of identifying ourselves. The author, however, fails to categorize or elaborate on those phases of human life. It is ill-conceived to regard our life as one monotonous, tedious and variance-deprived chapter. On the contrary, life is fraught with changes and unexpected occurrences. Those episodes compel us to utilize different approaches to understand ourselves and acquire an appropriate sense of identity. In the nascent stage of our lives, we strive to understand the world through communication with others. It is this communication that helps us to gradually gain a more complete picture about the world and what it means to us. In the prime of our lives: we have decent jobs, building our careers with a group of confidants, and we start families, sharing joy and sorrow with the ones we love. Jobs and family enable us to define ourselves as qualified employees, partners and parents. However, when we approach the end of our lives, we achieve a relatively exclusive status: we most frequently think about the past, both the miserable and happy times. We become introspective of what we have been through; such history belongs to us alone and it is through these experiences that we complete the final self-identification stage. If there was no such introspective life ritual, how pale would our lives be?

To sum up, while it is reasonable to establish positive connections with others and define ourselves through such connections, in most cases I argue that we can go further and self-identify only by forming and possessing a strong and independent ego. (605 words)

中文翻译

"自我认定"通过"非自我"（即与社会团体产生联系）的方式来完成，而非"自我认同"。借用"self"这个词根，作者提出了一个有趣且深奥的议题。诚然，通过参与外界的社会团体以及从中寻求自我认定，我们将自身与其他动物区分开来。正是通过这一系列社会活动——上学、参加派对、加入各类志愿活动，我们实现个体价值并找准自我定位。然而，我认为在许多、甚至是大多数情况下，在帮助我们实现自我认定的时候，社会团体扮演了一个令人失望的角色。在一些极端的情况中，我们甚至被剥夺了恰当的自我认定，进而被任意地放逐在社会的乱流中。

首先，在许多案例中，我们完全无法通过与其他社会组织的互动来实现自我认定，而作者对此视而不见。确切的说，它们可能是一段失败的婚姻、一次不成功的求职经历或者一次比赛中的惨败。这些与他人的互动不但无法使我们获得满意的自我认定，更为严重的是，这还有可能剥夺了我们未来人生中宝贵的自信，从而阻碍我们获得积极的自我认知。

另外，在帮助我们获得自我认定的层面，作者忽略了"空间"所扮演的核心角色。尽管与他人保持联系着实重要，但同样重要的还有：为我们的灵魂保留独立的空间。独立空间在这个充斥着拥挤与喧嚣的现代社会中显得尤为重要。购物商场、酒吧、公园，这些场所对于需要活跃社交的人来说几乎就是天堂。然而，一间僻静的自习室，乡村的一间小屋，或者纽约街头的一隅，却能为我们提供进行自我审视的绝佳场所。通过这些自省，我们能将自己从外界的各种干扰因素中解放出来，并进一步获得一些平静。这些平静在我们这些都市定居者的内心中占据着不可替代的位置。

最后，随着我们步入不同的人生阶段，我们注定要尝试各类实现自我认知的方式。然而，作者不但没能区分并充分解释这些不同的人生阶段，反而将我们的生活视为单调的、乏味的以及缺乏变数的断篇，这是一种缺乏妥善考量的想法。其实，生活充满了变化与未知的变数。这些小插曲能迫使我们采用各种不同的途径来理解自身，从而实现合理的自我认知。在生命最初的阶段，我们通过与外界的交流来认知世界。正是通过这些交流，我们逐渐获得一种对于这个世界及其真实含义的、更为完整的认识。当步入壮年，我们拥有体面的工作、与一众伙伴知己打拼职场、建立家庭并与深爱的人同甘共苦。工作和家庭促使我们成为更为合格的员工、伴侣和父母。然而，随着我们步入晚年，我们开始进入一种相对独立的状态：我们更多的是回忆过去，回味那些愉快与不愉快的时光。我们开始对自己走过的岁月进行自我审视；这些历史专属于我们，并且通过这些经历我们完成了最终的自我认同。如果缺失了这一段宝贵的自省，那我们的生命将多么苍白？

总的来说，通过这些联系来与他人建立正面的联系并实现自我认定，具有一定合理性；然而，在更多的情况中，我坚信只有先努力打造并拥有一个强大且独立的"自我"，我们才能够更加深入并且最终实现自我认知。

⚑ 文章解析与点评

这道题目比较抽象，题目本身的难度也比较高。这篇文章给大家提供了不错的思路。

一方面，我们确实可以通过和其他社会团体的联系来定义自我。比如上学、参加派对、参与志愿活动，都为我们提供了各种和他人接触的机会，在这种接触中我们也有可能完成自我的认定。

但是，和他人的接触并不一定能保证正面的自我认定。比如，不幸的婚姻体验、失败的求职经历等，不一定能够帮助我们认识自我，甚至可能让我们失去生活的信心。

另外，虽然和他人的交流有助于自我认定，但同时我们也需要一些个人的空间来完成一种朝向内心的审视。一件僻静的自习室、乡村的一间小屋，或者纽约街头的一隅，都为我们提供了完成自我对话和认知的绝佳场所。

最后，人在不同的阶段可能会诉诸不同的方式来完成自我认定。人在青少年以及壮年时期，可能都需要广泛地和他人以及诸多社会团体接触,但进入老年之后,人更多地和过去的自我对话,而这种对话是排他的,因此不需要社会团体和他人的介入。

除了思路之外,这篇文章的开头也值得借鉴。这篇文章的开头采用了一种"文字游戏"的方式来展开。Self-definition is gained through association with social groups, but is not achieved through self-identification. By arguing this, the author puts forth an interesting puzzle concerning the morphology of the root "self". (作者借用"self"这个词根,提出了一个有趣的议题:"自我认定(self-definition)"不是通过"自我",而是通过"非自我"(即社会团体)的方式来完成的。)

---

66 People who are the most deeply committed to an idea or policy are also the most critical of it.

Write a response in which you discuss the extent to which you agree or disagree with the statement and explain your reasoning for the position you take. In developing and supporting your position, you should consider ways in which the statement might or might not hold true and explain how these considerations shape your position.

The author of this issue reveals an interesting dilemma in which people claim to struggle with passionate commitment to and simultaneous discontent with an idea or policy. While those appear mutually exclusive, life and history are replete with such examples. Einstein, celebrated for his atomic theories, engaged wholeheartedly in the science field of study and with it, assisted the Allies to conquer the Nazis in World War Two. Nevertheless, he became a fierce opponent of utilizing nuclear weapons later in life after realizing their insidious danger.

While commitment to an idea may trigger the very awareness of its faults, and that awareness may ultimately lead one to deviate from allegiance, I argue that this is not necessarily the case in most circumstances.

To begin with, not everything is complex or ambiguous enough to provoke both commitment and criticism. That is to say, our view of one idea or policy is, in many cases, plain and simple: we are either highly enthusiastic about it or deeply critical of it. For supporting examples, a myriad of discoveries come to mind which have already been proven true and will remain so for a relatively long period of time. People would therefore have utter trust in such facts. For example, educated people nowadays do not dispute the fact that the Earth is round, nor would anyone deny the relationship between the Moon and the ocean waves. These things are sufficiently supported by scrupulous scientific evidence and will therefore provoke little criticism.

Moreover, I disagree with the assumption that someone who is committed to an idea could later become most critical of it. In many cases, once a person becomes faithful to an idea, he or she would ignore any voice that disputes it. This is demonstrated by fanatically religious cults which are blind to criticism. Moreover, even when people are aware of the disadvantages of an idea or policy, it is highly unlikely that these shortcomings would outweigh its advantages so people would remain loyal to it. Roosevelt's New Deal policy, among various examples, greatly supports my argument. While Roosevelt had a thorough understanding of what detrimental influence, which derives from government regulation, could be brought about upon capitalists and market economy, he adhered to such a policy, which later contributed to revitalization of American economy from the Great Depression. The very reason why he did so is that he was well aware that the potential desirable consequences resulting from the policy would ultimately outshine the undesirable ones.

Even if people understand both the advantages and disadvantages of an idea or policy, and even if the latter outweigh the former, we cannot conclude that they will become critical of it. People's behaviors are determined by a variety of factors. Of those factors, the potential profit resulting from a policy plays a paramount role. Consider factories which produce an exorbitant amount of waste every year which seriously jeopardizes the natural environment. Do employees have no idea how detrimental this waste is? Perhaps. Are the factory owners unaware of the deleterious consequences that may be invited? I highly doubt that. The owners have much better knowledge than anyone else of the potential threat of the waste, but this in no way hinders their behavior, but on the contrary, galvanizes it. The reasons for this are the benefits that can be gained by such behavior. These owners are exactly the ones who are most committed to their policy while not at all critical of it.

To sum up, while it is interesting to assert that contradictory attitudes to an idea may occur simultaneously, I believe that in most cases, an idea or policy is not ambiguous or complex enough to provoke an ambivalent position. Even if it is, other factors may sway our position as well, such as the information we possess regarding the policy, as well as the possible profits we may obtain from it.
(649 words)

中文翻译

　　题目的作者揭示了一个有趣的困境：面对同一个观点或政策，人们同时体现出强烈的"热爱"与"批判"两种对立的情绪。虽然（这两种情绪）表面上呈现互斥的关系，但生活和历史中不乏这样的例证。爱因斯坦，因其原子学而闻名于世，全身心投入科学领域并展开深入研究，在二战中帮助盟军一举击溃纳粹。然而在他的人生后期，尤其是当他意识到核武器的巨大杀伤力时，他变成了使用核武器的强烈反对者。

　　尽管对某一个观念的热衷可能会触发人们对其缺陷的认识，并且这种认识将最终破坏其支持者原有的忠诚，但我仍认为这并不适用于大多数情况。

首先，并不是所有事物都能复杂或模糊到足以使人产生"热衷"与"批评"两种情愫。也就是说，我们对于一个观点或政策的态度，在大多数情况下，是直白而简单的：我们要么热烈拥护，要么深恶痛绝。就像我们对待许多被证实且在相当长时间内难以被撼动的发现一样，我们对它们深信不疑。比如，当今受过教育的人不会去质疑"地球是圆的"这一事实，也不会去否认"月球与潮汐存在联系"。由于经历了充分且严谨的科学论证，这些事实很少遭受质疑。

此外，我也无法认同作者的这样一个假设：对某一个观点无比热爱的人会在之后转而批判它。因为在很多情况下，一个人一旦忠于一个观点，他/她就会对反对这个观点的声音充耳不闻。那些无视批评的狂热的宗教分子就充分地说明了这一点。另外，即使人们充分地了解到了一个观点或政策的缺点，这些缺点的数量可能也少于优点的数量，人们也就因此会保持对这一观点的忠诚。在众多的例子当中，罗斯福新政的例子很好地支持了我的观点。虽然罗斯福非常清楚政府管制会给资本家及市场经济带来什么样的影响，他依然坚持着自己的政策，而这一政策在之后也让美国经济从"大萧条"中得以复苏。罗斯福之所以这样做，是因为他清楚地知道这一政策可能带来的好处会远远多于坏处。

即便人们了解一个观点或政策的优、缺点，甚至意识到后者的影响可能超过前者，我们也不能贸然推断人们将会反对这一政策。人们的行为受到一系列因素的影响。在众多因素当中，这项政策中背后的"潜在利益"其实扮演着最为重要的角色。比如，工厂每年超标排放着严重破坏自然环境的废气废水。工厂员工没有意识到这些废物的危害程度吗？有可能。工厂老板没有意识到此举所带来的负面影响吗？绝无可能。工厂老板比谁都清楚这些废物的潜在威胁，但这却无法阻止他们这样的行为；相反，还加剧了他们的这一行为。他们之所以这样做的原因恰恰是这种行为所带来的利润，而这些工厂老板正好就是那些热衷于这些政策但完全不会批评这些政策的人。

总的来说，"对于一种观点同时存在对立态度的情况确实存在"，但尽管这种说法很有意思，我却认为在大多数情况下，一种观点或政策很难做到足够模糊或复杂，以至让我们对它产生两种对立的情绪。就算能产生，其他因素也能左右我们的态度，比如我们对于某一政策所持有的信息，以及我们可能从中获得的利益。

文章解析与点评

这道题目的难度几乎可以算是现行 Issue 题库中最高的。题目本身的意思就非常耐人寻味。题目描述了一种矛盾的心理状态的普遍存在：commitment and criticism。即，"又爱又恨"。

这种矛盾状态有时是存在的，比如爱因斯坦。他专注于核武器的研究，但当他意识到核武器可能带来的危害时，他转而对核武器的使用进行了严厉的批判。

但是，在大多数情况下，作者所描述的矛盾心态并不存在。

首先，并非所有事物都复杂到足以让我们对它们持有一种矛盾心态。比如诸多已经被验证为真的理论，我们对它们奉若圭臬而绝不怀疑。

　　并且，在一些情况下，当我们开始信奉某一个观点时，往往很难对其进行批判。一方面这是因为人们可能听不进任何反对这个观点的言论，比如一些狂热的宗教徒对任何反对的声音都置若罔闻；另一方面，即便我们能听进那些反对的言论，但权衡之下，对于这个观点的喜爱支持之情可能仍然占主导，这时我们依然会坚持这个观点，比如罗斯福新政。

　　最后，就算我们知道一个观点的弊大于利，有时我们依然会坚持这个观点。这是因为对这个观点的评判既可以从道德上展开，也可以从利益层面进行。例如，有些工厂排废水这件事，从道德上看自然是不正确的，但废水厂的老板依然我行我素地排着废水，就是因为左右他 / 她的不是道德判断，而是利益衡量。

② "因果类" Direction

> Write a response in which you discuss the extent to which you agree or disagree with **the claim and the reason** on which that claim is based.

🖣 中文翻译

　　写一篇文章，在这篇文章中讨论你在多大程度上同意或者不同意题目中的**结论以及**支持这个结论的**理由**。

🖣 讲　解

　　这类 Direction 对应的是新 GRE 写作中的一种全新题型，题干由两部分组成，一部分叫作 claim，也就是一个观点或者结论，另一部分叫作 reason，也就是支持这个结论的理由。这种题型所对应的 Direction 我们称之为"因果类"Direction，**它要求我们既谈到题目中的结论（claim），又提到题目中支持结论的原因（reason）**。在谈到原因时，我们还应该注意：就算原因成立，但它是否是构成该结论的原因？也就是说，有没有其他原因也可以推出该结论？

　　对于这种 Direction，希望大家注意：**我们对题目中原因和结论的态度到底是同意还是反对其实并不重要**，因为正如第一种 Direction 的讲解里说到的，ETS 并不在意我们的立场。

🖣 讲解浓缩版

　　既要提到题目中的原因，又要提到结论。

🖣 学术写作拓展

　　在将来的学术写作中，如果我们只是单纯地对某一论断或者看法表示同意或反对，未免显得肤浅和片面。更多时候我们应该透过这种看法，找寻它背后的原因或理由，全面理解得出这种看法的分析或者论证过程。对这种 Direction 的备考应该就会为我们以后的学术分析能力奠定基础。

例如，当我们在阅读别人的某一科学实验报告时，我们不能只是对其实验结果进行同意或反对，我们还要顺着结果找到其理论依据或方法论指导并对其进行评价。"因果类" Direction 恰好就是这一分析模式的微型缩略。

例题举证

Claim: Researchers should not limit their investigations to only those areas in which they expect to discover something that has an immediate, practical application.
Reason: It is impossible to predict the outcome of a line of research with any certainty.

Write a response in which you discuss the extent to which you agree or disagree with the claim and the reason on which that claim is based.

这道题的 reason 部分说：我们不能准确预测研究的结果；claim 部分说：研究者不能只是把他们的研究放在那些会有立竿见影的效果或应用的领域。其实这道题的推理思路是：正是因为研究结果无法预测，所以可能出现意料之外的惊喜，进而我们不能只关注那些可以知道结果的领域，也应该关注那些我们暂时还无法预测结果的领域。

一个可供参考的提纲如下：

> **总立场**：有保留地反对题目
>
> **分论点 1**（同意 reason）：一些科技研究的结果我们确实无法预知。（举例：核能、克隆技术等的研究初期，结果是不明朗的。）
>
> **分论点 2**（反对 claim）：当我们资金一定时，我们确实只能去关注那些结果可知且有立竿见影效果的领域。
>
> **分论点 3**（反对从原因到结论的推理过程）：我们是否关注一个领域的研究，可能不是取决于其结果是否可预知，而是取决于其是否能最终造福人类。

这个提纲的前两个分论点分别讨论题目中的 reason 和 claim，**这就已经照应了 Direction 的要求**。而第三个分论点讨论了从 reason 到 claim 的推理过程，**这一点其实是锦上添花的一点。我们建议有余力的考生可以对其进行一番思考。**

题库范文

44 Claim: It is no longer possible for a society to regard any living man or woman as a hero.

Reason: The reputation of anyone who is subjected to media scrutiny will eventually be diminished.

Write a response in which you discuss the extent to which you agree or disagree with the claim and the reason on which that claim is based.

In modern society where media coverage is ubiquitous, there is a claim that no living men or women can be regarded as heroes because their reputations, when subjected to media scrutiny, will eventually be diminished. In my opinion, it is undeniably true that media scrutiny is capable of deteriorating one's reputation; however, such abilities do not necessarily mean a hero's positive image will collapse. Even if heroes' imperfections are revealed, society may still regard living men or women as heroes.

In the first place, no man is perfect and "to err is human", says Alexander Pope. Therefore, if every aspect of one's life is exposed to the public by the media, his or her reputation could certainly be compromised. Some of his or her behaviors may not be accepted as the moral standard for a hero. For example, a brave, heroic firefighter who is willing to risk his own life to save others' might be committing adultery, which, if revealed, would result in his reputation being defamed. Also, the media may exaggerate a hero's negative side in order to gain more publicity. In such extreme cases, media scrutiny could focus on a hero's derogatory remarks and bias public opinion towards him or her.

That being said, the argument above assumes that the media will excessively probe into the heroes' personalities in details and/or focus on the negative. This assumption, however, could be wrong. With regard to the first part, media may not be willing to invest time and resources discovering every negative aspect of a hero's life due to limited resources and perhaps weak public resonance it can provoke. Furthermore, it would be unfair to assume that every media source is biased in this way. Thanks to the First Amendment, there are many independent media sources in the United States providing information from different angles. Even if politically motivated, it would be almost impossible to require or force all media to dedicate its coverage to a hero's dark side.

Even if a hero's reputation is diminished to some extent by media scrutiny, it is still necessary for society to regard him or her as a hero. To understand this claim, we need to revisit the definition of hero. Heroes are those who possess essential qualities which are admired by people. In other words, it is those particular qualities, such as valor, self-sacrifice, and commitment to public interest, that make a man or woman a hero. Therefore, as long as those key qualities are not falsified by the media, heroes can exist despite negativity concerning their personalities. Let's return to the aforementioned imaginary firefighter who has extramarital affair. If he indeed saves other people's lives by sacrificing his own in a blaze, it's not surprising at all that he will still be regarded as a hero. It is the valor and commitment demonstrated through him paying the ultimate price that outweigh the stain on his character and earn him the title of hero.

To summarize, it is true that media scrutiny has the potential to diminish one's reputation. Because men are inherently imperfect, the media could deliberately focus on the negatives but this cannot be guaranteed. The media may not necessarily broadcast only negative aspects intended to destroy a hero's positive image. Even if the media did so, the public would still accept them because they possess key characteristics that define them as heroes. (565 words)

中文翻译

在现代社会中，媒体报道无处不在，有人声称没有任何在世的人会被视为英雄，因为媒体监督最终会降低他们的声誉。在我看来，不可否认的是，媒体监督确实可以让一个人臭名昭著，然而这并不意味着英雄的积极形象会土崩瓦解。即使媒体揭露了英雄的瑕疵，社会仍然会视这些在世的人为英雄。

首先，人无完人，亚历山大·蒲柏云，"人非圣贤，孰能无过"。因此，当媒体把一个人生活的每一方面都暴露给公众，他/她的声誉肯定会受到损害。按照对英雄所设的道德标准，他/她的一些行为可能会不被接受。例如，一名英勇的消防员可能与他人通奸，如果这种行为被揭露，他的声誉会受到损坏。此外，媒体可能会夸大英雄的消极面以吸引公众的注意力。在这种极端情况下，媒体监督可能会着重发表贬损英雄的评论并让舆论对他/她心存偏见。

话虽如此，上面的论证假设了媒体会过分详尽地探究英雄的个性并聚焦于负面之上。然而，这个假设可能是错误的。就前者而言，媒体可能不会愿意投入时间和资源来发掘英雄生活的每一处消极面，因为他们的资源是有限的，而这么做也许激不起什么公众反应。此外，假设每家媒体都存在偏见也是不公平的。多亏《第一修正案》，美国有许多独立的媒体来源，从不同角度为人们提供信息。即使存在政治动机，要求或迫使所有媒体都致力于报道英雄的黑暗面几乎是不可能的。

即使媒体监督一定程度上降低了英雄的声誉，社会仍然需要将他或她视为英雄。要理解这个说法，我们需要重新审视英雄的定义。英雄是那些拥有人们崇敬的本质的人。换句话说，正是这些品质，诸如勇气、自我牺牲和献身公益，让一个人成为英雄。因此，只要这些关键品质没有被媒体篡改，尽管他们的性格有消极的一面，英雄仍然存在。让我们回到前文所说假想的有婚外情的消防员。如果他真的为了拯救别人的生命而牺牲了自我，那他被视为英雄是很自然的。他通过付出最高昂的代价展现了自己的英勇和承诺，正因此，这些品质盖过了他品格上的污点，并且让他赢得了英雄的称号。

总而言之，媒体监督确实有可能降低一个人的声誉。因为人们生来就不是完美的，媒体可能会故意专注于负面，但这并不是绝对的。媒体不一定会传播旨在破坏英雄积极形象的负面新闻。即使媒体这么做了，公众仍然会接受他们，因为他们拥有那些被定义为英雄的关键品质。

文章解析与点评

这篇文章给大家示范了如何既快速又保险地展开对"因果类"Direction 的照应。该类 Direction 对我们有一个基本要求：既要提到题目中的 claim，又要提到 reason。而我们对 claim 和 reason 分别是什么态度却并不重要。因此，我们可以完全同意 claim，也可以部分同意 claim；对待 reason 也是同理。假设我们对 claim 部分的分析分为两段，一段是同意其合理部分，一段指出其不合理的部分；对 reason 部分也可以有同样的处理方式。这样一来，我们对 claim 和 reason 的分析就达到了四段。而绝大部分情况下，三个中间段已经足够。

这篇范文采取的策略是：对 reason 部分同意反对参半，对 claim 持反对态度。具体内容如下：

中间段 1：同意 reason 的合理部分。因为人总是不完美的，因此当一个人的方方面面都被媒体曝光，他 / 她的形象必然会受损。并且有时媒体还会故意夸大报道对象的缺点以此来博取眼球，这种情况下被报道对象的形象必然也会受损。

中间段 2：反对 reason 的不合理部分。并非所有媒体都以丑化报道对象为目的，因此，并非所有的媒体曝光都会让被报道对象的名誉受损。

中间段 3：反对 claim。就算某些社会公众人物或群体确实因为媒体的曝光而名誉受损，这也可能不妨碍社会继续将他们当作偶像。因为社会所推崇的并非"完美"，而是某些特定的珍贵品质。只要这些人物或者群体依然保有这样的品质，他们就仍然会被当作偶像一样受人尊敬。

---

8 Claim: In any field—business, politics, education, government—those in power should step down after five years.

Reason: The surest path to success for any enterprise is revitalization through new leadership.

Write a response in which you discuss the extent to which you agree or disagree with the claim and the reason on which that claim is based.

Charismatic leadership surely comprises an irreplaceable role in any enterprise's endeavor to success; nevertheless, sometimes a leader's charisma is relentlessly tarnished by stains which seem indelible. Sloth, misconduct and corruption are such stains that are at odds with a leader's usually positive image.

While those blots might exert a detrimental influence on the leader's image, I have to emphasize their infrequency. As a result, from my perspective, the author of the issue may be so pessimistic that he/she arbitrarily equates those sporadic blemishes with predestined failure and therefore fiercely advocates the revitalization of leadership every five years.

In the field of politics, or more specifically in government, delinquency and crimes do occur. Such delinquency and crimes most likely derive from persistent power maintenance and greatly hinder political achievements. Therefore, revitalization through new leadership is highly desired for success. New leadership, once introduced, will bring about strict restrictions, if not a deadly crack down, on the old bureaucracy. Those restrictions will further witness a balance of power between the new and old politicians. As a result, a harmonious working ethic within the government is birthed and subsequent success can be expected. The regular presidential election in the United States, as well as in many other countries, exemplifies the significance of leadership revitalization within the political field. While many considerations contribute to such revitalization, the preclusion of corruption and other dishonest behaviors is no doubt one of the most important considerations.

When we turn to the field of education, however, the situation is appallingly different. When it comes to education, I disagree with this issue in terms of both its reason and claim. I contend that the surest path to success in universities, high schools and other education institutions, is not through the revitalization of leadership but rather through educators' (including the presidents and teachers of those schools) insightful decisions about vital policies. This insight, in most cases, springs from an accumulation of teaching experience. A sufficiently long teaching history further requires that the educators maintain position stability, which frequently exceeds a period of five years. For supporting examples, we can only imagine a university undergoing a steady change of department directors, even presidents within a short period of years, or, perhaps even several months. This leadership fluctuation would definitely lead to an interruption of educational policies with students being the victims. However, if the leaders of the university are insightful and experienced enough to bring the university to a higher level, their tenure can be extended.

Finally, if we switch our attention to the field of business, we find that changes in leadership are much more flexible. All that a new leader should be equipped with is the potential or capability to bring maximum profits. In the business world, unanticipated bargaining success could endow an unsung Joe with widespread reputation which even a much older businessman would covet. However, it is of equal possibility that an eminently respected entrepreneur could lose his/her crown overnight for an unexpected failure in a regular negotiation. From this perspective, neither the reason nor the claim of this issue stands tenable in the business field. Leadership hinges on profits—this allegation may sound harsh, but few would dispute its validity.

While every enterprise should strive for success, the means via which the enterprise should utilize is conditional on more thorough considerations. As a result, whether a leader should step down after five years requires further deliberation. (570 words)

中文翻译

　　毫无疑问，任何团队想要取得成功，魅力型的领导力总是占据极为重要的位置；然而，领导的非凡魅力却时常受到一些污点的困扰。一般来说，懒惰、管理不善和贪污会破坏领导人的高大形象。然而，尽管深知这些污点可能带来的负面影响，我也不得不强调它们其实发生得并不频繁。因此在我看来，持这个观点的作者可能太过悲观，他/她将这些偶然出现的污点与注定发生的失败武断地划上等号，并为此激进地倡导"以五年为限"对领导人进行更替。

　　在政界（更为确切的说，在政府），渎职或犯罪行为确有发生。这些渎职和犯罪行为极有可能来源于长时间的权力维系，并进一步阻碍了政治方面的任何可能的成就。因此，领导力更替对于一个团队的成功来说至关重要。一旦引入，新的领导力即便无法打碎，也至少能够有效地制约陈腐的官僚作风。这样的限制还将见证新老政治家之间的权力平衡。因此，政府内部和谐的职业道德将因此被催生，随之而来的成功也指日可待。包括美国在内的许多国家，定期举行的总统选举便很好地印证了在政治领域里的领导力更替的重要性。尽管疾呼领导力更替的理由有很多，但"杜绝腐败以及其他不诚实行为"无疑是最为重要的动力。

　　然而，当我们转向教育领域时，情况则大不一样。换句话说，当谈到教育行业时，不论是从原因和结论来看，我都反对这种观点。在大学、高中或其他教育机构，我认为获得成功的最为保险的路径，不是对领导力进行更替，而是教育者（包括该校的校长和老师）对于核心政策的睿智判断。这种洞察力，在大部分情况中，来源于教学经验的积累。一段足够长的教学经验需要教育者能够稳定地处在一个职位上，而这一般需要超过五年的时间。举例来说，如果一个大学经历了系主任的持续更替，或者不到一年、甚至只有几个月的持续校长更替，这种领导人的替换势必导致教育政策的紊乱，并最终使学生成为受害者。然而，如果大学领导人具备足够的洞察力以及经验，来进一步提升大学的水准，那么他们的任期则可以被延长。

　　最后，如果我们将注意力投向商界，我们会发现"领导力更替"这个话题将变得更为灵活。一位新领导最应该具备的是带来最大收益的潜力或能力。在商界，一场不经意的成功交易可能使一个无名小卒在一夜之间享有极高的、让打拼多年的商场老手也垂涎不已的名声。然而，同样可能的是，因为一场普通交易的惨败，一位驰骋商界多年的老手在一夕之间失掉他/她的"王冠"。因此，从商业角度来看，作者的说法，无论是理由还是结论都无法站稳脚跟。"领导力取决于利润"，这话虽然直白，但极少有人质疑。

　　虽然每个团队都想获得成功，但每个团队选取的途径应该得到更多的考量。因此，在五年的任期之后，领导人是否应该卸任？这个问题值得更加深入的探讨。

这篇文章为大家示范了在遵守 Direction 要求的前提之下如何把题目拓展得更加丰富。

这道题目的 Direction 要求我们既要提到题目中的 claim，又要提到题目中的 reason，只要满足了这一要求，我们的文章就越过了 3 分的雷区。在做到这一点的基础上，大家可以看到我们是通过"按领域讨论"的破题思路来展开文章的。我们讨论了在政界、教育界和商界中题目成立与否的情况。

在政界，不法行为来源于领导者久居其位且这种不法行为会阻碍领导者的成功。因此，领导层定期的更新换代是必要的。从这一层面上看，在讨论政界的情况时，该段既同意题目中的 reason，也同意题目中的 claim。

而在教育界，我们既不同意题目中的 reason，也不同意题目中的 claim。因为在教育界，成功的关键不在于领导的更替，而在于领导者的见识和经验，而这样的见识和经验通常又以较长的在职年数为依托。所以，只要领导者具备足够的见识和经验让大学的水平更上一层楼，其在职年限不必拘泥于五年这一特定数字。

在商界，成功的关键在于是否赚取利润，而利润的多寡并不取决于领导者的在职期限，而在于其潜力和能力。名不见经传的新手也能在商界声名鹊起，而经验老道的专家也可能马失前蹄。从这一层面上讲，题目中的 reason 和 claim 都站不住脚。

如上，文章从三个领域讨论了题目的 reason 和 claim，在遵守 Direction 的同时还丰富了文章的内容。希望大家可以借鉴学习。

79 Claim: The best test of an argument is its ability to convince someone with an opposing viewpoint.

Reason: Only by being forced to defend an idea against the doubts and contrasting views of others does one really discover the value of that idea.

Write a response in which you discuss the extent to which you agree or disagree with the claim and the reason on which that claim is based.

To bestow an argument, idea, contention or assertion with value, we must attempt to persuade those who hold contrasting views. Once we manage to convince our opponents, our argument seemingly gains fresh significance. This inclination to persuade others with our ideas presumably derives from the action embodied in the verb "argue": to persuade people with relevant reasons that we are correct. While this might be one way to prove our argument's validity and value, we do not always need to resort to this method. Additionally, sometimes attempts to persuade might even prove futile.

To begin with, I must express my appreciation for the reason part of this issue. It is exactly at the moment when we are forced to defend an idea against doubts and contrasting views that we begin to form a comprehensive understanding of the idea's value. It is also at such a moment that we should grasp the opportunity to show our rivals the advantages of our argument and earn their approval. This perspective is emphasized by how a debate takes place. In a debate, speakers strive to elucidate the advantages or the disadvantages of an issue in order to convince their opponents, as well as the audience of their point of view. It is also during this phase that the audience comes to establish a holistic understanding of the topic and its value. In addition, even though the debaters may not be utterly convinced by their opponents, they ultimately benefit from questioning their opponents and defending their own views, and further build up an unprecedented understanding of their argument's value.

However, tenable as the assertion may hold in most circumstances that an idea receives value by overshadowing its opponents, I contend that the value of an argument can be also realized in other ways. Consequently, this raises doubt about the issue's reason. Since we do not argue exclusively to disprove our rivals, but also to clarify our own principles, or support allegations, we do not always have to start a battle in which one argument is bound to knock down another. Academic papers serve as a simple but persuasive example. It is not difficult to find out that not all the articles we read, write or cite attempt to disprove others, but in more circumstances concentrate on either clarification of the methodologies the paper itself utilizes, or on supplementary explanation to similar studies. One semester I read a series of articles written by archeologists, historians and anthropologists regarding ancient Chinese rituals. Despite their contrasting arguments, these scholars did not focus on discrediting each other's work. On the contrary, they simply offer different interpretations of the same issue. The value of these papers is therefore achieved through their interpretations rather than through contention between the authors.

What is more, the writer's over-optimistic attitude is betrayed in the claim of the issue, which is supported by an unsubstantiated assumption: everyone can be convinced by an opposing viewpoint. This assumption further theorizes that an absolute truth exists, or to put it in another way: everything can be explained in only one way. Clearly, this is not true. The example previously discussed about three different interpretations of one issue support my opinion. Since academic research is based on different methodologies, scholars can never be truly convinced by each other; otherwise they would have used identical systems but not diverse ones. In addition, in some circumstances, the superficial debate between two arguments actually reveals an irreconcilable conflict, which concerns more fundamental factors, such as benefits. For exemplifications, we can look at strife between political parties all over the world. Due to the irreconcilable contention about respective interests, their quarrels never cease, and probably no one can foretell the day when they will actually convince each other.

To sum up, while I partly agree with the issue's reason, I reserve my approval of both the claim and its assumption. That is to say, the value of an argument may be realized through debate with someone holding a contrasting viewpoint, yet we cannot rely on that to always be true. (677 words)

中文翻译

为了赋予一个论点、观点、主张或声称以价值，我们必须试图去说服那些持相反观点的人。一旦我们成功地说服对手，我们的论点似乎就获得了更多的重要性。这种试图用我们的观点去说服对方的倾向，可能来自于动词"辩论"所蕴含的动作：用相关的理由去让对方相信"我方正确"。虽然这可能是一条提升我们论证有效性和价值的路径，但我们不一定非要采用这样的方式。此外，"尽力说服对方的做法"有时被证明是一种无效的尝试。

首先，我对这道题目的 reason 部分表示赞同。每当我们被迫去辩护一个受到质疑或存在对立看法的观点时，其实已经就这个观点的价值形成更为全面的认识。也就是这个时候，我们会抓住机会向我们的对手展示己方论点的优势，并尝试获得他们的认同。这种思维在辩论中体现得最为明显。在一场辩论中，为了说服对手以及他们的支持者，发言者就一个问题努力阐明其优势与劣势。也正是在这个阶段，观众对这个话题和它的价值建立起更为完善的认识。另外，尽管辩论者并未完全被他们的对手说服，但他们也终将通过质问对手、辩护己方立场而获益，从而进一步深化他们对己方论点的价值的认知。

然而，通过征服对手来使观点获得价值，尽管这种说法在大多数情况中都具说服力，但我依然认为一个论点的增值还可以通过其他方式获得，这也就质疑了这道题目的 reason 部分。由于我们争论的目的并不只是为了推翻对手，同时还有阐释我方的原则，或者支持我方的论点等目的，所以我们就没有必要总是掀起一场"只有一方能够幸存"的论战。比如说，学术论文是一个简单且富有说服力的例子。不难发现，并不是所有我们看到的、写的、引用的文章都是以推翻其他文章为目的；相反，在更多的情况下，这些文章专注于对论文本身采用的方法论的阐释，或者对相似研究进行的补充说明。记得有一个学期，我阅读了一系列由考古学家、历史学家和人类学家写作的有关古代中国仪式的文章。尽管这些文章的观点各不相同，但文章的作者并未执着于推翻彼此的观点。相反，他们只是就相同的问题提出不同的解释。因此，这些论文的价值来源于其各自的阐释而非对彼此观点的推翻。

另外，这个题目的 claim 部分还暴露了作者过度乐观的态度，因为 claim 部分被一个未被证实的假设所支持：每个人都能被相反的观点说服。这个假设还进一步假定：绝对真理存在于世，或者说，所有事物都只能有唯一的解释。很明显，这并不正确。前文讨论过的对同一话题的三种不同解释的例子能够支持这一观点。由于学术研究基于不同的方法论，所以学者之间并不能完全说服彼此；除非他们采用相同的系统。另外，在一些情况下，两方之间一次肤浅的争论也可能揭示出无法调和的冲突，而这种冲突往往与更为基本的元素相关，比如利益。举例来说，我们可以关注世界各地的政党间的冲突。因为基于各自利益的不可调和的争论，它们之间的争吵永不停息，并且也无人能预测到他们能够说服彼此的那一天。

总的来说，尽管我部分同意题目的 reason 部分，但我对这个题目的 claim 和 assumption 仍持保留态度。也就是说，论点的价值可能通过说服对立观点来获得，但我们也需要意识到，这并不是唯一的途径。

文章解析与点评

这道题目本身的内容比较抽象，而"claim—reason"的形式也使得破题难度进一步提高。但是，按照我们之前的讲解，大家只需要对题目的 reason 部分和 claim 部分分别讨论即可。

对于 reason 部分，文章用两段的篇幅既表示了赞同，也表示了反对。

首先，文章部分赞同了 reason 的观点。因为当我们尝试用一个观点去说服对立观点时，我们确实能发现这个观点的价值。辩论赛作为一个常见的例子，很好地支持了这个观点。因为辩论赛的双方都是在尝试说服对方和观众的过程中发现自身观点的价值。

然而，要认识并实现一个观点的价值，并不总需要试图用它驳倒对立的观点。从这个层面上讲，文章是反对 reason 的观点的。例如，我们经常遇到的学术论文就并不总以攻击或者说服观点相反的论文为写作目的的，而更多的时候，我们写论文是为了阐明自己的理论或者方法论，或者深化、支持我们的同盟者的观点。在这里，文章列举了作者在学习中遇到的一篇关于中国古代宗教礼仪的文章。这个事例非常贴近生活，并不是所谓的"名人名例"，但依然能很好地支持文章的观点。

最后，文章质疑了题目的 claim 部分。指出 claim 部分所依赖的假设有问题："所有对手都能够被说服"；或说，"所有事情只能用一种方式来解释"。然而，事实并非如此，在这里，文章又诉诸于之前所提到的宗教礼仪的文章，指出：很多论文虽然讨论的话题是类似的，但使用的方法论却是不同的，因此这些论文的作者在一定层面上讲并不能完全地说服其他人，亦或是被其他人说服。在这里，文章对相同的例子进行了不同侧面的解析，展示出批判性思维的辩证的特点。另外，有一些表面上的不同实则是掩盖着更加深层次的不可调和的矛盾，比如不同政党之间的无休止的斗争。像这样的诸多观点，是很难被彼此说服的。

③ "两种看法类" Direction

Write a response in which you discuss which view more closely aligns with your own position and explain your reasoning for the position you take. In developing and supporting your position, **you should address both of the views presented**.

中文翻译

写一篇文章，在这篇文章中讨论哪个观点和你的立场最接近，解释你所采取的立场的理由。在发展和支持你的观点立场的过程中，**必须考虑到双方观点**。

讲　解

这类 Direction 对应的是新 GRE 写作中的第二种全新题型，题干包含两种观点，这两种观点可能是相互排斥的，也可能在本质上并不是矛盾的。**相对应的 Direction 要求我们在写作时不能只提到题目中的一种观点，而要兼顾两种观点。**对于这种 Direction，有这样两点注意事项：

① Direction 中虽然要求我们明确说明哪个观点和我们的立场最接近，但真实情况完全可以是"两种观点和我们的立场一样接近"，因为正如之前所说，我们的立场并不重要。

②我们虽然要提到两种观点，但以多长的篇幅去提及却并没有要求。例如我们的中间段有三段，我们可以用两段讨论一种观点，用一段讨论第二种观点；而如果我们的中间段有四段，我们可以分别用两段谈论两种观点。

讲解浓缩版

题目中的两种观点都要讨论。

学术写作拓展

这种 Direction 的要求其实是在照应我们在学术写作，特别是论文写作中的"文献综述（Literature Review）"部分。在学术写作中，我们总会遇到很多他人和前人的看法，这些看法可能和我们的看法相似，也可能相斥，而这些看法之间还可能存在相似或相斥之处。如何看待、处理这些看法，是我们必须应对的问题。ETS 借用这样一个 Direction 其实是希望我们对这种问题提前做好准备。

例题举证

Some people believe that college students should consider only their own talents and interests when choosing a field of study. Others believe that college students should base their choice of a field of study on the availability of jobs in that field.

Write a response in which you discuss which view more closely aligns with your own position and explain your reasoning for the position you take. In developing and supporting your position, you should address both of the views presented.

参考提纲如下：

总立场：认为两种看法并不矛盾

分论点 1（同意第一种看法的合理之处）：兴趣是学习的动力，而天赋能够让学生在自己擅长的领域迈出更好的第一步。

分论点 2（同意第二种看法的合理之处）：大学是学生从学生身份向社会人转化的重要场所，工作是社会人的重要属性之一，因此学生应该在选择专业之时考虑就业情况。

分论点 3（这两种看法其实并不矛盾）：首先，一些学生所喜欢并擅长的专业可能就是社会需求量大的专业；其次，就算学生根据自己的兴趣和爱好所选择的领域并非社会需求量最大的专业，也可以通过努力让自己成为本专业最出色的人才，这样一来仍然不会缺少工作机会。

分论点 1 和分论点 2 分别探讨了第一种看法和第二种看法，**这就已经照应了 Direction 的要求**。而分论点 3 辩证地探讨了这两种看法的关系，**这一点属于锦上添花，建议大家可以尝试着思考**。

题库范文

86 Some people believe that government officials must carry out the will of the people they serve. Others believe that officials should base their decisions on their own judgment.

Write a response in which you discuss which view more closely aligns with your own position and explain your reasoning for the position you take. In developing and supporting your position, you should address both of the views presented.

Which criterion should be given more weight when assessing government officials, their determination to carry out the will of the people they serve or their ability to stand by their own decisions? While some designate government officials as public servants, others appreciate officials' resolution to make their own judgment, with public's will relegated to a secondary concern. While both of these views have merit, I argue that they are not necessarily mutually exclusive.

On the one hand, I concede that government officials are created by the demands from the people they serve and therefore officials should behave in accordance with the will of those people. First, government's central role in regulating its nation's affairs obliges officials to work for their citizen's benefit. In addition, government officials are simultaneously citizens themselves, which gives them unique insight and understanding of citizen request. While Abraham Lincoln has perished in history long ago, we could still see every generation of government officials bestirring themselves indefatigably at their positions, echoing Lincoln's prestigious motto "of the people, by the people and for the people". Those officials prioritize what the public desire not only because they derive their power from the public, but also because they are citizens themselves and accordingly benefit from their own achievements.

In great contrast, people who believe that officials should base their decisions on their own judgment assign little importance to the will of the people. From this perspective, officials' individual preference takes absolute precedence. While this claim might initially sound somewhat implausible and might even remind us of obdurate bureaucracy or headstrong leaders, it can in some circumstances serve the greater good. Officials confronted by dilemmas which force them to choose between the public's wishes and their own judgment may choose to sacrifice the former for the latter. We cannot call those officials tyrannical, however, since their actions are based on the long-term interests which will benefit the majority. Roosevelt's New Deal sufficiently exemplifies my argument. Had Roosevelt not subordinated capitalist interest and conjured up a marriage between market economy and government regulation, current Americans might still be suffering from the effects of the Great Depression. Even though Roosevelt implemented a series of policies in spite of business opposition, we do not judge him to have acted irresponsibly or autocratically. On the contrary, we applaud his policies because they stemmed from comprehensive concerns of what would benefit Americans overall. In this way, Roosevelt well embodies an efficient leader who struck a harmonious balance between the public's wishes and his own decisions.

The above-stated examination of the two views discloses my appreciation for both of them. Nevertheless this is not to say that I suggest appraising these two perspectives in isolation. Rather, I would like to view the process of policy-making of government officials as a continuum that includes public voices and officials' individual decisions. An insightful official should and is able to make decisions on the basis of the will of the people he serves; meanwhile citizens should attempt to understand that those policies have undergone thorough consideration regarding the potential benefits and consequences. The ideal world I depict is one in which leaders and public enjoy a harmonious relationship and both benefit from policy decisions. (535 words)

中文翻译

当评价政府官员时，"践行人民意愿"与"坚持个人决策"，到底哪种应该被给予更多的重视？尽管有人将政府官员视为公仆，但也有人欣赏那些坚持己见而把公众意志放在第二位的官员。虽然这两种观点各有所长，但我并不认为它们的关系一定是互斥的。

一方面，我认为政府官员（这个角色）是由人民的需求所创造的，因此官员的决策应该符合人民的意愿。首先，由于政府在国家事务中扮演着核心角色，所以政府官员必须为人民谋福利。另外，政府官员同时也是人，这赋予了他们独特的视角以及对人民需求的了解。尽管亚伯拉罕•林肯是一位相当久远的历史人物，但至今我们仍能看到每一任政府官员都在不厌其烦地引用他的至理名言以激励自己："民治、民有、民享"。这些政府官员之所以重视人们的需求，不仅是因为他们的权力来源于大众，还在于他们自身也是人民，并将最终受益于自己的政绩。

相反，有些人认为官员应该根据自己的判断做决定，所以不必太在意人民的意愿。这种观点认为，官员个人的偏好理应享有优先权。尽管这种说法乍听之下显得有些不可思议，甚至会让人想起那些刚愎自用的官僚机构或自大顽固的领导人，但在某些情况下，它确实可以带来更广泛的益处。到底听从公众的意愿还是个人的判断？面临这样的困局，一些官员们会选择牺牲前者而选择后者。然而，我们不能将这些官员视作蛮横暴虐，因为他们的所为是从长远利益出发的，并将最终造福大多数人。其中，罗斯福新政便能充分印证我的论点。如果罗斯福当时没有压制资本家的利益，并创造性地将"市场经济与政府干预"结合起来，当今美国可能仍在大萧条的泥潭中苦苦挣扎。尽管罗斯福不顾商业界反对，实施了这一系列政策，我们也很难将他的决策视作不负责任或独裁。相反，我们称赞他的政策，因为它脱胎于对美国未来整体利益的综合考量。这样看来，通过平衡公众意愿与个人决策之间的关系，罗斯福成功地展现了一位高效领导人所具备的素质。

对以上两个观点的检视揭示了我对两个观点的欣赏。但这并不是说，我认为应该分裂地夸赞这两个观点。确切地说，我更愿意将政府官员进行政策决断的过程视作一个统一连续体，它同时包括了大众的声音与官员的判断。一位富有洞察力的官员需要并且能够做到以民意为基础来决定政策；同时，人民也应该试着去了解这些政策，毕竟这些政策都考虑到了潜在的益处与结果，并经过领导者反复斟酌才得以推出。我能想象的理想世界是，领导和人民处于一种和谐的关系，并且因为政策制定而共同受益。

文章解析与点评

这篇文章为大家提供了以下几个参考的方面。

第一，文章的开头。这篇文章的开头运用了一个典型的开篇技巧：改写题目。这样的方式比较节约思考的时间，同时也能扩充字数。大家也经常使用这个技巧进行写作，不过在我们看到的同学习作中，大家普遍存在一个问题：不是对题目进行改写，而是几乎照抄题目。这样的改写显得比较呆板，不能充分体现大家对语言的驾驭能力。而这篇文章的开头就为大家提供了改写题目的参考范例。

如，这道题的题目其实是在比较两个概念：领导者自己的意愿和民众的意愿。相对应的，文章的开头段就用到了一系列表示比较、权衡两个事物的表达，如："Which criterion should be given more weight..."；"While some designate...as..., others appreciate..., with...relegated to a secondary concern."

第二，文章对于 Direction 的处理方式。这道题的 Direction 要求我们提到 A、B 两种看法。一种非常常见并且方便的处理方式：用一段写看法 A，一段写看法 B，一段写看法 AB 之间的关系。这样的处理方式既容易展开，同时也比较辩证。

第三，这篇文章为大家提供了两个很常见的政治类的例证：林肯和罗斯福。林肯的著名宣言 "of the people, by the people and for the people" 充分体现了政府和国家领导人为人民服务的精神；而罗斯福的"新政"政策的内涵十分丰富，既可以体现罗斯福作为领导人的全局观和长远眼光，也可以体现领导人面对民众意见有分歧时果敢的处理态度。这两个例子如果能够用好，几乎可以算是 Issue 中以一当十的例证。建议大家把有限的例子作多角度的切入，使其能够适用于尽可能多的 Issue 题目。

151 Some people claim that the goal of politics should be the pursuit of an ideal. Others argue that the goal should be finding common ground and reaching consensus.

Write a response in which you discuss which view more closely aligns with your own position and explain the reasoning you position you take. In developing and supporting your position you should address both of the views presented.

What is the ultimate purpose or goal of politics supposed to be? There are two seemingly contradictory views on this question. One side argues that the ultimate goal of politics should be pursuing ideals, while the other regards finding common ground and reaching consensus as the goal. I tend to give my support to the former view based on the nature of politics, while I object to the latter since it may result in many negative consequences.

Firstly, the ultimate goal of politics in my opinion should be constructing a world in which people can enjoy their lives and can fulfill their dreams by utilizing their talents and potentials to the maximum. In this light, this world is certainly idealistic. To understand why such an ideal world should be the goal of politics, one must first understand what politics stands for and where it originates. Politics rose from a contract between governors and citizens, where the people authorized the governors' power and governors, in turn, provided essential services to the people. To promote the well being of the people was the ultimate intended goal of this contract, and it is through this contract that politics came into existence. Politics has inherited this contract's goal and should therefore strive to serve the people by constructing an ideal world.

On the contrary, it is dangerous to abide by the view that the goal of politics should be finding common ground and reaching consensus. When there is no ideal principle to guide our behavior, our moral ground becomes shaky. For example, in this pragmatic ideology, we may sacrifice innocent people for the sake of so-called consensus. Throughout human history, there are many incidents in which the countries collude in reaching peace and consensus, but at the cost of other small nations and in violation of the moral principles. From a humanitarian perspective the result is undeniably tragic.

That being said, finding common ground and reaching consensus are still pivotal in politics. Without these, pursuing ideals could have disastrous political consequences. Similar examples can be readily found in the sporadic turbulence of the current society. These examples demonstrate how dangerous it can be when we commit ourselves to an ideal zealously without proper controls. Modern democracy based on negotiation and finding common ground, on the other hand, shows us the power of compromise and consensus.

To conclude, I believe that the goal of politics should be pursuing ideals rather than finding common ground and reaching consensus. However, even though common ground and consensus should not be the goal of politics, it does not mean that they are of no significance. On the contrary, common ground and compromise are essential in controlling zealousness and help us realize our ideals.
(454 words)

中文翻译

政治的最终目的或目标应该是什么？在这个问题上，有两个看似矛盾的观点。一方认为，政治的最终目标应该是追求理想，而另一方认为目标应当是找到共同点并达成共识。基于政治的本质，我倾向于支持前一种观点，并反对后一种观点，因为它可能会造成许多消极后果。

首先，我认为政治的最终目标应该是建设一个人们可以最大限度地发挥他们的才能和潜力，从而享受生活、实现梦想的世界。就此而论，这个世界当然是理想主义的。要理解为什么这样一个理想的世界是政治的目标，人们首先要理解政治代表的意义和它的起源。政治起源于统治者和公民之间的契约，人民授予统治者权力，而统治者反过来为人民提供必要的服务。促进人民的福祉是这项契约的终极预定目标，正是通过这项契约才诞生了政治。政治继承了这项契约的目标，因此应该通过建设一个理想的世界为人民服务。

相反，坚持政治目标应该找到共同点和达成共识的观点是危险的。当没有理想的原则指导我们的行为时，我们的道德之地就变得摇摇欲坠了。例如，在这种务实为上的意识形态中，我们可能会为了所谓的共识而牺牲无辜的民众。人类历史上充满了大国之间为了实现和平和达成共识而密谋牺牲小国利益的故事，这显然是有违于道德准则的。从人道主义的角度来看这无疑是一个悲剧。

话虽如此，找到共同点和达成共识在政治中仍是至关重要的。没有这些，追求理想可能会产生灾难性的政治后果。现代社会中偶有发生的动乱也是很好的例子。这些例子表明，当我们在没有适度控制的情况下，一头热地献身于理想是多么危险。另一方面，基于谈判和寻找共同点的现代政治制度向我们展示了妥协和共识的力量。

总而言之，我认为政治的目标应该是追求理想，而不是找到共同点、达成共识。然而，即使共同点和共识不应该被当作政治的目标，但这并不意味他们没有意义。相反，共同点和妥协在避免过度热情、帮助我们实现理想上至关重要。

文章解析与点评

这篇文章有两个点可供大家借鉴。

第一，这篇文章开头段对题目的改写。对于两种看法类的题目，我们可以有一个特定的改写模式。即：1. 抛出一个问题；2. 同义改写题目中的两种看法；3. 陈述自己对两种看法的态度。这样的模板方便快捷，可以让大家在较短的时间内写出较多的字数。但需要注意的是，一定要改写题目，而不是照抄。

第二，这道题目中的两种看法其实可以看作围绕领导者到底应该（should）追求什么这一问题的两条建议。针对这两条建议，我们可以从不同的侧面来考虑是否应该实施这样的建议，如：建议的必要性、充分性、可能带来的后果等。这篇文章即是从建议可能带来的后果层面来讨论的。

不过，我们需要注意，当一道题目的 Direction 是"建议类"的两种 Direction 之一时，我们就需要把重心放在对建议的后果的讨论上，否则会被判为偏题。

67 Some people believe that society should try to save every plant and animal species, despite the expense to humans in effort, time, and financial well-being. Others believe that society need not make extraordinary efforts, especially at a great cost in money and jobs, to save endangered species.

Write a response in which you discuss which view more closely aligns with your own position and explain your reasoning for the position you take. In developing and supporting your position, you should address both of the views presented.

With the growing influence of environmentalism, many consider the conservation of endangered species a moral obligation that humankind must acknowledge and fulfill. Some even argue that society must strive to save every plant and animal species at any cost, while there is a conflicting view. Society should not, such a view insists, expend too many resources, which could otherwise be used to create wealth and jobs, trying to save endangered species. My stance is slightly more aligned with the former, though my argument contains the specific prerequisite that society must save endangered species only if a species' extinction would lead to economic loss greater than the cost of saving that species.

Before elaborating on my reasoning, it is necessary to address a number of potential objections based on the nature of my view. I expect initial emotional responses to likely be negative from the public. Environmentalists, for example, would strongly condemn my position and argue that driving a species to extinction is a crime against nature, since every species is equal and humans are not entitled to slaughter other species. However, extinction is not new to nature. It has happened throughout Earth's long geologic history, long before modern humans occupied every continent except Antarctica.

Geological discoveries inform us of five major extinction events in the last 400 million years; in this short geological period, more than three quarters of life on Earth was wiped out. Consequently, human beings are not morally bound to preserve the status quo of Earth's current biological diversity. We should not save every species without considering their socioeconomic consequences.

This does not necessarily mean we should never take action to preserve endangered species. If the resulting loss from a species' extinction exceeds the cost of saving it, we should definitely protect it. Consider the following three examples. We appreciate pandas so much that the loss of these species would be regarded as a heavy emotional loss. We support the protection of raptors, such as eagles and falcons, because their extinction would allow rodents to proliferate and result in significant crop losses. And some endangered species have genetic and research value, which could lead to cures for diseases like cancer. The definition of loss in these cases encompasses broader social consequences rather than being solely financial.

Another reason we should save a species is that it provides a relatively objective and measurable benchmark to assess our policy. What would happen if we spared no expense to save every endangered species? What if the resources expended saving them could be used to save refugees of wars and famine? It may be acceptable to deem humans and other species as equal but when they are in conflict should other species take priority over human life? Assuming responsibility for the protection of all species is dangerous and violates basic human principles, which are the foundation of modern civilization. Therefore, we must utilize reasonable methods when deciding whether or not to save a species from extinction.

The real challenge is how to evaluate the loss of a species. This is not a question that can be sufficiently addressed in this short response, but simple classification into four categories can elucidate how the value of a species is ascertained. The first is direct economic value associated with domesticated species. The second is economic value associated with the ecological function of a species, exemplified by raptors which prey on rodents. The third is a species' research value. And the final category is cultural, religious, and aesthetic value, though this is admittedly more difficult to determine.

To summarize, I do not advocate allowing all endangered species to go extinct but believe it is unwise to strive to rescue every endangered species out of vague moral obligations. We should take action only when the loss of an entire species outweighs the costs associated with saving it. (641 words)

中文翻译

随着环保主义的影响越来越大，许多人认为保护濒危物种是人类必须认同并实现的道德义务。有些人甚至认为，社会必须不惜一切代价保护每一个动植物物种。然而，也有人持相反观点。

这些人坚持，社会不应该花费太多的资源拯救濒危物种，这些资源本可以用来创造财富和工作岗位。我的立场稍稍偏向前者，虽然我的论点其实是：只有在一个物种的灭绝所带来的经济损失大于拯救该物种的成本时，社会才必须保护濒危物种。

在阐述我的论证前，有必要先基于我的观点的本质来讨论一些潜在的反对看法。我预计最初的负面反应可能来自公众。比如，环保主义者就会强烈谴责我的观点，他们认为让某一物种灭绝是对自然的犯罪，因为所有的物种都是平等的，而人类没有权利屠杀其他物种。然而，对大自然来说，灭绝并不是什么新鲜事。灭绝贯穿于地球漫长的地质历史中，早在现代人类占领除南极洲以外的每个大陆之前就有。地质发现告诉我们在过去的四亿年中发生了五次重要的生物集群灭绝；在这短暂的地质时代，地球上四分之三以上的生物灭绝了。因此，人类在道德上并不一定要保护地球生物多样性的现状。我们不应该不考虑社会经济后果去保护每一个物种。

但这并不意味着我们不应该采取行动保护濒危物种。如果一个物种灭绝造成的损失大于保护它的成本，我们当然应该保护它。让我们来思考下列三个例子。我们如此喜欢大熊猫，每只大熊猫的死亡都让我们十分痛苦。我们支持保护猛禽，例如鹰和猎鹰，是因为它们的灭绝将使得啮齿动物变多、危害农作物。一些濒危物种具有遗传学或其他研究价值，也许能让我们治愈疾病——比如癌症。这些案例中"损失"的定义囊括了更广泛的社会结果，而不是仅仅指经济损失。

我们应该保护物种的另一个原因是，它提供了相对客观和可量化的基准来评估我们的政策。如果我们不惜代价地拯救每一个濒危物种，会发生什么事？如果节省这些花掉的资源可以用来拯救战争和饥荒中的难民呢？也许我们会接受万物平等的观点，但当人同其他生物互相冲突时，其他物种的生命优于人命吗？认为保护所有物种是人类的责任是危险的，违反了作为现代文明基础的基本的人道原则。因此，我们必须运用合理的方法来决定是否应该拯救一个濒危物种。

真正的挑战在于如何评估物种的损失。这篇短文中无法充分讨论这个问题，但简单的四分类法可以帮助阐明如何确定一个物种的价值。第一类是与驯养物种相关的直接经济价值。第二类是同一个物种的生态功能相关的经济价值，例如捕食啮齿动物的猛禽。第三类是物种的研究价值。最后一类是文化、宗教、审美价值，虽然这个类别确实更加难以确定。

总而言之，我不主张任由所有的濒危物种自生自灭，但我认为出于模糊的道德义务去拯救每一种濒危物种是不明智的。只有当整个物种的损失超过我们拯救它的成本时，我们才应该采取行动。

文章解析与点评

这一道题涉及一个建议："我们是否应该拯救濒临灭绝的动物"。这篇文章主要是站在后果的层面来论述的，提到了拯救这些动物可能付出的代价，以及拯救它们之后可能给人类带来的一系列价值，包括生态方面、经济方面、研究方面，甚至是情感方面的。

对于这个建议，我们还可以从更加宽广的层面考虑它的必要性、充分性、可行性、可能带来的后果等。可以思考的具体角度如下：

必要性：情况是否危急（不拯救这些动物的话，是否会威胁到人类的生存）？是否有义务这样做（这些动物的濒危是否由人类造成，如果不是，人类是否有道德上的义务去拯救这些动物）？

充分性：人类的拯救是否可以行之有效？

可行性：人类是否有能力（人力、物力、财力等）进行拯救行动？

可能带来的后果：拯救动物的付出是否会超过它们灭绝之后产生的损失？是否会打破生态平衡？不拯救的话是否会影响更大群体的安危？

以上就是对思考角度的罗列。大家从中挑选三到四个点进行发展就可以写出一篇立意还不错的文章了。但在写作中要注意，一定要照应 Direction 的要求，即对题目中的两种看法都提到。

④ "敌方看法类" Direction

Write a response in which you discuss the extent to which you agree or disagree with the claim. In developing and supporting your position, **be sure to address the most compelling reasons and/or examples that could be used to challenge your position**.

中文翻译

写一篇文章，在这篇文章中讨论你在多大程度上同意或者不同意题目中的观点，解释你所采取的立场的理由。在发展和支持你的立场的过程中，**注意讨论那些可以被用来反驳你观点的有力理由和 / 或例子**。

讲 解

这种 Direction 要求我们不仅阐明自己的观点，还要讨论那些可能被用来反对我们立场的观点。即，要提到"敌方"的观点。

比如，针对题目"国家需要让全国学生在进入大学之前学习相同的课程"，如果我们的观点是"国家**不需要**让全国学生在进入大学之前学习相同的课程"，而这时所谓的"敌方观点"则是："国家**需要**让全国学生在进入大学之前学习相同的课程"。由此可以看出，"敌方观点"是什么这一问题是由**我们的观点**决定的，而不是由题目决定的。

对于这样一种 Direction，有以下几点需要注意：

① 我们建议大家针对一种敌方看法展开一段论证，至于全文要提到多少敌方看法，即写多少段，这个是无关紧要的。**但至少应该有一段是在讨论敌方看法。**

② 大多数考生在讨论敌方观点时是这样的：简略提到敌方观点，然后再驳倒。其实，这种写法往往很难写多。

针对这种 Direction，我们建议大家采用以下的思维模板进行思考：

"敌方看法 + 我对敌方看法的分析 + 我对敌方看法的评价"

从这个思维模板可以看出，我们不一定要反对敌方的看法，也可以承认其合理性，亦或是站在辩证的立场上，既反对又同意，甚至说敌方看法和我的看法在本质上是不矛盾的。另外，我们还应该在草率地对敌方看法做出评价之前，对其进行分析，分析对方为什么会反对我、他的出发点和依据是什么。这样的分析和评价过程，才会让我们对这种 Direction 照应得既饱满又深刻。大家可以详细参照对例题的解析。

讲解浓缩版

参照思维模板提到敌方观点。

学术写作拓展

在学术写作，或者在一次学术会议，甚至是班级讨论中，我们必然会遇到那些反对我们的声音。对于这些声音，我们不仅要坦然面对，还要对其进行深刻的分析和全面的评价。针对不同学科里的那些反对的声音，各科目的回应方式在细节上略有不同。但不论是什么专业的考生，都可以参照我们给出的思维模板，在 GRE 写作的备考中迈出第一步，为以后的学术写作奠定基础。

例题举证

Universities should require every student to take a variety of courses outside the student's field of study.

Write a response in which you discuss the extent to which you agree or disagree with the claim. In developing and supporting your position, be sure to address the most compelling reasons and/or examples that could be used to challenge your position.

参考提纲如下：

总立场：不同意题目观点
分论点 1（我的看法）：学生精力不够，无法同时兼顾专业和专业外的学习。
分论点 2（我的看法）：如果贸然开设丰富多样的课程，学校的师资、物资可能捉襟见肘。
分论点 3（敌方看法）：有人可能会反对我的观点。他们认为：学生的确应该选择专业之外的课程（**对敌方看法的陈述**）。他们之所以这样认为，一来可能是因为希望学生拓宽知识面；另一方面可能是因为这样做能够让学生借鉴不同学科的方法论，从而加深对本专业知识的理解。（**对敌方看法的分析**）但是我认为，虽然这样的看法具有一定的合理性，但并非所有学生选择了课程就一定能认真听讲并且充分消化知识，最后做到灵活运用。而如果要中和两种看法的矛盾，我们可以为学生提供选修课的机会。（**对敌方看法的评价**）

分论点 1 和 2 都是"我的看法"，**而真正照应 Direction 要求的应该是分论点 3。**其实这里的分论点 3 已经不是提纲了，而我们之所以把这一点展开得如此详尽，是希望大家看到应该如何应用我们的思维模板。

在这一段中，我们不仅陈述了敌方看法，还分析了敌方为什么会有这样的看法，以及我们对敌方看法的评价。**考生应该尤其注意评价的部分，**因为我们不仅承认了敌方看法的合理性，也看到了其局限性，最后还提供了一种解决方法以解决敌方看法和我方看法的矛盾。这种思考模式就比大家之前的思考模式更全面，也更深刻。

题库范文

104 To be an effective leader, a public official must maintain the highest ethical and moral standards.

Write a response in which you discuss the extent to which you agree or disagree with the claim. In developing and supporting your position, be sure to address the most compelling reasons and/or examples that could be used to challenge your position.

A leader is elected to lead the government and serve the people. The personalities of leaders have always been the center of political discussions. Some people claim that an official must maintain the highest ethical and moral standards in order to be an effective leader. From my point of view, people with high moral standards will be more inclined to be effective leaders but these high standards do not necessarily achieve effectiveness. In some cases, remaining loyal to high moral principles without any chance of compromise will weaken a leader's effectiveness.

Before going any further, it is necessary to clarify the definition of "effective". Since the mission of a political leader, in my view, is to unite the people, distribute limited resources, and make important decisions to ensure social prosperity. Simply put, an effective leader must promote the welfare of the people he or she serves. With this definition, we can now discuss how moral standards impact a leader's effectiveness.

Maintaining high ethical and moral standards can definitely promote a leader's effectiveness because his or her personality will attract support and cooperation from the public. In other words, his or her political views are more likely to be accepted by the people, making political goals more likely to achieve. For example, in Chinese history an emperor with high moral standards was usually admired and loved by his people. People were more willing to execute the emperor's orders, facilitating the accomplishment of his political goals. That is why strong, prosperous dynasties, such as those of the Han, Tang and Song, were founded by emperors with high moral principles.

However, effectiveness does not necessarily originate in the moral standards. The possession of high moral standards cannot guarantee a leader will be effective nor can a leader's effectiveness be denied if he or she does not possess superior moral qualities. For instance, imagine a country plagued by terrorism. One of the primary goals of the country's leaders in this scenario is to defend the people they serve. If they could lead the nation to win the war on terror, despite some immoral means taken to achieve the goal, they must be considered effective. Some may argue that without high moral qualities, leaders will be despised or even overthrown. How can a leader be effective when he or she is not in power? Leaders may lose power if they are morally despicable but they are not required to have the highest moral standards. People can be quite tolerant when it comes to their leader's morality. As long as a leader's moral qualities do not jeopardize the people's interests, minor defects can be ignored. After all, given the definition of effectiveness above, an immoral leader may accomplish his or her mission if he or she is able to identify critical social goals and has the skills to coordinate governmental operations. These are the true sources of effectiveness.

In addition, in some cases adhering to the highest moral standards actually backfires, because some high moral principles, such as honesty and integrity, require actions that place national interest in jeopardy. If, for example, a nation's leader is asked to reveal confidential and sensitive information concerning national defense, he or she ought to, from a purely moral perspective, be candid and not withhold any information. However, we could easily recognize the danger of revealing such information to the public, which could be abused by terrorists. Some may argue this example is too absolute and rare and thus cannot serve as compelling evidence. This scenario, however, reflects the inherent conflict between moral ideology and reality, in which compromises are often required. Such conflict is ubiquitous in the real world.

To summarize, it is evident that high moral qualities do not equate to effective leadership. In some cases a leader's loyalty without exception to high moral principles can create serious problems and even harm social interests. That being said, possessing high moral standards can help leaders achieve their political mission, because such qualities will help them earn people's trust and support and facilitate governmental efficiency. (675 words)

中文翻译

人们选举领导人来领导政府并服务人民。领导人的性格一直都是政治讨论的中心。有些人声称，官员必须保持最高的道德标准，才能成为一个有效力的领导者。在我看来，虽然拥有高道德标准的人更有可能成为有效力的领导，但这些高标准并不一定能实现效力。在某些情况下，保持忠于高道德标准而没有任何折中妥协将会削弱领导者的效力。

在进一步展开论述之前，我们有必要澄清"有效力"的定义。在我看来，由于政治领袖的使命是团结人民、分配有效资源和做出重要决策以确保社会繁荣。简单说来，有效力的领导必须提升他/她所服务的人民的福祉。在这一定义下，现在我们可以讨论道德标准如何影响领导者的效力了。

维持高道德标准当然可以提升一位领导者的效力，因为他/她的性格将会吸引公众的支持和合作。换句话说，他/她的政治观点更有可能被人接受，更有可能实现政治目标。例如，在中国历史中，一位高道德标准的皇帝常常受到子民的欣赏和爱戴。人们更愿意执行皇帝的命令，加快完成他的政治目标。这就是为什么强大而繁荣的王朝，如汉、唐、宋，都是由具有高道德原则的皇帝建立的。

然而，效力并不一定来源于道德标准。拥有高道德标准并不能保证领导者一定有效力；若一位领导者并不具有高道德素质，我们也不能否认他/她的效力。例如，假想一个饱受恐怖主义困扰的国家。这个国家领导人的主要目标之一就是保卫人民。如果他们能够带领国家赢得反恐战争的胜利，那么即便在这个过程中他们采取了不道德的手段，他们也应该被认为是卓有成效的领导人。有些人可能认为没有高道德素质的领导者会被鄙视乃至推翻。如果一个领导者没能上台，他/她还如何发挥效力呢？道德卑下的领导者可能会失去权力，但他们并不需要有最高的道德标准。在领导者道德的问题上，人们可以相当宽容。若领导者的道德素养不会损害人民的利益，人们会忽视他们的小缺陷。毕竟，鉴于上述对效力的定义，如果一个不道德的领导者能确定关键的社会目标并具备协调政府运作的能力，他/她也能完成自己的使命。这些才是效力的真正来源。

此外，在某些情况下，坚持最高的道德标准会适得其反，因为有些高尚的道德原则，如诚实和正直，要求采取使国家利益受损的行动。例如，如果一个国家的领导者被要求披露有关国防的机密和敏感信息，从纯粹的道德角度而言，他/她应该坦诚相待、不隐瞒任何信息。然而，我们很容易认识到向公众披露这些信息的危险性，因为这些信息可能会被恐怖分子所滥用。或许有些人会说这个例子太极端罕见了，因此不能作为令人信服的例子。然而，这种情况反映了道德和现实之间的内在冲突，这种冲突往往要求妥协。这样的冲突在现实世界中是普遍存在的。

总而言之，虽然高道德素质不能等同于有效力的领导。在某些情况下，始终忠于高道德原则的领导者可能会造成严重的问题，甚至危害社会利益。话虽如此，拥有高道德标准能帮助领导者实现政治使命，因为这些素质可以帮助他们赢得人们的信任和支持，并提升政府的效率。

文章解析与点评

这篇文章为大家提供了两点思路层面上的参考。

首先，下定义。这篇文章首先对领导者的 "effective" 下了定义，将其定义成 "团结人民"、"分配资源" 和 "确保社会繁荣"。而之后的文段都是围绕这些概念来展开的。"下定义" 的方法经常在 Issue 文章中被使用，其主要的好处有二。其一，是缩小自己的论证范围，不会让文章显得大而空；其二，能够体现出我们充分认识到了题目的复杂性。正是因为题目所涉及的概念太过复杂而无法在一篇短短的 Issue 文章中被讨论透彻，所以我们需要对题目的核心概念做一个窄化的定义。值得注意的是，不同于我们之前在高中说明文或大学论文中接触到的 "下定义"，Issue 中用到的 "定义法" 不需要我们提出极为准确、无懈可击的定义，而只需要规定一个我们希望进行论证的范围即可。比如，如果要对领导者的效能 "efficiency" 或是否有成效 "effective" 进行正式定义，那应该从政治学、社会学、人类学等诸多领域下手，每个领域对其的定义必然是各不相同甚至相互龃龉，而这就不是我们需要或者应该关注的范畴了。毕竟，GRE 写作是不考查大家的专业能力的。

第二点，这道题目实则是讨论了两个概念之间的相互关系，即 "effective" 和 "moral standards"。在讨论 A 和 B 的关系时，我们经常可以从 "因果关系" 或 "充分必要关系" 入手。这道题即是如此。本文认为，"high moral standards" 是 "effective" 的必要条件，但 "highest moral standards" 却不是；同时，"high moral standards" 也不是 "effective" 的充分条件，有时为了顾全大局我们甚至需要牺牲一些 "moral standards"。

比如，Issue 第 61 题讨论了 "冒险行为" 和 "深思熟虑" 之间的关系。"People should undertake risky action only after they have carefully considered its consequences." 我们也可以从 "充分必要关系" 的角度入手讨论二者的关系。在一些情况下，深思熟虑是我们进行冒险行为之前的必要条件，因为人是理性的动物；而另一些情况下，我们却并不需要深思熟虑，因为我们进行行为活动并非全是为了收获所谓的成功，或是追求利益最大化，有时失败也是一种宝贵的经验和回忆；另外，不论在什么情况下，深思熟虑都不是冒险行为最终能带来成功的充分条件，因此，即便我们在深思熟虑之后再进行行为活动，活动的结果也可能不如人意。

13 Universities should require every student to take a variety of courses outside the student's field of study.

Write a response in which you discuss the extent to which you agree or disagree with the claim. In developing and supporting your position, be sure to address the most compelling reasons and/or examples that could be used to challenge your position.

After undergoing a marathon journey from primary to high school and then to university, students are confronted by another dilemma: how to strike a balance between their majors and courses in other fields. A similar quandary must have perplexed educators for decades as they grappled with designing university courses. While at first glance it may seem appealing to require students to take various courses outside of their fields of study, I remain doubtful of such a proposal. If we hastily carry out the advice, it would probably jeopardize education's purpose of facilitating students' well-roundedness.

Advocates of this claim will reject my position. They argue that knowledge gained from other fields contributes to innovative approaches to understanding the majors. The blending of different methodologies from various fields exemplifies this argument. For supporting examples, we can no further turn to the cooperation of linguistics and literature and the combination of math and economics. What bind these pairs are similar methodologies. By transferring a methodology from one field to another, students are able to understand the essence of both fields and this leads to the emergence of creative ideas and more profound understanding. However, not all fields relate as readily as the aforementioned pairs, so we cannot expect to apply principles from any field to another. Therefore, only when the courses share similar methodological principles can the author's recommendation come into effect.

Opposition to my argument also comes from current students' limited range of knowledge and narrow horizons. From this point of view, university students should be equipped with holistic capabilities in diverse fields so that they can better accustom themselves to diverse work in the future. In modern society, we are not surprised to encounter a professional lawyer who excels at public speaking; nor will it shock us when a mathematician assumes the role of a philosopher. An abundance of these generalists demonstrates the very advantage of a mastery of comprehensive skills and expertise. Nevertheless, I argue that generalists choose to be excellent, but are not required to be. It is their insatiable desire for knowledge that drives them to conquer new fields one after another, and it is their proficiency in the previous fields that enables them to excel in the new ones. Students nowadays are exceedingly short of time and universities should foster, in most circumstances, specialists rather than generalists. Consequently, while we welcome generalists, it might be more reasonable if we step back from the decision requiring students to choose courses in various disciplines, and adopt an alternative policy: encourage them to take extra courses and do whatever we can to facilitate this process.

Although I maintain that encouraging course selection may function better than a mandatory requirement, some people may dispute my position. They claim that the latter overshadows the former in terms of efficiency, since sluggishness is human nature and it is only through compulsory course requirements that students will really make progress in their major fields. The beginning of every course, they argue, inevitably stumbles on questioning and even emphatic repudiation; however, such questioning and repudiation will be followed by subsequent acceptance and students will quickly absorb new knowledge. Consistent might this claim appear with the reality, I tend to say that students do not learn for the sake of learning, and instead they learn in order to pass tests. Whatever form is used to test students, be it an exam, a paper submission or group work, students always tend to focus on the test itself, but not on the accumulation of knowledge. Without adjusting students' attitude towards learning, the introduction of various new courses will remain well-intentioned but will inevitably result in a meaningless struggle against the exam-oriented education system.

Taking extra courses outside one's original field goes far beyond the decision of whether or not to take them, but raises more fundamental and far-reaching issues. We may tentatively implement the issue's recommendation, but a complete change in the design of university courses requires more careful consideration. (662 words)

中文翻译

从小学到中学再到大学，在经历完这一段马拉松式的艰辛旅程之后，学生们遇到了另一个难题：如何在本专业与非专业课程之间寻得平衡。几十年来，类似的困境也让那些设计大学课程的教育工作者感到纠结不已。尽管乍看之下，要求学生选修各类非专业课程显得格外诱人，但我却对这个建议持怀疑态度。如果贸然推行这条建议，那么我们将很可能破坏教育的初衷——促进学生的综合发展。

这条建议的拥护者可能会反对我的观点。他们也许认为，从其他专业获得的知识能够为学生深入理解其专业贡献新的途径。各领域的方法论的综合似乎能够佐证这一观点。其中，最为恰当的例子莫过于语言学与文学的穿插、数学与经济学的交织。相似的方法论将这些组合成功勾连起来。通过将一个领域中的方法论转移到另一个领域，学生们能够同时理解这两个领域的精髓，并在此基础上进一步催生各类新颖的观点以及更为深刻的理解。然而，并非所有领域都如前面列举的组合那般紧密相连，我们不能期望任何领域之间的原理都能相互适用。因此，只有在方法论原理近似的科目之间，作者的建议才能产生实际意义。

反对我的观点还可能会提到：当今学生的有限知识与狭窄视角。从这个角度来看，大学生确实应该具备多种领域的综合能力，以便于他们未来能够更好地适应各种工作。在现代社会，如果遇到一名职业律师精通公开演讲，我们不会感到惊讶；同样，如果看到数学家能像哲学家一样思考，我们也不会诧异。大量的通才向我们反复证明掌握多门技巧和专长的益处。然而，我认为通才的产生是自行选择的结果，而非强制要求使然。正是由于知识本身永不满足的欲望，使其能够不断征服新的领域；也正是因为对前一领域知识的精通，帮助其在后续领域中占据优势。当今学生的时间已然十分有限，在大部分情况下，大学应该培养专才而非通才。因此，尽管欢迎通才，但更为合理的做法是：我们放弃要求学生选修大量非专业课程的决定，转而采取另一条政策：鼓励学生选修非专业课程，并尽一切可能帮助他们加速成为通才。

尽管我认为鼓励而非强制学生选课会达到更好的效果，但有人可能会站出来反对我的观点。从效率来看，他们认为后者明显强于前者，因为懒惰是人类的天性，所以只有通过强制选课，学生们才能在其本专业领域取得进步。他们可能相信，一开始这些课程会不可避免地遭遇学生们的质疑甚至怨怼；但是，这样的质疑或斥责将逐渐被接纳所取代，随后学生将开始迅速吸收新的知识。然而在我看来，与这条建议更为相符的现实是：学生并不会为了学习而学习；相反，会为了通过考试而学习。不论以任何形式出现的考试：测验、个人作业或者小组作业，学生们总是会注重测试本身，而非任何知识上的积累。如果不对学生的们学习态度进行调整，而贸然引入各类非专业课程，那么此举只能停留在好心办坏事的层面，并最终使学生身陷以考试为导向的教育系统中，做着毫无意义的挣扎。

选修非专业课程，其探讨意义已经超出了是否应该这样做，进而牵涉到了更为根本且深刻的问题。我们可以试探性地尝试题干所给出的建议，但对大学课程设计进行彻底的修改，仍需要我们更为妥帖的考量。

文章解析与点评

这篇文章很好地回答了一个被经常问到的问题：面对"敌方看法（他人看法）"类的Direction，我们需要用多少篇幅去写那些反对我们立场的观点？

将本文与其他两篇敌方看法类的文章相结合，我们可以得出结论：面对敌方看法类的Direction，我们少则用一段，多则可以用三段（假设中间段有三段）来讨论敌方看法。

也因为这篇文章的中间段三段都在照应 Direction，这也给我们提供了很好的思维模板和语言素材。比如，在陈述敌方看法时，这三段分别用了这样的句式：

1. Advocates of this claim will reject my position. They argue that...

2. Opposition to my argument also comes from...

3. Although I maintain that..., some people may dispute my position.

而每一个中间段在陈述了他人看法之后，还对他人看法做了进一步的分析和评价，这些部分的内容和语言也值得大家学习。

另外值得一提的是本文的观点。在面对"大学是否应该要求学生选修多种多样的课"这一话题时，同意这个建议的考生最容易想到的观点是"多样的课程能拓宽学生的视野，增强他们的综合素质"；而反对者最容易诉诸的观点则是"学生没时间，精力不够"。这些观点不是不可以，只是很多考生都写，便很难出彩了。而这篇文章给大家提供了一些新的思路，如：

1. 学习其他课程可能会加深对本专业知识的理解，但这仅局限于方法论相似而且可以互相借鉴的学科。

2. 大学不排斥通才，但更应该培养专才。

3. 当学生被要求选很多课时，他们看似学到了很多知识，但只是在应付考试而已。

106 In most professions and academic fields, imagination is more important than knowledge.

Write a response in which you discuss the extent to which you agree or disagree with the claim. In developing and supporting your position, be sure to address the most compelling reasons and/or examples that could be used to challenge your position.

In regard to the magic code to success in professions and academic fields, the statement assigns more significance to imagination rather than knowledge and expertise. However, I tend to argue that in most circumstances, imagination and knowledge are not necessarily mutually exclusive, but more complementary to each other; therefore, it is of greater importance to strike a favorable balance between imagination and knowledge rather than to weigh their value and then give up either of them. The fields of literature, art and science, sufficiently support my claim.

In the world of literature, professional knowledge serves as the cornerstone of the credibility of works while free imagination contributes to polishing the story and refining the plot. Should there be no professional knowledge or expertise supporting the details, the whole work would be no more than a flamboyant corpse deprived of the fundamental validity of stories. On the contrary, the lack of imagination within the stories would only lead to readers' loss of appetite to go on with the books. To have a brief scan of the previous literature world, all the masterpieces benefit from a successful marriage of unfettered imagination and reliable knowledge. In "Anna Karenina", Leo Tolstoy successfully created a classical character Anna, whose legendary life is replete with reflections of the nineteenth century of Russia. These reflections are trustworthy because they are based on the author's authentic and vast knowledge of that period of time. In addition, what renders the character so distinguishable from other characters is the writer's unrestrained imagination. It is not difficult to imagine how less sparkling this work would be if the writer had been less knowledgeable and had poorer imagination.

While in the field of art, the combination of imagination and knowledge appears even closer. Artists temper their professional knowledge and skills by learning from the previous masters; however, in order to make innovative achievements, they unavoidably tend to break the chains of tradition and stimulate their imagination by all possible means. For example, from the prestigious work Last Supper by Leonardo Da Vinci, one of the greatest painters in the Renaissance period, we can observe the painter's insightful understanding and professional knowledge of the mid-century European religions. However, it was not until the birth of one of his another works Mona Lisa, which is not only a great reflection of the artist's imagination, but also stirs the viewers' illusions, did he reach his peak in the field of art. Likewise, another well-known artist Monet also owes his success as an important impressionist to his vast knowledge about the shadowing of objects under light, as well as to his unfettered imagination of the relocation of all the objects on the same piece of paper.

Even the universe of science, which is famous for its rigorous demonstration and scrupulous observation, also derives substantial benefit from the cooperation of knowledge and imagination. It is imagination that inspires scientists to explore the unknown world, and it is the professional knowledge that enables them to pave the way to such an unknown world. History has witnessed countless examples: the invention of the microwave oven, the first use of radar, the creation of dolphin-like ships, all of which would still be in the vacuum without their inventors' fertile imagination, as well as the experts' knowledge and gallant endeavor.

Conversely, someone might oppose my argument, drawing attention to the frustrating fact that nowadays people sometimes rely too much on the existing resources of information and knowledge, such as the Internet, books, libraries, but are reluctant to think for themselves. Admittedly, students who overpay their attention to knowledge but cease to brainstorm would become nerds; scholars who overlook the importance of imagination would end up mediocre; society that only relies on existing knowledge would come to an overall standstill. Nevertheless, it is exactly the contribution of such discouraging facts that convince us of the necessity of combining imagination and knowledge and employing them to help us go further on the road to the mysterious world.

To briefly sum up, while imagination and knowledge might play different roles in our life and career, it behooves us to regard them as inseparable and interdependent factors. Only equipped with both imagination and knowledge, are we able to walk faster and further. (708 words)

中文翻译

在大多数职业与学术领域中，谈论什么才是获取成功的秘诀时，题目似乎更愿意强调想象力而非知识和专长的作用。然而，我个人倾向于认为，在大多数情况下，想象力与知识并不互斥，反而相互补充；因此，更为重要的是在想象力与知识之间求得更为有利的平衡，而非在权衡轻重之后舍弃掉其中的任何一方。文学、艺术以及科学领域皆（有例证可）有力支持我的观点。

在文学世界里，专业的知识对于作品的可信度而言起到了奠基石的作用，而自由的想象力能将故事与情节打磨得更加精致。如果没有知识或专长来支撑细节，那么整部作品将不免沦为一具花哨的、失去基本可信度的干尸。相反，如果故事缺失了想象力，那么读者也就失去了继续把书看完的兴趣。简要地扫视一下此前的文学世界，几乎所有的伟大著作都受益于自由的想象与可靠的知识这两者的成功结合。在《安娜·卡列尼娜》一书中，列夫·托尔斯泰成功刻画了一位经典人物——安娜，她富有传奇色彩的生命旅程中充满了有关19世纪俄国的真实写照。由于这种写照是建立在作者对那段历史真实且广博的知识积累上的，所以它们都是可信的。与此同时，真正将这个人物与其他人物区别开来的是作者天马行空的想象力。不难想象，但凡作者缺少一点点知识或想象力，这部作品都将会因此而黯然失色。

在艺术领域，想象力与知识的结合显得更加紧密。通过向前辈高人学习，艺术家们能够打磨他们的专业知识和技能；而为了取得新的成就，他们也不可避免地需要打破传统的锁链，并通过一切手段来刺激自己的想象力。比如，列奥纳多·达·芬奇，文艺复兴时期最伟大的画家之一，从他创作的传世作品《最后的晚餐》中，我们可以观察到这位画家对中世纪欧洲宗教的深刻理解与专业知识。而使他步入艺术巅峰的是他的另一部巨作《蒙娜·丽莎》，该画不仅完美反映了画家的丰富想象，更强烈激起了读者的想象。同样，作为重要的印象派画家，另一位知名艺术家莫奈的成功很大程度上在于：一方面他熟知光线下物体的阴影变化，另一方面他不受拘束的想象帮助他在同一张纸上对所有物体进行完美地重新排布。

即便是以严谨的实证和仔细的观察而闻名的科学领域，也会因知识与想象力的结合而广受裨益。想象力启发了科学家去探索未知的世界，而专业知识则辅助他们走进这个未知的世界。历史见证了无数的例子：微波炉的发明、雷达的首次使用、海豚状船只的发明，如果不是发明者们丰富的想象，以及专家们博学而勇敢的努力，那么这一切仍是一片虚无。

然而，有人可能会反对我的观点，他们会指出一些令人沮丧的事实：人们当下时常会过分依赖已知的信息和知识资源，如互联网、书籍、图书馆等，自己却不愿思考。不可否认，如果过分关注知识而停止活跃思考，学生就会变成书呆子；如果忽视想象，学者终将沦为平庸之辈；如果只是依赖现存的知识，社会则会陷入整体停滞。不过，正是这些令人沮丧的事实，有效地促使我们看到将想象力和知识结合，以及通过付诸实践使我们进一步深入未知的世界的必要性。

简要来说，尽管想象力和知识在我们的生活和工作中可能扮演着不同角色，但我们也需要认识到它们不可分割且相互依赖的一面。只有同时身兼想象力与知识，我们才能在未来走得更快、更远。

文章解析与点评

这篇文章有四个地方值得大家借鉴。

第一，文章的展开方式。大家可以发现，文章是对题目中的 "field" 这个词进行了分类讨论，分成文学、艺术和科技领域。这种分类讨论的思想在 Issue 题目中经常用到，非常便于展开全文的讨论。大家一看见 "field"，几乎就可以立刻用到分类讨论的思想，将其分成政治、文学、艺术、科技、教育、历史等领域来思考。

第二，文章的例子。很多考生都对例子的积累非常发愁。但事实上，为了应对 Issue 题目，我们只需要在遇到相关题目时才需要去准备例证，而不需要单独背很多的例子。这篇文章其实就已经为大家提供了文学、艺术和科技领域的数个例子，而大家只需要再去准备政治、教育、历史等几个领域的数个例子即可。毕竟，真正能够帮助我们进行以后的学术写作的不是现在积累的例子，而是借用例子对道理进行论证的能力。

第三，文章语言的多样性。在遇到相同概念的表达时，这篇文章充分体现出了同义改写的能力。如：在表达 "领域（文学领域、艺术领域和科技领域）" 这一概念时，三个中间段分别用了 "world"，"field" 和 "universe" 这三个词；而在表示想象力和知识的 "结合" 之时，这篇文章又用到了 "marriage"，"combination"，"cooperation" 等不同的表达。这种同义改写的做法能够很大程度上丰富文章的用词。

第四，对 Direction 的照应。这道题目的 Direction 要求我们提到敌方看法，不少考生会把敌方看法的这个段落当成让步段来写，写法是：草草提到敌方看法，然后用一句话反驳它。这种写法是不能满足要求的。而这篇文章的倒数第二自然段就为大家提供了讨论敌方看法的一个很好的事例：既有对敌方看法的陈述，也有对敌方可能引用的事例的列举和讨论，还有对敌方看法合理性的承认，以及最后对敌方看法的评价。这样的写法就比较丰富了，同时也能彰显出我们对于敌方看法的透彻分析。

5 "建议类" Direction（一）

Write a response in which you discuss the extent to which you agree or disagree with the recommendation and explain your reasoning for the position you take. In developing and supporting your position, describe **specific circumstances** in which adopting the recommendation **would or would not be advantageous** and explain how these examples shape your position.

中文翻译

写一篇文章，在这篇文章中讨论你在多大程度上同意或者不同意题目中的建议，解释你所采取的立场的理由。在发展和支持你的立场的过程中，描述一下你认为这个建议**有利或者不利的具体情况**，并且解释这些情况如何影响你的立场。

讲 解

这种 Direction 对应的题目都是一条建议。Direction 要求我们讨论这条建议在什么时候有利（advantageous），什么时候不利（not advantageous）。很多考生在写这类题目的时候，谈了很多该建议的"必要性"、"紧迫性"、"充分性"等等。然而，我们只有在谈论建议所产生的结果之时，才会用"有利"或"不利"来形容。**因此，这种 Direction 其实是要求我们谈谈在什么情况下，该建议会产生什么样的结果。所以，如果一旦偏离"结果"的范畴，我们也就偏离了 Direction 的要求。**

讲解浓缩版

讨论什么情况下会产生什么有利或不利的结果。

学术写作拓展

在谈论一个建议时，我们不能只是单纯地谈论我们对它或推崇或抵制的态度，而应该列举出具体的情况，说明这个建议在该情况下会带来什么样的结果，这样才能以理服人。在学术写作中，我们也会遇到各种各样的研究方法和理论。同样的，我们不能单纯地对某个理论示以好恶，而应该说明这个理论在什么样的情况之下会带来什么样的结果，而正是这些或好或坏的结果决定了我们在研究中是否应采用这种理论或者方法论。这样的启示也适用于下一条 Direction。

⚱ 例题举证

A nation should require all of its students to study the same national curriculum until they enter college.

Write a response in which you discuss the extent to which you agree or disagree with the recommendation and explain your reasoning for the position you take. In developing and supporting your position, describe specific circumstances in which adopting the recommendation would or would not be advantageous and explain how these examples shape your position.

参考提纲如下：

> **总立场**：有保留地同意题目观点
>
> **分论点 1**（题目建议会带来的有利结果）：全国学生学习一套课程，可以保证考试内容相同，这样更方便高校录取人才，促进教育公平。
>
> **分论点 2**（题目建议会带来的有利结果）：全国学生学习一套课程，方便教师的培训和备课。这就客观促进了教师资源的可流动性，方便不同地区间教师的相互补给。
>
> **分论点 3**（题目建议会带来的不利结果）：全国学生学习一套课程，可能导致区域间的多样性匮乏，学生千人一面，缺少个性。

分论点 1 和 2 是在讨论题目中建议有利的情况，分论点 3 是在讨论不利的情况。而不论是哪一个分论点，都紧紧扣住了题目中建议可能产生的"结果"，也因此很好地照应了 Direction 的要求。

题库范文

39 College students should be encouraged to pursue subjects that interest them rather than the courses that seem most likely to lead to jobs.

Write a response in which you discuss the extent to which you agree or disagree with the recommendation and explain your reasoning for the position you take. In developing and supporting your position, describe specific circumstances in which adopting the recommendation would or would not be advantageous and explain how these examples shape your position.

Should college students be encouraged to take classes that truly interest them or select courses that seem most likely to increase their competiveness in the job market? From my point of view, pursuing interests should be prioritized over practical concerns but students with financial difficulties may find it more desirable to take courses that will lead to decent jobs. It is also worth pointing out that students can take courses based on Interest while also taking classes specifically to improve their employment prospects.

Interest is the most powerful motivator in students' academic endeavors so pursing subjects which interest them may lead to greater academic achievements. When students face challenges in their classes, they must have a firm belief to carry on or they might simply quit. Although the prospect of a well-paid job may seem like a strong motive, it is actually far less effective than personal interest. This is because when students strive for decent careers, it takes a long time for their efforts to pay off. Consequently, their motivation could fail whereas personal interest could sustain them. Therefore, in order to make greater intellectual achievements, students should be encouraged to enroll in classes that interest them.

Behind the claim that students should take courses likely to result in jobs is the assumption that it is possible to determine whether or not a specific class is capable of doing so. This assumption may not always hold true because the job market changes quickly and can be hard to make accurate prediction. For example, in the field of computer sciences, there are incessant changes in prevalent programming language. A few years ago, C was the industrial standard so courses in that language would have been helpful when searching for a job. It did not take long, however, for Java and Python to become dominant and knowledge in C is no longer valuable. In short, such "useful" courses can become obsolete by the time students graduate because of the short timescale of changes in the job market. This is clearly not a desirable outcome for students.

However, students experiencing financial difficulties may depend on a promising career to improve their (or their family's) economic situation. They may prefer to place more emphasis on courses that can earn them a better job than what they are interested. In this particular scenario, the argument that a future career is not strong motivation does not hold true because the desire to change one's fate can be extremely powerful.

Finally, it is also necessary to address the underlying assumption in this debate that courses which interest students are different from those conducive to finding jobs. This is problematic and does not always hold true. Even for those classes that seem to have few practical connections to the real world, they can still teach students vital skills needed to secure decent jobs and succeed in their careers. For example, advanced theoretical physics involving abstruse ideas and mathematics may seem useless in the job market at first glance, but these courses teach students how to think critically, simplify complex systems in a model and acquire solid mathematical skills essential in the financial world. Firms on Wall Street are actively seeking job candidates with solid background in math, physics and computer sciences, which is a compelling piece evidence that courses of interest can also lead to jobs.

In conclusion, it is beneficial for students to pursue subjects that interest them but students should take their financial situation into consideration when selecting courses. Job availability and students' interest do not constitute an irreconcilable dichotomy: classes can be both interesting and beneficial in the job market. (607 words)

中文翻译

应当鼓励大学生参加他们真正感兴趣的课程，还是让他们选择那些最可能提升他们在就业市场上竞争力的课程？在我看来，追求兴趣的优先级高于对现实的考虑，然而经济困难的学生可能更想要上那些能让他们得到体面工作的课程。此外，还应指出的是，学生可以基于兴趣选择课程，同时也可以选择专门提升他们的就业前景的课程。

兴趣是学生学术活动中最有利的激励因素，因此让学生追求他们最有兴趣的学科能带来更大的学术成就。当学生在课堂上面临挑战时，他们必须怀有坚定的信念才能继续下去，不然他们可能就会放弃。虽然高薪工作的前景似乎是一个强烈的动机，但它事实上远不如个人兴趣有效。这是因为当学生为体面工作而努力时，他们的努力需要很长时间才能获得回报。因此，他们的积极性可能受挫，然而个人兴趣却可以让他们继续。因此为了取得更大的智力成就，我们应当鼓励学生参加他们感兴趣的课程。

主张学生参加有助于就业的课程的背后是这样一个假设：我们可以确定某门课程有这个作用。这一假设并不一定总是正确的，因为就业市场变化很快，很难作出正确的预测。例如，在计算机科学领域，流行的编程语言正在不断变化。几年前，C 语言是工业标准，因此 C 语言课程对找工作是有帮助的。但好景不长，Java 和 Python 变成了主流语言，C 语言知识不再有价值。简而言之，因为就业市场时常发生变化，这些"有用"的课程在学生毕业的时候可能会过时。这对学生而言显然不是一个理想的结果。

然而，财务困难的学生可能需要一份有前途的工作来改善他们（或他们的家庭）的经济情况。他们可能更喜欢把重点放在那些能为他们赢得更好工作的课程，而不是他们感兴趣的课程上。在这种情况下，"未来职业并不是强烈的动机"的论点就不成立了，因为一个人想要改变自己命运的愿望可能非常强烈。

最后，还有必要解决争论中的潜在假设：让学生感兴趣的课程和有助于他们找到工作的课程是不同的。这个假设可能是有问题的，并不总是成立。即使是那些看起来和现实世界没有多少实际联系的课程，他们仍然可能教给学生得到体面工作和在职业生涯中成功的重要技能。例如，乍一看涉及深奥思想和数学知识这些高级理论的物理学在就业市场中毫无作用，但这些课程教导学生如何批判地思考、在模型中简化复杂问题，并让他们获得在金融界十分必要的坚实的数学技能。华尔街的公司正在寻找那些具备数学、物理和计算机科学背景的求职者，这是一个强有力的证据证明凭兴趣选择的课程也能赢得好工作。

总而言之，让学生选择他们感兴趣的课是有益的，但学生们选课时也应当考虑他们的财务情况。能不能找到工作和学生的兴趣并不构成不可调和的分歧：课程可以既是有趣的又是对找工作有益的。

文章解析与点评

这道题目相对来说比较简单，也是涉及两个概念作比较。我们在破题的时候，也可以采用之前提到的方式行文。这篇文章即是如此，既谈到兴趣对选择职业的重要性，也谈到现实因素，如经济实力的不可抗性，还谈到兴趣和现实因素的结合。

下面，我们帮助大家拓展一些在对两个概念做比较时经常用到的表达。

A 比 B 重要：

A should take precedence over B.

A should be given/assigned priority over B.

A overshadow/outshine/dwarf B.

B is subordinate/inferior to A.

B lose luster in front of A.

B pale/lag in significance in comparison with A.

A 和 B 不可比：

A and B are not comparable.

It is ill-conceived to draw a parallel between A and B.

A 和 B 不矛盾：

A does not necessarily contradict B.

A and B are not mutually exclusive.

A is compatible with B.

We have to admit the coexistence of A and B in some circumstances.

---

54 In order to become well-rounded individuals, all college students should be required to take courses in which they read poetry, novels, mythology, and other types of imaginative literature.

Write a response in which you discuss the extent to which you agree or disagree with the recommendation and explain your reasoning for the position you take. In developing and supporting your position, describe specific circumstances in which adopting the recommendation would or would not be advantageous and explain how these examples shape your position.

The author of this issue task seems to have experienced little hesitation before establishing the link between students' comprehensive development and the study of imaginative literature, such as poetry, novels and mythology. Indeed, this attributes, the capability to think freely, or, to put it more directly, to emancipate one's thinking from stale research frameworks, lay the foundation for a college student's academic performance. Before arriving at a final decision about whether to render imaginative literature courses mandatory, however, we should consider several specific circumstances in which this recommendation could be either advantageous or disadvantageous.

Unlike various scientific courses, such as mathematics, physics or chemistry, which require meticulous observation and scrupulous computation, imaginative literature is renowned for the free domain it gives students for it does not require them to rigidly adhere to one methodology or unique principle. In addition, we can even predict the generation of an innovative marriage of unrestrained creativity and discreet academic attitude. Such a combination will surely exert a positive influence upon science students and further facilitate the process of becoming well-rounded individuals.

Courses utilizing imaginative literature are intended to encourage creativity, yet this can be jeopardized by circumstances—which go beyond students' schedules and teaching resources available to them. First of all, reading novels and poetry is thought to offer students a temporary respite from the onerous assignments in other courses, and it is exactly because of this that students are relaxed enough to appreciate the beauty of imaginative literature. However, if compulsory literature courses have as strenuous a workload as major courses, then students' passion is bound to languish. Their consequent reluctance to participate in the class will further impede creative thinking. Moreover, it is difficult to imagine enrollment proliferation in literature courses in the absence of sufficient teaching resources. One way to ensure course accessibility is by requiring teachers to take on more Direction, but the teaching quality, as well as teachers' attention to each student, cannot be guaranteed. In such circumstances, the issue's recommendation fails to provoke students' wholehearted engagement with the material, which ultimately lies at the root of well-rounded individuals.

While I sympathize with the author's desire to enhance college students' creativity, I argue that he/she hastily equates students' enrollment in literature courses with increased innovative thinking. As is often the case, however, the improvement of thinking ability is subject to various factors, such as students' ability to absorb new information, attitudes toward assignments and frequent review of material. What matters most, however, is the potential link between literature courses and other courses students take. Not all fields are easily connected in terms of methodologies. Consequently, while imagination assumes a significant role in literature, and may serve an important methodological purpose, it cannot be used in other majors in exactly the same way. Even if it could, it does not mean that students are capable of understanding such an approach, let alone mastering its application and using it in their major fields. Therefore, instead of taking literature courses, student may benefit more from taking courses where methodologies are easily transferrable and can thus be utilized in other fields. This alternative policy is more focused and thereby more efficient. (529 words)

中文翻译

　　"学生的综合发展"与"包括诗歌、小说和神话的想象文学"，在这二者之间建立联系时，题干作者似乎没有丝毫的犹豫。的确，这种特质——这种自由思考，更确切的说，这种将人的思维从死板的研究框架中解放出来的能力，是大学生优秀学术表现的坚实基础。然而，"是否将想象文学课提升为必修课？"在得出最终决定之前，我们必须设想一些确切而可能的后果，以进一步考量这条建议的优、劣之处。

　　数学、物理和化学，这些学科往往要求严谨的观察和精准的推算；然而不同于这些学科，以自由无边而闻名的想象文学，并不要求学生呆板地遵守任何一条特定的方法论或原理。另外，"天马行空的创造力"与"一丝不苟的学术态度"，我们甚至可以乐观地预测这种新奇的结合以及进一步的代际延伸。极为可能的是，这样一种结合会给科学专业的学生带来十分正面的影响，并且使他们加速成为更加全面发展的个体。

　　尽管想象文学这门课被设计来鼓励创新，但其正面影响还有可能受到一些负面后果的干扰，比如学生课业压力因此而超负，或者师资不足。首先，不少人认为，读小说、诗歌可以将学生暂时从其他学科的繁重课业中解救出来；正因为这样的特点，学生才能做到足够放松以欣赏想象文学的美。然而，如果文学课上升成主要学科，这将造成繁重的课业负担，那么学生对此的热情势必衰减。因此，随之而来下降的出勤率将进一步瓦解创新思维带来的积极影响。另外，在缺乏充足教学资源的情况下，我们也很难想象文学课的选课率会激增。而为了保证正常开课，任课教师只能承担更多的任务，那么教学质量、教师对学生的关注度也就无法保证了。在这些情况下，题目所提供的建议便未能使学生全心投入到对课程的学习中，但这恰好又是一个全面的个体得以养成的重要前提。

　　尽管我能够理解作者希望提高大学生创造力的愿景，但将"选择文学课程"与"提高创新思维"贸然划上等号，我认为他/她过于草率。事实上，思考能力的提高还受许多因素的影响，如学生吸收新信息的能力、对待作业的态度以及对课程内容的反复咀嚼。然而，更为重要的是，文学课程与学生所选其他课程的潜在关联。并不是所有学科的方法论都是相通的。因此，尽管想象力在文学中不但占据重要地位，更起着方法论的重要作用，但它却很难适用于其他学科。即便能适用，这也并不意味着学生能够完全理解这样一种能力，更别提熟练掌握并且将其运用在其他主要的学科。因此，相较于选修文学课程，学生更可能通过选修其他课程而受益，因为这些课程的方法论适于转化，且更容易被应用到其他学科当中。这条替代性的策略更有针对性，因此也更加有效。

文章解析与点评

这道题目本身不难，但是大家很容易忽略 Direction 的要求。题目是在谈论是否应该选择跟想象文学有关的课，对于这个建议，我们可以考虑它的必要性、可行性、充分性和可能产生的后果等等，但最后落在纸上的，却只能是这个建议可能带来的后果。这是由 Direction 的要求所决定的。

所以，本文的中间段三段都是围绕结果展开的。

中间段第一段，肯定这个建议可能带来的有利结果。比如，因为文学课中并不要求学生固守一个方法论，所以学生可以在文学课上自由思考。并且，学生还可能受到这种课程的启发，将这种自由的方法论和自己本身严谨的治学态度相结合。这将特别有利于科学专业学生的学习，促进他们的全面发展。

但是，题目中的建议也会产生很多的负面结果。学生紧张的课程安排和有限的师资都是这个建议的拦路虎。如果强行将想象文学设为必修课程，可能导致学生兴趣的下降，以及教师对每个学生精力分配的涣散，这些都不利于学生的全面发展。这在第二段中讨论得比较详尽。

另外，由于一系列其他因素，题目中的建议不一定能够带来正面的结果。比如，学生对待作业不认真，吸收能力差等等。并且，并非所有课程的方法论都是可以互相借鉴的，因此即便学生在想象文学的课程上学有所得，也不一定能够把这种方法论运用在别的课程中。这在最后一段有详细的讨论。

值得注意的是，在很多和课程设计或者跟教育有关的 Issue 题目中，我们都可以讨论课程中所涉及的方法论。相对于课程本身的知识和内容，对方法论的讨论会更能触及教育和课程的本质，也因此更加深刻。

最后值得一提的是，本文并没有传统意义上收束、总结全篇的结尾段。在这里我们想告诉大家，只要前文对所有问题的讨论都很清楚并且圆满，Issue 文章并不一定需要结尾段。

---

61 People should undertake risky action only after they have carefully considered its consequences.

Write a response in which you discuss the extent to which you agree or disagree with the recommendation and explain your reasoning for the position you take. In developing and supporting your position, describe specific circumstances in which adopting the recommendation would or would not be advantageous and explain how these examples shape your position.

Thinking ability, both analytical reasoning and rational decision-making, has always marked the human species and therefore distinguished human beings from other animals. Accompanying such abilities is an intense sense of pride and the obligation to contemplate actions before carrying them out. When it comes to potentially risky decisions, we strive to know all the possible consequences ahead of time and then use these consequences to define standards of behavior. While any action frequently requires thorough consideration of the possible consequences, I maintain that this principle is not carved in stone, and abundant cases exist wherein we are not able to and, indeed should not consider the consequences of risky actions.

I acknowledge that in general circumstances, initiative, one of the most conspicuous characteristics that differentiate humans from other animals, coincides with the comprehensive thought about the consequences of our actions. Confronted with particularly complex or risky issues, we are constantly expected to make sensible judgment and predict potential results. Experience accumulating, in most cases we are able to perform systematic analyses of the circumstances we encounter and make rational decisions accordingly. Almost all research in any professional field are premised on a researcher's attempt to make accurate predictions of actions they undertake; and once such a prophecy is confirmed, we regard the action as being worthwhile and acquire experience that may be applied in subsequent situations.

As we become increasingly accustomed to this "think-move" style, however, we simultaneously suffer from the stereotypical assertion that "think" will definitely lead to predictable consequences and such a prediction equals success. Unfortunately, neither of these is guaranteed. Since we make predictions based on previous experiences and these experiences can be surpassed by a variety of issues we have never encountered, we sometimes fail to account for the unknown and therefore fail in our attempts to make positive or successful decisions. In order to address new challenges, we need to keep observing until we accumulate sufficient information to make an accurate prediction. Nevertheless, it may be also during this process of observation, the very chance to take prompt action roars past us. This is why so many business magnates frequently manage to seize and greatly profit from fleeting and seemingly dangerous opportunities. While some may attribute this to their insight and vision, what really motivates those businessmen to grasp opportunities is their awareness of how little they will achieve if they solely rely on previous experiences to address new problems as well as how disappointed they will be if they hesitate and miss their chance.

In addition, what I find most questionable with this issue is its underlying assumption that we should always undertake action consistent with the consequences. While a utilitarian (specifically one who seeks practical benefits) might warmly applaud this principle, I find that the sole pursuit of consequences deprives our lives of fun. We should at least occasionally, to put it bluntly, do crazy and dangerous things without caring about the consequences. It is indeed satisfying when we formulate a thorough plan which leads to a positive result; but will we mourn the unexpected result that comes from acting according to our hearts? Probably not. Wise men may base decisions on the consequences, but others can just follow their hearts.

As human beings, we must contemplate the consequences our actions may have. Contemplation, however, does not suffice to generate success. Moreover, we are proud of our rationality, but we should also restrain it so that it would not jeopardize our true feelings, another significant feature of human beings. (586 words)

中文翻译

思考能力，包括分析推理和理性选择，不但是人类的重要特征，更将人类与其他动物区别开来。与这种能力相伴而生的还有人们在行动前预测后果的强烈的自尊感和责任感。当涉及潜在的冒险决策时，我们总是尽力去提前了解所有可能的后果，并据此对我们的行动划分等级。尽管任何行动都需要事先对其可能的后果进行详尽的思考，但我仍不认为这是一条铁板钉钉的准则；有大量的例证能够说明：我们不能也不应该考虑冒险行动的可能后果。

我承认，一般来说主观能动性，这个最能将人类与其他动物区分开来的特征，和我们对行动后果进行周全思考的能力是相伴而生的。遭遇特别复杂或冒险的问题时，我们总希望做明智的判断并预测潜在的后果。随着经验的累积，在大多数情况下，我们能够就遇到的情况进行系统性的分析，同时相应地做出理性的决策。几乎所有职业领域的研究都是以此为基础，研究者希望对其研究对象的行为进行精准的预测；一旦这种预测被证实，我们便将这种行为视为有价值的，并且将这段经历应用到后续的研究当中。

然而，随着我们越来越习惯于这种"先想后动"的模式，我们便同时受限于一种陈腐的观点：只要"想"，就能"预测"，并且只要"预测"就能"成功"。不幸的是，这两种说法都站不住脚。由于我们的预测一般以先前的经验为依据，但先前的经验极有可能被未知的事情推翻，所以我们有时无法解释这类未知的事情，因此我们也无法试图做出正向或者成功的决策。而为了应对新的挑战，我们需要保持观察，直到我们积累起足够多的信息以作出精确的预测。然而，也许就是在我们观察的过程中，宝贵的机会正从我们的身边呼啸而过。这也能解释为什么这么多的商业巨头能够频繁地抓住，并受益于这些短暂且貌似冒险的机遇。尽管有人将这种成功归因于他们的洞察力和远见，但真正促使这些商人抓住机会的推动力是他们深知：如果只是依赖老经验来解决新问题，自己将颗粒无收；而如果因为迟疑而错失了机会，自己也将无比失望。

另外，我最不能接受的是题干的观点所暗含的假设：我们应该总是采取以结果为导向的行动。尽管实用主义者（特别是逐利者）可能热衷于这条原则，但我认为仅仅以结果作为前进路上的唯一参考条件将剥夺我们生活中的乐趣。我们应该至少，说得再直白点，偶尔做一些疯狂、危险且完全不计后果的事。当我们做了一个详尽的计划并因此而取得了正面的结果，这确实是一件令人满意的事情；但我们会为那些因"随心而动"而产生的未知结果而感到后悔吗？可能不会吧。贤人可能倾向于"依脑行事"，但普通人"随心而动"也未尝不可。

作为人类，我们必须要去预测自身行为所带来的后果。然而，仅仅预测并不足以保证成功。诚然，我们为人类的理性感到骄傲，但我们也需要对此进行适当的克制，以防它损害人类另一种重要的特征——真实的情感。

文章解析与点评

Issue 题库中有不少关于"思考能力"或"思考方式"的题目，这道题目就是其中一道。这篇文章的开头就提供了一个针对这种题目的套路式语言：Thinking ability, both analytical reasoning and rational decision-making, has always marked the human species and therefore distinguished human beings from other animals.（思考能力，包括分析推理和理性选择，不但是人类的重要特征，更将人类与其他动物区别开来）。但是，在这种套路式的语言之后，大家一定要把它和题目相结合。比如这篇文章的首段在写出这句话之后，就继续把人类的思考能力细化为题目所讨论的"预测行为的结果"的能力。这种具体化的做法大家需要学习。

另外，这道题从思路层面也给大家提供了参考。

一方面，我们承认题目建议的合理性，预测行为的结果并且依据该结果行事是人类区别于其他动物的显著特点。我们正是通过"预测—行动—检验预测"的方式不断将之前的经验应用于之后的行动中。

然而，预测只是一种思考过程，这并不代表预测本身总是正确的或者预测总会带来成功。一方面，我们总是依据之前行事的经验来指导之后的行为，而新情况总是层出不穷，因此旧经验有时也会失效。另一方面，我们要积累足够的信息进行预测，这就需要我们对事态进行一段时间的观察，但就在这种观察的过程中，机会可能和我们擦肩而过。

最后，虽然有时结果是不可预测的，我们也会"随心而动"。随心而动可能不会产生预期的结果，甚至不会带来正面的结果，但我们也不一定会因此后悔，因为贤人依脑行事，而普通人随心而动即可。

---

81 All parents should be required to volunteer time to their children's schools.

Write a response in which you discuss the extent to which you agree or disagree with the recommendation and explain your reasoning for the position you take. In developing and supporting your position, describe specific circumstances in which adopting the recommendation would or would not be advantageous and explain how these examples shape your position.

Unlike past education, which exclusively concerned educators, current education involves anything or any person responsible for educating children. Naturally, the duty of teaching shifts from sole teachers to various subjects; parents, among these subjects, are of no doubt an indispensable one. Thus, it is both reasonable and necessary to call for a school-family partnership. Active parent engagement with school activities therefore gains unprecedented significance. However, I tend to argue that such an engagement, may include, but in no way equals time engagement; and when this engagement becomes a mandatory task, the healthy school-family partnership is jeopardized.

I welcome parents' engagement at school. A dilemma constantly exists: children spend most of time receiving education at school, but it is limited in preparing them to face the outside world. Such a discrepancy leads to criticism upon educators. While even now we can do little to change the fact that students are restricted to classrooms when receiving education, we can establish a connection between children and the world by bringing in outside factors. Parents are reasonably among the first group of guests schools show hospitality to. By participating in triangular activities involving children, parents and teachers, parents can gain a better understanding of the methods teachers use and subsequently utilize these methods when teaching their children at home. In such sense, teaching extends beyond the classroom.

However, parents' commitment to their children's education cannot be merely measured or fulfilled by the amount of time they volunteer at their children's school. Firstly, how well parents comprehend the nature of formal education hinges primarily on what aspects schools reveal to them and how perceptive they are. In addition, measure of parental involvement in their children's education is determined by the total time they spend with their children, both at school and outside the classroom. For instance, we cannot claim a mother to be irresponsible regarding her child's education if we have no idea how wholeheartedly she assists her son at home with his assignments; nor is it fair to praise a father who we observe picking up his daughter from school every day if we are unaware that he leaves her unsupervised all night while he is out with friends. Thirdly, a vivid communication between parents and school requires far more than time. The amount of information and knowledge children absorb depends on how often and well their parents informally teach them using their own life experiences and knowledge gained from their careers. From this perspective, parents who merely participate at their children's school hardly bestow on their children information they cannot learn in the classroom. Parents should also study with their children, admittedly in a very different way, so that they can provide appropriate lessons when the opportunities arise.

Moreover, although we emphasize the importance of parents' participation at their children's schools, when this participation becomes mandatory, it may have a detrimental effect. If parents are required to be present on specific dates, their children will intuitively link their parents' presence with how much they are loved, and will become depressed when their parents are absent. In addition, teachers may attempt to impress parents by behaving in ways they normally would not if parents were not present. For instance, it is not difficult to imagine a copiously weeping girl glaring at all the other parents and whining about her busy mother's absence; we can also readily visualize a scene in which a normally severe teacher acting in an effusively flattering manner because parents are present. In both of these scenarios, the real being of schools is not concealed and the parents' volunteer activity occurs merely for its own sake.

To summarize, while I deeply sympathize with the proposal that parents should actively participate in their children's education, how parents participate is still subject to further deliberation. (632 words)

🖉 中文翻译

过去的教育模式以教育工作者为绝对中心，但当今的教育模式关注任何与教育孩子有关的人和事。因此，教育的重任自然从教师开始向各类主体转移，其中父母无疑是不可或缺的存在。因此，呼吁"学校—家庭协作关系"既是合理又显必要。至此，家长对学校活动的积极参与开始获得空前的重要性。不过，我更倾向于认为：这样一种参与，可能包括，但绝不仅仅包括时间上的投入；另外，当这样一种参与变成强制的任务时，健康的"学校—家庭协作关系"便会受到损害。

我个人欢迎家长对学校活动的参与。这是因为，这样一个困境一直存在：一方面孩子们花费大量时间在学校接受教育，但是另一方面这却不足以让他们更好地应对外部世界。这样一种不平衡经常使教育工作者遭受非议。尽管目前我们仍难以改变孩子们长时间被限制在教室中接受教育的这一事实，但我们可以通过引入外界的因素来建立孩子们与世界的联系。家长，理应是学校热烈欢迎的第一拨客人。通过参与涵盖学生、家长和老师的三角互动，家长能够更好地理解老师所教授的方法，并且随后在家中将此运用于对孩子的教育。这样看来，教学得以延伸出教室。

然而，父母参与学校志愿活动时间的长短，并不是衡量家长对子女教育投入的唯一标准。首先，家长能在多大程度上理解正式教育的本质，取决于学校在多大程度上愿意向他们展现真实的教育现状，以及家长自身的观察力。另外，对父母参与子女教育的时间的衡量，取决于他们在孩子身上花费的总时间量——既包括校内也包括校外。比如，如果不了解一位母亲在家中是多么投入地辅导孩子完成作业，那么我们便无法认定这位母亲是不负责任的；同样不公平的还有：夸赞一位每天接女儿放学的父亲，而我们不知道他随后将孩子独自留在家里，而自己整晚出去与朋友鬼混。第三，家长与学校之间的有效沟通需要的远远不止是时间。孩子吸收信息与知识的多少取决于，父母能否频繁且有效地以非正式的方式向他们传授取材于自己职业生涯的生活经验。这样看来，如果只是参加学校活动，父母很难向子女传授那些难以从外界获得的信息。尽管以一种全然不同的方式，父母也应该同孩子们一起学习，以便在恰当的时机向他们提供合适的经验。

另外，尽管我们强调父母参与的重要性，但当这种参与一旦被强制化，那么它将产生不利的影响。如果父母被要求在特定的日期访校，那么他们的孩子将本能地把父母的出席与自己多大程度受到父母的关爱相勾连；换句话说，如果父母缺席，那么孩子将倍感痛苦。另外，为了给父母留下良好印象，老师们也可能采取一些平日里不会采取的行为。比如，不难想象一个女孩一边眼泪汪汪地看着其他孩子的父母，一边抱怨着因工作繁忙而缺席的母亲；我们也很容易在脑海中刻画出这样的场景：因为父母的出现，一位平日里严厉的老师摆出一副热情谄媚的嘴脸。不论是哪种情况，学校的真实情况都将被隐藏，而家长参与校方的志愿活动也将仅仅流于形式。

总的来说，"父母应该积极参与子女的教育"，尽管我十分理解这个建议，但切实参与的方式仍待我们进行更深层次的探讨。

文章解析与点评

这道题目相对来说比较简单，但是如何写出深度却是难点。那么，应对看似简单的题目，如何在立意层面做得更好呢？

首先，这篇文章关注到了题目背后的本质问题。如，题目所阐述的是"是否应该要求家长去学校"这一话题，而更加本质的问题应该是学校和家长的协同教育（school-family partnership），或者老师、学生和家长之间的三角互动（triangular activities involving children, parents and teachers）。

此外，文章的第二段认识到了学校教育面临的一个困境，即"学生虽然在学校接受教育，但他们要面临的是整个世界（A dilemma constantly exists: children spend most of time receiving education at school, but it is limited in preparing them to face the outside world.）"。既然我们无法改变这一现状，那一个解决办法就是将学校之外的元素引入学校之内，而家长就是这些元素之中极为重要的一个。

文章第三段的内容比较丰富，但都围绕一个中心论点：家长对孩子教育的参与不能只由其在学校出现的时间来衡量。首先，家长能多大程度参与教育，这取决于学校在多大程度上愿意向家长展示学校真实的教育现状；其次，家长对教育的参与应该包含其在校内以及校外的参与；最后，家长对教育的参与不应该只付出时间，还应该以其他方式对孩子进行潜移默化的正面影响。如果不做到这些，那么家长的参与将会毫无意义。

文章的第四段主要讨论了题目中建议可能带来的不良后果。一方面，孩子可能把家长的缺席当作冷漠；另一方面，校方可能因为家长的到来而大献媚态。不论是哪一种情况，"家长参与"都会流于形式，而不能让家长见到真实的教育状态。

6 "建议类" Direction (二)

Write a response in which you discuss your views on the policy and explain your reasoning for the position you take. In developing and supporting your position, you should consider **the possible consequences** of implementing the policy and explain how these consequences shape your position.

中文翻译

写一篇文章，在这篇文章中讨论你在多大程度上同意或者不同意题目中的政策，解释你所采取的立场的理由。在发展和支持你的立场的过程中，考虑一下你认为**这个政策可能产生的结果**，并且解释这些结果如何影响你的立场。

讲 解

这种 Direction 对应的题目是在谈论一个政策（policy）。政策和建议在本质上是类似的，只不过政策显得更加强硬，实施主体也通常是国家、政府、学校等。而 Direction 中的 "consequence" 这个词明确地告诉我们，**我们应该把文章的论述重点放在这个政策可能带来的结果上**。所以，与上一个 Direction 类似，如果考生通篇都在论述政策的 "必要性"、"紧迫性"、"充分性" 等，就偏离了 Direction 的要求。

由此看来，这种 Direction 和上一条 Direction 对我们的要求几乎一致：**都是要谈题目中建议所带来的 "结果"**。唯一的细微差别是：上一条 Direction 还要求我们阐述不同结果产生的情况，但这条 Direction 并没有对此作明确要求。但可以想见，如果我们能在论述结果之时也对该结果产生的情况加以说明，无疑可以使我们的论证更加完善。

讲解浓缩版

与上一条 **Direction** 的要求基本一致，要讨论政策可能带来的结果。

例题举证

Nations should pass laws to preserve any remaining wilderness areas in their natural state, even if these areas could be developed for economic gain.

Write a response in which you discuss your views on the policy and explain your reasoning for the position you take. In developing and supporting your position, you should consider the possible consequences of implementing the policy and explain how these consequences shape your position.

参考提纲如下：

> **总立场：** 有保留地反对题目
>
> **分论点 1**（题目建议会带来的有利结果）：国家只有用法律手段限制野生区域的开发，才能杜绝一些个人和企业为了自身利益而对野生区域进行无限度的开发利用，进而防止生态失衡。
>
> **分论点 2**（题目建议会带来的不利结果）：有一些野生区域已经基本不存在任何植物或动物，对这些区域的保护可能费时费力，最后得不偿失。
>
> **分论点 3**（题目建议的延伸）：对一些野生区域，我们可以把经济开发和自然保护结合起来，如将其发展为野生植物园等。这样既能促进自然环境良性发展，还取得了经济效益。

分论点 1 是讨论题目建议可能产生的正面结果，分论点 2 是在讨论负面结果，而分论点 3 则是对原题目中建议的延伸，以替代建议的方式提供了一种双赢的结果。但不论是哪一个分论点都紧紧围绕着"结果"二字，这也正是 Direction 的要求。

题库范文

100 Colleges and universities should require their students to spend at least one semester studying in a foreign country.

Write a response in which you discuss your views on the policy and explain your reasoning for the position you take. In developing and supporting your position, you should consider the possible consequences of implementing the policy and explain how these consequences shape your position.

Spending at least one semester studying in a foreign country is an appealing and realistic proposal for driven university students. Whether or not this should be a mandatory high-education requirement, however, greatly depends on how they regard the opportunity. Will they focus exclusively on their studies or will they assume the role of ambassadors for their countries?

If we want students to expand their academic and non-academic experiences, we should encourage them to study in a foreign country for at least one semester, but should not make it a compulsory requirement. Not all students are well-suited to study abroad. Assimilating into a foreign culture entails a comprehensive understanding of that culture. This is unlikely if the student lacks language proficiency. However, acquiring sufficient language proficiency so as to have little difficulty communicating, both academically and in their daily lives, is incredibly time-consuming. This makes overseas study a desirable choice exclusively for those already proficient in the target language. For example, while an English major student might benefit tremendously from immersion in an English-speaking country, requiring a Japanese Literature major student, who is Japanese, to pursue his/her study in an English-speaking country is unreasonable when he/she would receive better Direction in his/her own country. It may even be disastrous to compel an American freshman to study in a Chinese university, if his/her rudimentary Chinese language skills would preclude him/her from a wholehearted immersion in Chinese culture and consequently inflame his/her eager of returning to his/her home country.

On the other hand, if we are discussing whether to require every student to become an exchange student, the issue is far more complex and therefore necessitates a more thorough examination. Firstly, it is expensive to live and study in a foreign country. Even if the government assumed the expense, it would still be impossible to provide every student with such an opportunity. More importantly, exchange student programs are designed in the hope that students from two countries could contribute to the multicultural communication. Such a contribution depends on how well the students embody their country's most valuable characteristics and whether they are able to express and convey those in a friendly and explicit way. Moreover, exchange students should possess an intense passion for various cultures and an appreciation for multiculturalism. Therefore, colleges and universities should adopt a selection method that would provide only elite students who personify these characteristics with the opportunity to study abroad. As a result, the students selected would represent their nation well and also gain a wealth of experience in foreign countries. However, if we give this opportunity to students indiscriminately, the goal of multicultural communication will be jeopardized.

In addition, while communication with different culture is appealing and indispensable for a university student, not only does such communication result from an overseas experience, but it can be also achieved through introduction of foreign teachers into students' home country. This alternative policy demonstrates advantages when students cannot afford the expense of overseas study and is thereby presumably desirable in some developing countries.

To draw a conclusion, no matter how students perceive the opportunity to study abroad, they should always be asked whether or not they want to do so, as well as whether or not they are capable of doing so. Besides, when it comes to a case where exchange students are selected, we should guarantee that only those who sufficiently embody their countries are provided with opportunities. Moreover, when alternative options emerge, which outshine the proposed one in this issue task in terms of financial factors, we should better adopt the former ones. (595 words)

🖳 中文翻译

对于在校大学生来说，在国外度过至少一个学期的学习生活是一条诱人且现实的提议。然而，是否将这条建议上升为高等教育的一个强制要求，在很大程度上还取决于学生如何看待这个机会。他们将会以学习为主还是会承担起本国形象大使的角色？

如果希望丰富学生们的学术以及非学术经验，我们应该鼓励他们在外国学习至少一个学期；但我认为，不应该把这条建议当作一个强制要求。因为并不是所有学生都能很好地适应海外留学。融入一国文化需要对这种文化具备全面的理解。如果学生缺乏熟练的外语，那这点便不大可能实现。然而，在学习和日常生活两方面，掌握熟练外语以实现零障碍交流是极为耗时的。这就使得海外留学只针对那些熟练掌握外语的学生来说，才是一个可取的选项。比如，尽管能够浸染在一个英语国家对于英语专业的学生来说无疑是一个莫大的恩惠，但如果要求一个主修日语文学专业的日本学生，前往英语国家继续学业则是不合理的，因为他/她明明可以在自己国家接受更好的教育。如果强迫一个美国大学新生在一所中国大学里求学，其结果也可能是灾难性的，因为中文水平低将阻碍他/她吸收中国文化，并可能进一步刺激他/她想要回国的欲望。

另一方面，如果我们在讨论"是否要让每一个学生都成为交换生"，那么这个问题将变得极为复杂，因此需要更为详尽的检视。首先，在国外学习、生活开销不菲，即便政府承担费用，但为每一个学生提供这样的机会还是显得不实际。更为重要的是，交换生项目存在的初衷是：希望两国学生能够为多边文化交流的建立做贡献。这样一种贡献取决于学生能在多大程度上展现他们国家最为宝贵的特质，以及他们能否以一种友好且明确的方式将其表达与传递。另外，交换生应该对各类文化抱有极高的热情并且乐于欣赏多元主义。因此，各所学院和大学应该采取"只向精英学生开放"的甄选模式，因为他们能够通过海外学习的机会完美呈现本国的优秀特质。因此，被选中的学生将很好地代表自己的国家，并且在海外收获丰富的留学经历。然而，如果我们不加区别地向学生提供机会，多元文化交流的目标将因此而受损。

另外，尽管跨国文化交流是具有吸引力且不可或缺的，但对于大学生来说，这样的交流不是只能来源于海外留学，也可以通过引进外籍教师来实现。当学生们无法支付海外留学的费用时，这条替代性政策将显示其优势，并且因此可能在发展中国家受到广泛的欢迎。

总的来说，无论这些学生如何看待海外留学，他们都应该被问问：自己是否想去？以及自己是否能去？另外，如果进展到"留学生挑选"这个环节时，我们应该保证那些能够充分体现本国文化精髓的学生获得这样的机会。此外，从财政层面来看，如果替代性政策优于题干所提供的政策，我们最好还是选择前者。

文章解析与点评

这道题目应该算是 Issue 题库中比较简单的一道，讨论的是"大学生是否应该被要求在国外度过至少一学期的时间"这一常见的话题。但根据 Direction 的要求，我们应该着重讨论该建议可能产生的结果。因此，文章的中间段三段都是从这一角度展开的。

在做到按照 Direction 的要求来写的基础上，本篇文章还兼顾了题目的复杂性，提出：当学生作为普通留学生，或是公派的交换生时，我们应该对题目的建议采取不同的态度。

另外，本篇文章还提出了替代建议。考虑替代建议是一种常见的丰富"建议类"文章的做法，但大家要注意，我们在讨论替代建议时，也要从结果的角度出发，探讨替代建议是否比原本的建议带来的结果更有利。

---

73 Colleges and universities should require all faculty to spend time working outside the academic world in professions relevant to the courses they teach.

Write a response in which you discuss your views on the policy and explain your reasoning for the position you take. In developing and supporting your position, you should consider the possible consequences of implementing the policy and explain how these consequences shape your position.

Should universities and college require all faculty to spend time working outside the academic world in professions relevant to the courses they teach? I agree with this recommendation to a large extent because faculty's exposure to industries related to their fields of study can promote academic research and teaching. This recommendation, however, may not be applicable to instructors in all fields, so I cannot fully endorse the policy.

A professor's research can benefit from non-academic work experience due to an awareness of industrial needs and, thus, those of society. By working on the topics that have the maximum societal values, professors can not only gain more recognition but also make greater contribution to society. For example, if a faculty member from the biology department has the opportunity to work at a pharmaceutical company, he or she will have a more comprehensive understanding of the medical industry's current needs, perhaps reflecting the difficulties of battling certain diseases. Upon his or her return to the university, he or she can focus on pressing industrial demands and test more effective medicines to combat disease, thereby benefiting society. This line of reasoning also extends to other fields of applied science and thus scientific research would benefit by having professors work outside academia.

Benefits from understanding industrial needs also extend to teaching, which better prepares the students for job market. When instructors are fully aware of industrial needs, their students benefit by being better informed and thoroughly understanding the prospects of a certain career. A computer science faculty member actively participating in non-academic, industrial activities will certainly understand industrial requirements and what programming qualities are desired in this rapid-changing field better than colleagues who never leave the ivory tower. He or she will be able to share his or her insights with students, helping them become productive members of the community and gaining advantages and competitiveness. In short, professors working in industry become effective channels to relay employer demands to potential employees, which benefits their students.

Despite all the benefits mentioned above, I feel the need to point out that it is not always advisable to require all faculty members to work outside of the academic world. The connection between industry and some academic fields, such as pure mathematics and theoretical cosmology, is relatively weak. In this case, it may be difficult for faculty to find an appropriate job and if they do, the social benefit would be nominal if there is little industrial interest in their research. The nature of such fields makes students unlikely to find jobs that perfectly match what they learn. For example, there is no mathematical company that tries to solve the Goldbach's conjecture. It would therefore be unproductive in terms of time and resources to require faculty from those fields to work outside of academia.

In conclusion, research and teaching can benefit by requiring faculty members to work in the industrial world. On the other hand it may not be desirable or productive to compel faculty from disciplines with poor industrial connections to do so. Thus I do not fully agree with the recommendation but call for a careful consideration of its applicability. (524 words)

中文翻译

大学是否应该要求所有的教师在学术界以外从事和他们所教课程相关的工作？很大程度上，我同意这个建议，因为让教师投身和研究领域相关的行业可以促进学术研究和教学。然而，这项建议可能并不适用于所有领域的教师，因此我不能完全赞同这项政策。

教授的研究可以受益于非学术工作经验，因为他们会更为了解业界需求和社会需求。通过研究具有最大社会价值的课题，教授们不仅可以获得更高的认可，还可以为社会作出更大的贡献。例如，若生物系的教师有机会在制药公司工作，他/她会对医疗行业的当前需求有更为全面的了解——也许是同某些疾病斗争的困难。当他/她回到大学后，他/她可以专注于紧迫的业界需求，测试更多的有效药物来对抗疾病，从而使社会收益。这种推理也可以延伸到其他应用科学领域，因此科学研究将受益于教授在学术界之外的工作。

了解业界需求的好处也会扩展到教学，从而让学生更好地为就业作准备。当教员们十分清楚业界需求时，他们的学生会因更好更彻底地了解某一职业的前景而受益。与从未离开象牙塔的同事相比，一位积极参与非学术、工业活动的计算机科学教师，当然会更了解行业的需求以及什么样的编程素质在这一高速变化的领域中是必需的。他/她可以同学生分享他/她的见解，帮助他们成为社会中更有生产力的成员，获得优势和竞争力。总之，在业界工作的教授会成为有效的渠道，将雇主的需求转达给潜在的员工，这对他们的学生是有益的。

尽管有上述种种好处，我觉得有必要指出，要求教师在学术界外工作并不总是可取的。有些学术领域，如纯数学和理论宇宙学，和业界的关系相对较弱。在这种情况下，教师很难找到合适的工作，即使他们找到了，因为他们的研究没有什么工业利益，社会效益可能也是有名无实。这些领域的性质让学生不太可能找到和他们所学内容完全对口的工作。例如，没有试图解决哥德巴赫猜想的数学公司。因此，要求这些领域的教师在学术界外工作，无论在时间上还是资源上都是徒劳的。

总之，要求教师在业界工作可以使他们的研究和教学受益。另一方面，强迫同业界没什么联系的领域的教师这么做则可能不是理想的或没有成效的。因此虽然我并不完全同意这一建议，但要求认真考虑它的适用性。

文章解析与点评

这种"建议类"的 Direction 要求我们把论证重点放在建议可能产生的结果上，因此，很多同学看到这道题就会想到诸如"教师可能时间精力不够"，"不是每一个专业的教师都应该这么做"等观点可能就偏离要求了。因为这些点是围绕建议的可行性或必要性来展开的，而不是结果。但是，我们仍然可以从这些角度来思考，只不过要稍微调整一下，使其向"建议产生的结果"方向上靠拢。

为此，本文用到了一些表达或好或坏的结果的词或短语，大家对此应该有所积累。如"benefit by"，"benefit from"，"it is (not) advisable to..."等。此外，一系列可以表示"结果"的词语，如"consequence"，"result"，"ramification"，"outcome"，"aftermath"等，以及可以修饰这些词语的形容词，如"far-reaching"，"adverse"，"detrimental"，"devastating"，"beneficial"，"positive"，"desirable"等，大家也应该有所积累。

另外，Issue 题目中有很多会涉及教育问题，甚至细化到教师或者学生的题目。如本题，又如第 35 题（Educational institutions should dissuade students from pursuing fields of study in which they are unlikely to succeed）。

遇到这类题目，我们往往可以从以下几个层面来思考。

教师：教师的研究发展（development of research）；教师的专业技能发展（development of expertise）；教师的教学技能发展（development of teaching）等。

学生：学生的知识积累（accumulation of knowledge）；学生习得知识的技能发展（development of knowledge-acquisition skills）；学生的德育发展（ethical development）；学生的职业发展（career development）等。

第二节 Argument 具体性指令与范文精讲

和 Issue 类似，新 GRE 的 Argument 也新添了 8 种（四大类）Direction。我们分别将其称为"Assumption 类"，"Evidence 类"，"Explanation 类"和"Question 类"。对于"Argument"这个词，我们可以把它理解为"用论据论证结论的过程"。因此，每一道 Argument 的题目就是一个论证过程。而我们要做的，就是从上述四大类 Direction 的角度去评价该论证过程是否完善。

需要注意的是，Argument 的 177 道题目中，有一些题目的题干非常类似甚至完全相同，但 Direction 不一样，这也就决定了我们的破题角度不一样。

与 Issue 部分一样，Argument 的评分标准中也明确提到，如果对 Direction 照应得不够，文章的分数不会超过 3 分。而通过之后的讲解，大家会发现 Argument 的 Direction 对我们行文的影响更大，换句话说，与 Issue 相比，Argument 的 Direction 更加"危险"。

然而，大多数同学在备考 Argument 的时候，仍然把破题角度放在了所谓的"逻辑错误"上，如"错误类比"、"臆造因果"、"问题数据"等等。很多同学也背了不少针对每种逻辑错误的语言模板。然而，这些语言模板基本上没能很好地照应新 GRE 中 Argument 的 Direction。所以，即便大家能够清楚地识别出 Argument 中的逻辑错误并且用已经背熟的语言将其表达出来，最终可能仍然免不了 3 分的结局。究其原因，就是因为没有按照 Direction 来写。

Argument 的 Direction 对我们行文影响巨大，这既是 Argument 备考的难点，其实也让我们的备考变得更有针对性和高效。因为面对 177 道 Argument 题目，我们只需要掌握四种思维和语言模板，分别对应四大类 Direction 就可以了。相比于老 GRE 中的十多种"逻辑错误"，新 GRE 中的四大类 Direction 更简洁，也更贴近 Argument 的论证本质。

下面就是一道 Argument 题目所应依循的破题步骤：
1. 通读文章，准确定位文章当中的论据和结论。
2. 依据论据和结论，在纸上（或在脑中）用逻辑图的方式再现原 Argument 的推理过程。（这一点非常重要，会影响到大家的全文结构和段落组织！）
3. 依照 Direction 的要求对原 Argument 进行分析。

下面我们就用一道题来具体说明以上三个步骤。其中的步骤 3 会分散到每一种 Direction 的讲解中。

例题举证

The following was written as a part of an application for a small-business loan by a group of developers in the city of Monroe.

"A jazz music club in Monroe would be a tremendously profitable enterprise. Currently, the nearest jazz club is 65 miles away; thus, the proposed new jazz club in Monroe, the C-Note, would have the local market all to itself. Plus, jazz is extremely popular in Monroe: over 100,000 people attended Monroe's annual jazz festival last summer; several well-known jazz musicians live in Monroe; and the highest-rated radio program in Monroe is 'Jazz Nightly,' which airs every weeknight at 7 P.M. Finally, a nationwide study indicates that the typical jazz fan spends close to $1,000 per year on jazz entertainment."

Write a response in which you discuss what specific evidence is needed to evaluate the argument and explain how the evidence would weaken or strengthen the argument.

步骤 1：找出文章当中的论据和结论

> **结论：** 在 M 新开一个爵士乐俱乐部会很赚钱。
>
> **论据：**（在这道题中，很多同学把除结论以外的部分都称为证据，其实这还不够准确，我们应该对剩下的部分再做如下的细分）
>
> **分论点①：** 新爵士乐俱乐部在本地没有竞争对手。
>
> **分论点②：** 爵士乐在 M 很受欢迎。
>
> **分论点③：** M 存在相当数量的愿意把钱花在爵士乐俱乐部上的粉丝。

其中的分论点①（或称理论论据）是被"最近的爵士乐俱乐部在 65 英里之外"这个事实论据（即证据）所支持的；分论点②是被三个证据共同支持（十万人参加了去年的音乐节；有著名爵士音乐人住在本地；爵士乐广播节目在周中晚上收听率第一）；分论点③是被一个全国性调查所支持。

不难看出，分论点③并不是作者直接给出的，而是我们总结出来的。这种从证据中总结出论点的能力是大家需要培养的。

步骤 2：列出逻辑图

在步骤 1 中，我们不仅找出了证据和结论，而且已经把文章的论证框架进行了大致的梳理。下面我们通过逻辑图的形式让这一框架更加明显：

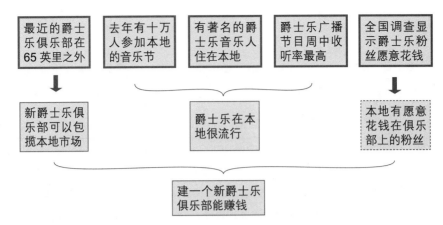

上图中，最上面一层的五个蓝色粗框代表作者给出的事实性的证据；中间一层的三个蓝色细框是作者由此推导而出的分论点，或称为理论论据，到这里作者一共做了三次推导，每次推导的结果就是一个新分论点的产生。其中最右边的蓝框用虚线表示，代表这是作者没有在题目中明确提到的论点；最下面的蓝框代表由三个分论点共同推出的文章的最终结论，在这里作者又做了一次推导。

无疑，每一次推导过程中都存在漏洞，使得文章的论证不够完善。而我们接下来的任务，就是根据不同具体性指令的特殊要求，从不同侧面对这道题的论证过程进行评价。

需要注意的是，每个同学列出的逻辑图可能都有所不同，特别是虚线蓝框的部分会因人而异，这不要紧，重要的是逻辑图能够帮助我们整理作者的论证框架。在本书中，我们给出的每一篇范文后面都附有一个逻辑图，这些逻辑图的画法并非唯一，而我们遵循的原则是：大家可以根据这个逻辑图读懂作者的论证逻辑，同时也可以根据逻辑图组织出篇幅适宜的文章。所以，我们的大部分逻辑图都是以让大家写出 3~4 个中间段为目标所构建的。

下面我们就来看一下如何根据逻辑图，按照不同 Direction 的要求来分析题目。

① "Assumption 类" Direction

Write a response in which you examine the stated and/or unstated assumptions of the argument. Be sure to explain how the argument depends on these assumptions and what the implications are for the argument if the assumptions prove unwarranted.

中文翻译

写一篇文章，在这篇文章中，考查该文章提到的或者没有提到的前提条件。解释这些前提条件是如何支持题目的，并说明如果这些前提条件没有被证实会产生什么结果。

讲　解

每一道 Argument 的逻辑漏洞都出现在其推理过程中。而推理过程之所以有问题，就是因为存在一些可能不成立的 Assumption。我们通常把 Assumption 翻译为"前提"或者"假设"，其实，我们可以更加简易地将 Assumption 理解为"poorly supported claim（没有被很好地支持的论断）"。

需要注意的是，根据这种 Direction，我们需要找出题目中的 Assumption，但这些 Assumption 可能是作者明确提到的（stated），也可能是作者没有明确提到的（unstated）。

在上文的例题中，作者根据"旧爵士乐俱乐部在 65 英里外"这一事实证据，直接得出了"新爵士乐俱乐部在本地没有竞争对手"这一论断。显然，这一论断不一定成立，因为它缺乏足够的支撑信息，而这一个论断就可以被看作作者明确提到的论断（stated assumption）。而这一论断，又是进一步被其他主观臆造的 Assumption 所支持的。比如：作者认为，人们没有车，所以会觉得 65 英里远，因此会去新开的爵士俱乐部；或者旧爵士乐俱乐部的服务、音乐品质等都不如新开的爵士乐俱乐部。而这些 Assumption，就属于作者没有明确提到的论断了（unstated assumption）。很明显，这些 Assumption 不一定成立，进而，作者的"新爵士乐俱乐部在本地没有竞争对手"这一论断也就不成立。此时，全文的最终结论"新爵士乐俱乐部能赚钱"也就被削弱了。

同理，作者还根据"十万人参加去年的音乐节"、"有著名爵士音乐人住在本地"、"爵士乐广播节目在周中晚上收听率第一"这三个证据得出了"爵士乐在 M 很受欢迎"这一明确提到的论断（stated assumption）；并且根据一个全国调查得出了"M 存在相当数量的愿意把钱花在爵士乐俱乐部上的粉丝"这一暗示性的论断（unstated assumption）。最后，作者得出了"新爵士乐俱乐部能赚钱"这一结论。这几个论断和结论都不一定成立，就是因为在这些论断和结论的推导过程中还存在可能不成立的 Assumption。而我们需要做的，就是像上面一段所演示的那样，找到这些 Assumption，指出其不成立的情况，并且说明这些 Assumption 一旦不成立，作者的最终结论就会被削弱。

值得注意的是，Assumption 的数量是不一定的，找多少 Assumption，能写多少 Assumption，这完全取决于考生的能力和考试时间。

那么，我们要写几个自然段呢？

很多考生在遇到一道题的时候，对如何组织每一个自然段，以及要写几个自然段都是不清楚的。往往在认定 Argument 中的一句话有逻辑漏洞时，会用一段来论述这个问题；接着发现另一句话也有逻辑漏洞，则开启新的一段来论述这个问题。那么如果文章中有五句话都存在漏洞，可能就会写五个中间段（如本题）。殊不知，有一些自然段是可以合并的。而合并的依据，其实就是逻辑图。从逻辑图中我们可以清楚地看到，作者一共做了四次结论的推导，其中三次是从证据推导出分论点，第四次是从分论点推导出总结论。既然作者做了四次结论的推导，那我们就可以写四个中间段，每一个中间段分别讨论作者的每一次推导是否合理，有何缺陷。至于如何讨论，那就要结合 Direction 了。比如这里，我们就需要从 Assumption 的角度来讨论。

至此，我们可以来总结一下如何应对 Assumption 类的 Direction：

如何写单段（每一段中都应包含下面所示的①②③，而不是①②③各成一段）：
① 找出原文中各论断或结论所依赖的 Assumption。
② 指出这些 Assumption 在什么情况下不成立。
③ 阐明这些 Assumption 一旦不成立，作者的结论就会被削弱。

如何把各个中间段组织起来：
根据逻辑图，作者做了几次结论的推导，就写几个中间段。

题库范文

132（微臣线下 325 班讲解文章）The following appeared in a letter to the school board in the town of Centerville.

"All students should be required to take the driver's education course at Centerville High School. In the past two years, several accidents in and around Centerville have involved teenage drivers. Since a number of parents in Centerville have complained that they are too busy to teach their teenagers to drive, some other Direction is necessary to ensure that these teenagers are safe drivers. Although there are two driving schools in Centerville, parents on a tight budget cannot afford to pay for driving Direction. Therefore an effective and mandatory program sponsored by the high school is the only solution to this serious problem."

Write a response in which you examine the stated and/or unstated assumptions of the argument. Be sure to explain how the argument depends on these assumptions and what the implications are for the argument if the assumptions prove unwarranted.

In the letter, the writer recommends an initiation of a high-school-sponsored driver's education course program and predicts that such a program will help solve the teenage driving problem in Centerville. While this program might be beneficial to some extent, the reasoning of this argument is unconvincing due to several unsubstantiated assumptions which, if proven unwarranted, will seriously challenge the author's recommendation.

First of all, the writer's recommendation relies heavily on the assumption that the driving problem involving teenage drivers in the town of Centerville is serious enough to require immediate measures be taken. Based on such an assumption, the writer therefore proposes formal Direction to ensure that these teenagers become safe drivers. However, this assumption is potentially problematic because we are not informed with the exact number of the accidents. Nor do we know whether the teenage drivers are to blame for these accidents. In addition, we even have no idea whether or not the teenage drivers are local. If it turns out that the accidents are not sufficiently serious, or they could be attributed to factors other than the local teenage drivers' negligence, then the author's argument for a proposed driver education program is unconvincing.

In addition, by stating that parents have either little time or funding to provide their teenagers with driving courses, the writer rules out alternative methods which could rival the proposed driving program. However, we need to re-examine the assumption that the driving program is the only solution to the teenage driving problem. It is likely that the so-called busy parents just use their unavailability as an excuse because they are reluctant to teach. It is of equal possibility that parents with limited budget make up only a minority of parents. In addition, government-sponsored driving courses could also serve as an alternative method. If any of these possibilities is true, then we are inclined to believe that other solutions could overshadow the one proposed to solve the driving problem.

Even if the assumptions mentioned above are valid, the writer's recommendation could be unnecessary due to the doubtful assumption regarding the efficiency of the proposed driving program. Claiming that this program will be effective, the writer might be too optimistic. It is unreasonable to assume that all parents, including those who would like to teach their teenagers personally, will readily accept such a school-sponsored mandatory driving Direction program. Also, the writer hastily comes to the conclusion that the local high school should sponsor this program but does not discuss whether the school is financially capable of doing so. Furthermore, we cannot be sure that there will be fewer accidents involving local teenage drivers after the implementation of the proposed recommendation. If this program provokes general discontent amongst parents or the school cannot afford such a program, then the recommendation may not be enacted and we cannot therefore expect a decrease in the number of driving accidents in Centerville.

To summarize, whether or not we should implement the writer's recommendation depends greatly on the validity of the assumptions in the argument. If these assumptions prove unwarranted, then the recommendation will be little more than the writer's wishful thinking, and accordingly we need to consider other solutions to the teenage driving problem in Centerville. (536 words)

📝 中文翻译

在这封信中，作者建议成立由本地高中资助的驾校项目，并预计该项目将帮助解决 Centerville 的青少年驾驶问题。尽管该项目在某种程度上可能不无益处，但是几处未经证实的假设使得这篇论证的推理并不可信，没有根据的假设将会严重削弱作者建议的可靠性。

首先，作者的建议很大程度上建立在这样一个假设上：发生在 Centerville 镇的青少年驾驶问题已经严重到需要立刻采取行动。基于这一假设，作者提出通过正式教学让这些青少年驾驶员学会安全驾驶。然而，这一假设可能是有问题的，因为我们并不知道事故的确切数目。我们同样不知道事故是否是青少年驾驶员的责任。此外，我们甚至无法得知这些青少年驾驶员是否是本地人。如果这些事故并不那么严重，或它们并非由于本地青少年驾驶员的疏忽而导致，那么作者提出建立驾校项目的论点就是没有说服力的。

不仅如此，作者认为家长们要么没有时间，要么没有钱让他们的孩子上驾驶课程，由此排除了驾校项目之外的替代方案。然而，我们需要考察驾校项目是否是解决青少年驾驶问题的唯一方案。那些自称很忙的家长有可能只是以此为借口掩饰他们不愿意教孩子的事实。经济捉襟见肘的家长可能只是一小部分人。此外，由政府资助的驾驶课程也可作为替代方案。假使真实情况符合上述任一可能性，其他解决方案可能会让作者的提议相形见绌。

即使上述假设是有根据的，若不能证明驾校项目是有效的，那么作者的建议也可能是没必要的。作者可能对项目的有效性过于乐观了。假定所有家长，包括那些想亲自教孩子的家长在内，都乐意接受这一学校资助的强制性驾校计划，是不合理的。另外，作者草率地总结本地高中应当资助这一项目，却没有讨论学校的财力是否足以承担。此外，我们无法确定建议实施后，本地青少年驾驶员所导致的事故数量是否会减少。如果此项目在家长中引发普遍不满或学校的财力无法承担，那么该计划将不会被推行，而我们也无法预测 Centerville 的事故数量是否会减少。

总而言之，我们是否会采纳作者的建议很大程度上取决于假设的可信性。如果这些假设并无根据，那么作者的建议可能只是一厢情愿，而我们需要思考其他的方案来解决 Centerville 的青少年驾驶问题。

文章解析与点评

这道题目讨论的是一个建议，我们在分析建议类的题目时通常可以从以下几个方面思考：建议的必要性、充分性、替代建议、建议可能产生的结果等。但不论是从哪一个方面分析，我们都必须结合题目本身的论证结构。

结合这道题目的逻辑图，我们可以有以下的思考：

1. 题目中建议的必要性值得怀疑。虽然作者提到近两年内，在 C 地及其附近发生了若干起青少年司机牵涉其中的事故，但是我们并不知道事故的数量和严重程度，也不知道事故发生是否应该归咎于这些青少年司机，我们甚至不知道这些青少年司机是否是 C 地的居民。因此，让 C 地的青少年学习驾驶课程的建议可能并不必要。

2. 题目中建议的必要性不高的另一种可能原因，在于替代方案的存在。虽然一些家长声称自己很忙因此无法亲自指导学生驾驶，而经济紧张的家长无法负担孩子去驾校学习的费用，但是我们并不知道前者是否真的很忙，也不知道后者占所有家长的比例。又或许，由政府出资赞助的驾驶课程也不失为一种解决方案。而作者正是在假设这些解决办法都不存在的基础上才推出了最终结论，因此当这些解决办法存在时，作者的结论就会被削弱。

3. 最后，题目中建议的可行性可能不高。并且，题目中的建议不一定能带来预期的后果。由于作者提到的驾驶课程是强制性的，所以不一定所有家长或学生都愿意参加，并且我们也不知道学校是否有相应的财力承担起课程所需的一切费用。最后，即使课程得以开展，所有学生也都参与其中，我们也无法预知最终的收效。

以上就是对题目问题的分析。在明确了写几段、每一段写什么的基础上，我们就可以结合Direction的要求，用与"Assumption类"Direction相对应的语言对这些问题进行描述和分析了。

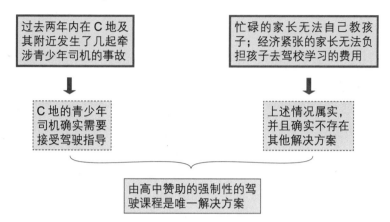

62 The following appeared in a memo from the director of a large group of hospitals.

"In a laboratory study of liquid antibacterial hand soaps, a concentrated solution of UltraClean produced a 40 percent greater reduction in the bacteria population than did the liquid hand soaps currently used in our hospitals. During a subsequent test of UltraClean at our hospital in Workby, that hospital reported significantly fewer cases of patient infection than did any of the other hospitals in our group. Therefore, to prevent serious patient infections, we should supply UltraClean at all hand-washing stations throughout our hospital system."

Write a response in which you examine the stated and/or unstated assumptions of the argument. Be sure to explain how the argument depends on these assumptions and what the implications are for the argument if the assumptions prove unwarranted.

In this memo, the author recommends supplying UltraClean to all hand-washing stations throughout the hospital system to prevent serious patient infections. To support his/her suggestion, the director presents two separate studies, one conducted in a lab and the other in the field. Although UltraClean may indeed help reduce the occurrences of infections, information currently available is not conclusive because there are several unsubstantiated assumptions in the author's reasoning. The director's recommendation will be seriously challenged if these assumptions prove to be unwarranted.

To start with, the laboratory study shows that a concentrated solution of UltraClean is excellent at reducing the number of bacteria. Based on an unstated assumption that the non-concentrated version of UltraClean is similarly effective, the director endorses the use of regular UltraClean in the hospitals. However, this assumption is potentially problematic because intuitively speaking a concentrated solution of UltraClean may naturally outperform the non-concentrated version. Even if we acknowledge this assumption, UltraClean may not necessarily be as effective as the liquid hand soap currently used in the hospitals. If this is the case, the director's assumption will not hold and his/her recommendation will be clearly weakened.

Additionally, the Workby hospital field study demonstrating that UltraClean use in hospitals can reduce cases of patient infections requires further examination. Whether or not UltraClean should be credited for this depends upon the assumption that Workby hospitals are comparable to those in other areas. For example, if the Workby hospital is extremely small and only receives a handful of patients each day, it would not be a surprise to see fewer numbers of infections. Moreover, the Workby hospital may be the best-staffed one in the region, and it is their attentiveness and expertise that keeps patient infections in check. For that reason, UltraClean may not necessarily be the key to few infections in the Workby hospital. As a result, the value of supplying UltraClean to other hospitals is debatable.

Even if we concede the aforementioned assumptions, the recommendation may still not be advisable because UltraClean is not shown to deal specifically with serious infections. The lab and field studies focused little, if at all, on serious infections. The director's recommendation here essentially relies on the two assumptions: (1) serious infections are caused by bacteria and (2) regular and serious infections are caused by a common agent which UltraClean can effectively eliminate. Both of these assumptions need more support. It is not impossible that serious infections are drastically different in terms of its pathological nature and are caused by viruses or parasites rather than bacteria. In this case, it is very questionable if UltraClean, which only proves to be able to fight bacteria and reduce normal level of infections, can satisfactorily prevent serious patient infections.

To sum up, whether or not serious patient infections can be prevented by the use of UltraClean is still questionable and worth further investigation. The answer could turn out to be positive, but only after the author can reasonably demonstrate the validity of his/her assumptions by offering more compelling evidence. (503 words)

中文翻译

在这篇备忘录中，作者建议为整个医院系统的洗手站提供 Ultraclean，以防止严重的患者感染。主任为了支持自己的建议，提出了两个不同的研究——一个在实验室中进行，另一个则在实地进行。虽然 Ultraclean 可能确实有利于减少感染的发生，但现有信息并不足以得出这一结论，因为在作者的推理中有几处未经证实的假设。如果这些假设被证明是不合理的，那么主任的建议将受到严重的挑战。

首先，那项实验室研究表明 Ultraclean 的浓缩溶液在减少细菌数量上表现出色。主任基于没有言明的假设，即 Ultraclean 的非浓缩版本同样有效，赞同在医院使用普通版的 Ultraclean。然而，这个假设可能是有问题的，因为就直觉而言，Ultraclean 的浓缩溶液自会优于非浓缩版本。即使我们承认这一假设，Ultraclean 也不一定像目前医院使用的液体洗手皂一样有效。如果是这样的话，主任的假设不能成立，他的建议也将被明显削弱。

此外，我们需要进一步考察 Workby 医院的实地研究，该研究证明在医院使用 Ultraclean 可以减少患者感染的病例。（患者感染的减少）是否归功于 Ultraclean，这取决于 Workby 医院和其他地区的医院是否有可比性。例如，如果 Workby 医院规模很小，每天仅接收少量患者，那么他们有更少数量的感染并不奇怪。此外，Workby 医院可能是该地区员工素质最高的医院，员工的专注和专业知识使患者感染得到了控制。因此，Ultraclean 不一定是 Workby 医院感染数少的关键原因。向其他医院提供 Ultraclean 的建议的价值是有争议的。

即使我们承认上述假设为真，该建议仍可能是不可取的，因为我们不知道 Ultraclean 是否能专门应对严重感染。实验室和实地研究几乎没有关注严重感染。主任的建议本质上建立在两个假设上：1）细菌导致严重感染；2）普通感染和严重感染都是由 Ultraclean 可以有效消除的同一媒介物引起的。这两个假设都需要更多的支持。就病理性质而言，严重感染是截然不同的，它可能是由病毒或寄生虫而不是细菌引起的。在这种情况下，只被证明能抗菌和降低普通感染的 Ultraclean 能否有效防止严重的患者感染是非常可疑的。

总而言之，使用 Ultraclean 能否防止严重的患者感染仍然存疑，并需要进一步调查。只有在作者通过更有力的证据、合理地证明其假设的有效性后，我们才能打消疑虑。

📝 文章解析与点评

这篇文章本身的逻辑结构比较简单，但我们需要还原出一些作者暗示的 Assumption（见原文逻辑图）。

值得一提的是文章的第四段，文章对于作者在论证过程当中存在的细微的逻辑问题把握得很到位。实验中明确说道：UltraClean 在对抗 bacteria 时是有效的，但题目最终的结论是 UltraClean 能够 "prevent serious patient infections" 这一结论。这之间的推理值得商榷，如：serious infection 是否只由 bacteria 造成？如果其他原因也能造成 serious infection，那么 UltraClean 是否依然有效？

另外，文章每一段的论证结构十分清晰，先指明问题和 assumption 所在，再解释原因，随即提出可能的反例，并最终分析 assumption 不成立时的后果，这种论证的步骤大家可以借鉴。

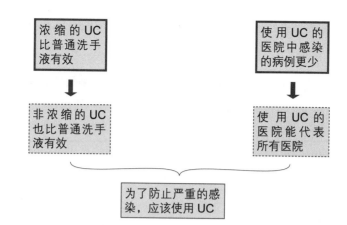

137 While the Department of Education in the state of Attra recommends that high school students be assigned homework every day, the data from a recent statewide survey of high school math and science teachers give us reason to question the usefulness of daily homework. In the district of Sanlee, 86 percent of the teachers reported assigning homework three to five times a week, whereas in the district of Marlee, less than 25 percent of the teachers reported assigning homework three to five times a week. Yet the students in Marlee earn better grades overall and are less likely to be required to repeat a year of school than are the students in Sanlee. Therefore, all teachers in our high schools should assign homework no more than twice a week.

Write a response in which you examine the stated and/or unstated assumptions of the argument. Be sure to explain how the argument depends on these assumptions and what the implications are for the argument if the assumptions prove unwarranted.

The author of this argument casts doubt on the recommendation of the Department of Education in Attra state about daily assigned homework. Data about the frequency of homework assignments and students' academic performance in the districts of Sanlee and Marlee, serve to demonstrate daily homework's minor contribution to a decent education. The author therefore claims that students in Attra should not be assigned homework more than twice a week. However, such a conclusion cannot be readily arrived at because of several unsubstantiated assumptions. If these assumptions prove unwarranted, the argument will be seriously undermined, thus compelling us to reconsider the significance of daily homework.

To start off, the author's conclusion fundamentally relies on the assumption that the frequency in assigning homework is equal to the amount of homework, or more specifically, the time students are expected to spend on homework. Even though the data reveals that a smaller number of teachers in Marlee assign homework three to five times a week, it is imprudent to assume that students in Marlee are thereby under less pressure than those in Sanlee. It is highly likely that even though teachers in Marlee assign homework less frequently, the formidable difficulty of this homework may cost students more time; it is of equal possibility that while students in Marlee may receive modest amounts of homework from their math and science teachers, such an amount is offset by that assigned by teachers in other subjects. If either of the previous scenarios turns out to be true, then the assumption that students in Marlee spend less time on homework is disproved and the suggestion to assign homework less frequently is unreasonable.

Moreover, the author unfairly assumes that students in Marlee generally excel at schoolwork based on overall better grades and less likelihood to repeat a year. However, these two factors do not necessarily represent excellent academic performance, let alone indicate a successful education system. If schools in Marlee and Sanlee adopt different, even distinct standards of grading their students, it is not surprising that there would be variations in students' scores. Additionally, Marlee district school may be attempting to prevent their academic reputation from declining by allowing students with poor academic performance to graduate. Both of these two cases serve to undermine the facts presented by the author as good indicators of students' excellence at school. If either of these circumstances proves to be true, then there is reason to doubt the validity of students' academic performance in Marlee. As a result, teachers in Marlee who assign less homework are not an example that we should follow.

Last, the author's argument also suffers from a questionable assumption which hastily generalizes the situation of high schools in Marlee to those in Attra. By recommending all high school teachers in Attra to follow the lead of their counterparts in Marlee, the author assumes that students in Attra share similar capabilities with those in Marlee. Nevertheless, teachers should be flexible when teaching and assigning homework and may therefore adjust the amount of daily homework, as well as the frequency of giving homework in response to their students' performance in their homework. If high school students in Attra absorb knowledge at a relatively slow rate but have strong desire to achieve improvement, they might need and even ask for more homework themselves. In such a circumstance, the author's proposal to assign homework no more than twice a week is not feasible, but theoretical at best.

To sum up, while homework does not necessarily play a paramount role in enhancing students' academic performance, we cannot readily ignore its significance. Thus, I propose examining the aforementioned assumptions in this argument before we accept the author's recommendation.
(613 words)

🕮 中文翻译

本文作者质疑了 Attra 州教育部对于每天留作业的建议。作者引用了 Sanlee 和 Marlee 两地关于作业布置频次和学生学业表现的数据来证明每天留作业对良好的教育无甚贡献。作者因此声称 Attra 州的老师每周不应该留超过两次以上的作业。然而，仅仅凭借若干未经证实的假设，这样的结论是不应轻易得出的。如果这些假设被证明是没有根据的，那么作者的论点将被严重地削弱，从而迫使我们重新考虑每日留作业的重要性。

首先，作者的结论基本上依赖于这一假设：留作业的频次等同于作业量的大小，或更具体而言，学生在作业上预计要花费的时间。虽然数据显示 Marlee 地区的教师很少一周布置 3~5 次作业，但就此假设 Marlee 学生所承担的压力比 Sanlee 学生更小是轻率的。很有可能虽然 Marlee 的教师更少布置作业，但作业的超高难度会让学生花费更多时间；还有可能虽然 Marlee 的数学和科学老师给学生布置的作业更少，但这一差距却被其他科目的老师布置的更多作业所抵消。如果任何上述情况为真的话，那么假设 Marlee 的学生花更少的时间做作业，从而认为应更少布置作业的建议是不合理的。

此外，作者基于更好的分数和更少的留级情况判定 Marlee 的学生课业表现更好的假设也是不当的。这两个因素并不一定能代表优秀的学业表现，更不用说表明教育制度是否成功。如果 Marlee 和 Sanlee 的学校采用不甚相同甚至大相径庭的标准来给学生评分，那么学生分数的不同也就不会让我们惊讶了。此外，Marlee 地区的学校为了捍卫学术声誉可能会允许学业不佳的学生毕业。这两种情况都会削弱作者以成绩和留级作为学生表现优秀与否的指标的可信度。如果上述任一情况被证明是真的，那么我们就有理由怀疑 Marlee 学生的学术表现。因此，布置更少作业的 Marlee 也就不是我们应当遵循的例子了。

最后，作者的论点还存在一个可疑的假设，那就是他草率地将 Marlee 高中的情况推而广之到整个 Attra 州的高中。通过建议 Attra 所有高中老师向 Marlee 的老师学习，作者假设 Attra 的学生和 Marlee 的学生的能力是相似的。然而，教师在授课、布置作业的量和频次时应当灵活应变，根据学生的表现进行调节。如果 Attra 的高中生吸收知识的效率相对较低但有强烈的进步愿望，他们也许会需要，甚至会主动要求更多的作业。在这种情况下，作者提议每周布置作业不要超过两次是不可行的，充其量不过纸上谈兵。

总之，虽然作业不一定在提高学生的学业表现中起着至关重要的作用，我们并不能轻易忽视它的重要性。因此，我提议在接受作者的建议之前我们要考察文中的上述假设。

⤵ 文章解析与点评

这道题目的推理过程很简单，作者根据两个现象，即：在 S 地区，86% 的老师报告说一周布置三到五次作业，而在 M 地区，不到 25% 的老师报告说一周布置三到五次作业；M 地区的学生的平均成绩比 S 地区高，学生留级率更低，得出结论："我们学校"的老师布置作业不能超过一周两次。这样的推理过程显然是有问题的，但如果我们单纯就这一个推理过程作出分析的话，文章的层次感会不太分明，组织也可能不够有逻辑。因此，我们找出了两条作者暗示的推论（如逻辑图所示）。

根据逻辑图，我们可以对文章的组织结构有以下思考：

1. S 地区学生花在作业上的时间不一定比 M 地区多。虽然 M 地区的大部分老师报告说他们一周布置作业的次数不会超过三次，但我们不知道每次作业的量以及难度。并且我们所知道的数据只是来自数学和科学这两个科目的老师，其他科目的老师如何布置作业，布置多少作业，我们都不了解。

2. M 地区学生的学术表现不一定比 S 地区好。虽然 M 地区学生的普遍分数比 S 地区高，但这很可能是因为两地的评分标准不一。而 M 地区更低的留级率也可能是源于校方的主观行为，让即便是学术表现欠佳的学生毕业，目的是为了维护学校声誉。

3. 就算 S 地区和 M 地区的例子能够证明：S 地区的学生作业多，但学业表现不佳，而 M 地区刚好相反，我们也不能草率地认为一定是大量的作业导致欠佳的学术表现。因此，作者认为他 / 她所在区域的学校也要控制布置作业的频率的这一建议还有待商榷。

以上就是一个可供参考的思路。可以讨论的点还有很多，但不论是分析哪一个点，大家都需要紧密地贴合 Direction 进行论证，尤其要注意语言上的照应。

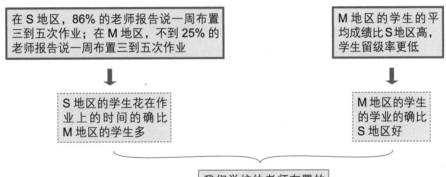

14 The following appeared as part of an article in a business magazine.

"A recent study rating 300 male and female advertising executives according to the average number of hours they sleep per night showed an association between the amount of sleep the executives need and the success of their firms. Of the advertising firms studied, those whose executives reported needing no more than 6 hours of sleep per night had higher profit margins and faster growth. These results suggest that if a business wants to prosper, it should hire only people who need less than 6 hours of sleep per night."

Write a response in which you examine the stated and/or unstated assumptions of the argument. Be sure to explain how the argument depends on these assumptions and what the implications are for the argument if the assumptions prove unwarranted.

In the article, the author describes a study concerning the average number of sleeping hours of 300 advertising executives and the success of their firms. The study shows a connection between sleep required (6 hours per night), and higher profit margins and faster growth. The author concludes that this link is a causal relationship and further suggests that business should exclusively hire people who need less than 6 hours of sleep per night. Astonishingly stimulating as this recommendation may sound, it suffers from several questionable assumptions, which, if not justified, would negatively influence the soundness of this argument.

First, when discussing the connection between the executives' sleeping hours and the financial performance of their firms, the author apparently assumes that these executives should receive most, if not all, the credit for the higher profits margins and faster growth. However, common sense informs us that any company's excellent performance derives from combined efforts of every single unit within that company. Although those in high positions, such as executives, may exert great influence over the company, dismissing other employee's contributions would be both unfair and unreasonable. Therefore, while I admit that the advertising executives might play an essential role in their firm's operation, once the participation of others also proves significant to the development of the firms, the assumption would be undermined that we should ascribe the healthy performance of these firms to their advertising executives, and the conclusion of this argument is also rendered in jeopardy.

Even if the advertising executives should be honored for their contributions to their firms' excellent financial performance, the validity of this argument may also be impaired by another dubious assumption, the one which attributes these executives' capabilities to the amount of sleep they require, namely, 6 hours per night. While we acknowledge the correlation between the length of sleep staff require and their work performance, we cannot easily see how 6 hours is applicable to everyone to perform their best at work. Therefore, we cannot rule out the possibility that arduous work tasks actually exhaust these executives that they cannot sleep longer than 6 hours; that is to say, even better performance may result if they sleep longer. If this is the case, then the previous assumption is unwarranted and we should thus vote against the author's proposal to only hire those who need less than 6 hours of sleep per night.

Even if we concede that the handsome financial performance of these films results from their executives' outstanding capacity and that this capacity is attributable to their 6-hour sleep per night, whether the author's suggestion is advisable highly depends on the soundness of the assumption that the executives' performance and that of their firms can be generalized to other staff as well as to business world. However, the executives' circumstances cannot be easily applied to staff who occupy different roles; likewise, it would be irrational to draw hasty generalizations based on one firm. If a business claims that a longer period of sleep is needed for both their workers' development as well as its prosperity, then the aforementioned assumption is defeated and the author's suggestion thus becomes absurd.

To draw a conclusion, while improved financial performance is always desirable, without any support, it is illogical to assume that the performance only springs from a limited amount of staffs' sleep. Also, we cannot expect the executives to bring their firms high profits on their own. Consequently, while the author's suggestion appears appealing, the questionable assumptions discussed above may deprive it of its feasibility. (588 words)

中文翻译

在这篇文章中，作者描述了一项关于 300 位广告业高管的平均睡眠时间和他们的公司是否成功的研究。该研究表明在高管所需的睡眠时间（每晚 6 小时）和公司更高的利润率及更快的增长率之间存在联系。作者认为这二者之间存在因果关系，并更进一步建议公司尤其应当雇佣那些每晚只需不到 6 个小时睡眠的人。尽管这一建议听起来振奋人心，但它的几处假设都存在问题；如果这些假设不能被证明为真的话，那么将会影响该论点的可靠性。

首先，在讨论高管的睡眠时间和他们公司的财务表现之间的联系时，作者想当然地认为更高的利润率和更快的增长率都应当归功于这些高管。然而，就常识而言，任何一家公司的优秀表现离不开公司里每个个体的共同努力。尽管身处高位的人，例如高管，可能会对公司产生更大的影响，但忽视其他雇员的努力既不公平，也不合理。因此，虽然我承认广告公司的高管在公司经营中可能扮演着关键角色，但若其他人的参与也被证明对公司的发展十分重要，那么"广告公司的强劲表现归功于他们的高管"这一假设就会被推翻，而从这一点推导出的论点也就站不住脚了。

即使广告公司的卓越的财务业绩得益于他们的高管，这一论点的有效性也可能被另一不确定的假设所削弱，那就是将这些高管的能力归功于他们所需要的睡眠时间，即每晚 6 小时。虽然我们承认员工需要的睡眠时长和他们的工作绩效之间存在联系，但并不能轻易地判定 6 小时的睡眠和最好的业绩之间的联系对所有人而言都是适用的。我们不能排除这样的可能性：费力的工作任务让经理们睡不足 6 个小时，使得他们精疲力尽；也就是说，如果他们睡得更长，他们本可以表现得更为出色。如果是这种情况，那么之前的假设是不合理的，我们应该反对作者关于只雇佣那些每晚所需睡眠时长短于 6 小时的人的提议。

即使我们承认这些公司出色的财务表现源自他们高管的杰出能力，且这一能力是因为他们每晚只需睡 6 小时，作者的提议是否可取很大程度上还取决于另一假设的可靠性：即高管的业绩可以推而广之到其他员工，他们的公司业绩也可以推而广之到整个商业界。然而，高管的情况不能轻易代表担任其他职位的员工；同样的，基于一个公司去概括业界情况也是不合理的。如果一家企业声称他们员工的个人发展和公司的繁荣都离不开较长时间的睡眠，那么上述假设就会被推翻，而作者的建议也会显得荒谬。

总之，虽然企业们都想要提高他们的财务业绩，在没有其他证据的情况下，假定出色的业绩来自于员工有限的睡眠时间是不合逻辑的。同样的，我们也不能指望高管们凭一己之力给公司带来高收益。因此，虽然作者的提议看起来十分有吸引力，我们指出的这些充满漏洞的假设让它不具备多少可行性。

文章解析与点评

这道题目的难点在于信息的表达太过简短，原文中只用了一句话交代和论证直接相关的事实信息：即，经理们报告说自己只需要不到 6 小时睡眠的那些广告公司的经济增长更快，利润更多。据此，作者得出结论：一个企业想要成功，就需要只雇佣那些需要不到 6 小时睡眠的员工。

而正是因为事实信息太少，原文的推理过程才显得漏洞百出。而这些漏洞，就是一些没有根据的 Assumption。在逻辑图中，我们用虚线构成的蓝框罗列出了一些 Assumption。如：

1. 作者认为，经理们报告说自己只需要不到 6 小时的睡眠，就代表他们一定只需要 6 小时不到的睡眠。然而，很有可能经理没有说实话。（Argument 当中经常会出现 report 这个词，这个词很具有麻痹性，因此考生容易忽略这个词。然而，report 这个词其实带有很大的主观性，我们需要考查 report 的主体到底有没有说真话。）

2. 作者认为，经理的卓越能力是来自他们不到 6 小时的睡眠。然而，经理如果能睡得更久，他们的表现可能会更好。

3. 作者认为，公司的良好业绩应该完全归功于经理。然而，其他员工也有可能对公司做出了贡献。

4. 作者认为，广告公司的情况也适用于其他类型的公司。

以上四点都是从逻辑图里归纳而出，这篇范文对其中的三点进行了详细的分析。大家可以仔细研读，认真学习。

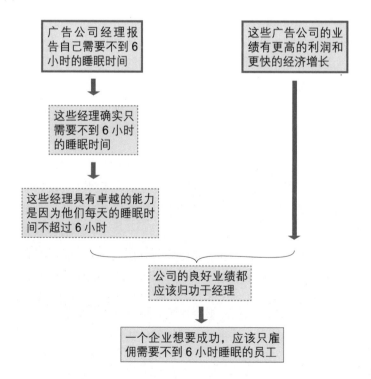

41 The following appeared in a health newsletter.

"A ten-year nationwide study of the effectiveness of wearing a helmet while bicycling indicates that ten years ago, approximately 35 percent of all bicyclists reported wearing helmets, whereas today that number is nearly 80 percent. Another study, however, suggests that during the same ten-year period, the number of bicycle-related accidents has increased 200 percent. These results demonstrate that bicyclists feel safer because they are wearing helmets, and they take more risks as a result. Thus, to reduce the number of serious injuries from bicycle accidents, the government should concentrate more on educating people about bicycle safety and less on encouraging or requiring bicyclists to wear helmets."

Write a response in which you examine the stated and/or unstated assumptions of the argument. Be sure to explain how the argument depends on these assumptions and what the implications are for the argument if the assumptions prove unwarranted.

In the newsletter, the author suggests that the government should assign priority to bicycle safety education instead of emphasizing the necessity of wearing a helmet while riding a bicycle. What underlies such a recommendation is the assumption that bicyclists feel safer because they are wearing helmets and therefore take more risks. This assumption is further supported by two more assumptions: one which advocates an authentic increase in the number of people wearing helmets during the past ten years and the second which assumes more frequent bicycle-related accidents during the same period. However, a thorough examination discloses that these assumptions suffer from the absence of critical information and are thereby liable to be invalidated. Once proved unwarranted, these assumptions would undermine the author's conclusion and consequently nullify the proposed recommendation.

To begin with, while we are informed of the significant increase in both the percentage of bicycle-related accidents and people who claim to wear helmets, we cannot safely assume that an increasing number of people began to wear helmets, nor can we confidently claim that people have a greater tendency to take risks while bicycling. First, whether or not the number of people who report wearing helmets, both in proportion and in number, has greatly increased depends on their truthfulness. Generally speaking, when interviewed about how to ride bicycles, people may allege safety awareness, by claiming to wear a helmet, for example. If it turns out that people lied about wearing a helmet, then the assumption that more people are wearing helmets while bicycling is unwarranted. Moreover, if the 200 percent increase in bicycle-related accidents results from an increase in bicyclists, which is highly likely given the ten-year time period, or if the accidents should not be ascribed to carelessness of the bicyclists, but instead to car drivers or pedestrian, then the assumption is untenable that bicyclists tend to take more risk. As a result, the author's recommendation is rendered questionable.

Even if the aforementioned assumptions remain tenable, it is worthwhile examining the soundness of another assumption that it is the helmets that led to bicyclists' likelihood to take more risks and finally result in more accidents. In this argument, the author clearly regards the increased percentages of people claiming to wear helmets and the bicycle-related accidents as a causal relationship. However, we just do not know whether the bicyclists, who are supposed to take responsibility for the accidents, wore a helmet or not when the accidents occurred. If it was the ones who did not wear helmets while bicycling that caused the accidents, then we should not find fault with the helmets and the author's recommendation deemphasizing the necessity of wearing helmets is obviously weakened.

Granted that wearing a helmet does increase a bicyclist's propensity to take risks and consequently gave rise to increasing accidents, we should still be cautious about the assumption that helmets contributed little to the protection of these bicyclists involved in the accidents; it is of equal significance that we remain alert to the assumption that educating people about bicycle safety functions well in reducing the number of serious injuries from bicycle accidents. If helmets excel at the protection of bicyclists from significant injuries, then we should maintain their use until better safety measures are found. In addition, if the education about bicycle safety turns out to be futile, then the author's proposal is undermined and we should therefore vote against such a recommendation.

To summarize, while people probably should receive more professional education about bicycle safety, we cannot readily assume that they will not benefit from wearing helmets while bicycling. Also, without concrete and reliable information, it is hasty to attribute the increased number of accidents to helmets, which in this argument are assumed to be responsible for bicyclists' penchant for risky behavior. (630 words)

中文翻译

在这篇新闻通讯中，作者建议政府应当优先考虑自行车安全教育，而不是强调骑自行车时戴头盔的必要性。该建议以这一假设为基础：戴头盔骑自行车的人们感到更安全因而更会冒风险。作者还列举了另两个假设来支持这一假设：一，过去十年里戴头盔的人数增长了；二，同一时期里发生了更多的自行车事故。然而，周密的考察让我们发现这些假设都缺乏关键信息，因而可能是站不住脚的。一旦这些假设被证明是没有根据的，就会推翻作者的结论并由此使作者的建议作废。

首先，虽然我们被告知自行车事故的比例和声称自己戴了头盔的人数都有大幅增长，我们并不能想当然地认为更多的人开始戴头盔了，同样我们也不能断言这些人在骑车时更倾向于冒风险。第一，是否有更高比例或更多数量的人戴头盔取决于他们的可信度。一般而言，在被问到如何骑自行车时，人们会用诸如称自己戴头盔来表现自己有安全意识。如果人们被证明在是否戴头盔上说了谎，那么关于更多的人骑车时戴头盔这一假设就不可信了。此外，历经十年之久，很有可能 200% 自行车事故的增长率是由于骑车人数的增长；自行车事故也可能不是因为骑车人的疏忽所导致，而应归咎于汽车驾驶员或行人。那么关于骑车人更倾向于冒风险的假设也就站不住脚了。作者的建议由此显得可疑。

即使上述假设仍然可以成立，我们也应当考察另一假设的可靠性，即头盔提高了骑车人冒风险的可能性，并最终导致了更多的事故。作者在文中明确认为更高比例的人戴头盔和自行车事故之间存在因果关系。然而，我们并不知道被假定为事故责任方的骑车人在事故发生时是否戴了头盔。如果是那些骑车时没有戴头盔的人造成了事故，那么我们就不能归咎于头盔，而作者认为应当弱化戴头盔的必要性的建议也因此被大幅削弱。

姑且假定戴头盔会增加骑车人冒风险的倾向从而增加了事故数量，我们也应当谨慎对待这一假设：头盔对遭遇事故的骑车人的保护微乎其微。我们还需对这一假设持警惕态度：教育人们自行车的安全功能可以显著降低自行车事故中的重伤率。如果头盔能有效保护骑车人免受重伤，那么我们在发现更安全的措施前都应当坚持使用。此外，如果自行车安全教育被证明是徒劳的，那么作者的建议是站不住脚的，我们也不应当赞成。

总之，虽然人们可能会接受更多的关于自行车安全的专业教育，我们不能轻易地假设骑车时戴头盔对他们是没有益处的。此外，在没有具体和可靠的信息前，像作者那样认为头盔导致了骑车人更倾向于冒风险，将事故的增长量归咎于头盔，是十分草率的。

文章解析与点评

在这道题目中，作者列举了两个事实性信息，即两个调查。一个调查显示十年间宣称自己在骑自行车时带了头盔的人数比例上涨了45%；另一个调查显示相同的十年间和自行车相关的案件数量上升了200%。根据这两个信息，作者得出了一个推论：人们正是因为带了头盔而更易冒险，所以才会有更多的事故发生。作者进而提出建议：为了减少事故所带来的伤害，政府应该更加强调骑行安全，而不是戴头盔的必要性。

在整个推理过程中，作者进行了两次明显的推理，每一次推理都有问题，而如果我们只针对这两次推理来组织文章的话，就只能写两个中间段，并且如果每一个中间段又展开得不够充分的话，这样的段落数就略显不够。所以，我们还需要去捕捉作者没有提到但又明显有暗示意味的其他推论。这些推论可能包括但不止于：

1. 人们接受调查时没有说谎。
2. 事故数量的上升等同于相同幅度的事故率的上升。
3. 事故的产生的确是因为人们掉以轻心，而不是其他原因。
4. 头盔在事故中对骑行者不会起到很大的保护作用，而安全教育可以。

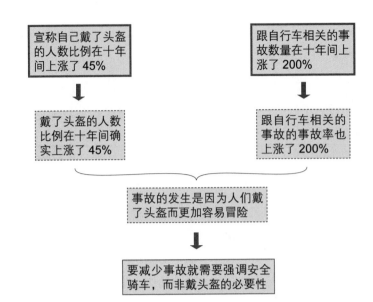

2 "Evidence 类" Direction

Write a response in which you discuss what specific evidence is needed to evaluate the argument and explain how the evidence would weaken or strengthen the argument.

中文翻译

写一篇文章，在这篇文章中，讨论一下需要哪些具体的证据来评价这个 Argument，解释这些证据将如何加强或削弱这个 Argument。

讲　解

其实，这种 Direction 的思路和 Assumption 类 Direction 的思路大体一致。原 Argument 的逻辑漏洞主要出在推理过程中，亦即原 Argument 的推理过程是不完善的。

如何不完善呢？我们无法确认其中的一些 Assumption 是否成立。

那为什么我们无法确认呢？因为重要证据不足。

所以，由于重要证据的缺失，我们还无法判断 Argument 的一些 Assumption 是否成立，也就因此无法判断其结论是否成立。

因此，我们现在还不能贸然使用一些评价性的词语来评论原 Argument 的结论是否成立或者正确。但是，在我们看到的同学习作中，95% 的同学都在使用诸如 "The conclusion of the argument is wrong/unconvincing/flawed" 一类的评价性的表达。这样一来，其实就偏离了 Direction 的要求。

　　既然现在我们无法评价 Argument 中的结论，我们需要怎么做呢？——我们需要完善推理过程。如何完善？——我们需要像 Direction 所要求的那样，提供新的具体的证据（specific evidence）。有了新的证据，我们就可以评价原 Argument 的结论了，并且，这种评价既可以是正面（加强其结论/strengthen）的，也可以是负面（削弱其结论/weaken）的。

　　还是拿那道题举例，为了更好地评价"新爵士乐俱乐部在本地没有竞争对手"这一论断是否真的成立，除了作者给出的"旧爵士乐俱乐部在 65 英里外"这一证据之外，我们还需要找出其他证据和信息。诸如：本地人的私家车拥有量；旧爵士乐俱乐部的服务质量、音乐品质、消费水平，等等。如果新证据表明本地人有车，或者旧的爵士乐俱乐部的服务好、音乐品质高、消费低，那么人们可能就不会去新开的爵士乐俱乐部，这样一来，作者的结论就被削弱了。如果新证据表明相反的内容，那么作者的结论就被增强了。

　　这道题剩下的部分，以及诸段落的组织方式，都可以参考上一种 Direction 的讲解。唯一的区别，就是我们现在要从 Evidence（证据）的角度来评价作者的结论。

　　让我们来总结一下如何应对 Evidence 类的 Direction：

　　如何写单段（每一段中都应包含下面所示的①②③，而不是①②③各成一段）：
　　① 指出我们现在还无法评价作者的某一个论断。
　　② 说明为了更好地评价这一论断，我们还需要什么样的新证据。
　　③ 用新证据削弱或者增强作者的这一论断。

　　如何把各个中间段组织起来：
　　根据逻辑图，作者做了几次结论的推导，就写几个中间段。

题库范文

25（微臣线下 325 班讲解文章）The following was written as a part of an application for a small-business loan by a group of developers in the city of Monroe.

"A jazz music club in Monroe would be a tremendously profitable enterprise. Currently, the nearest jazz club is 65 miles away; thus, the proposed new jazz club in Monroe, the C-Note, would have the local market all to itself. Plus, jazz is extremely popular in Monroe: over 100,000 people attended Monroe's annual jazz festival last summer; several well-known jazz musicians live in Monroe; and the highest-rated radio program in Monroe is 'Jazz Nightly,' which airs every weeknight at 7 P.M. Finally, a nationwide study indicates that the typical jazz fan spends close to $1,000 per year on jazz entertainment."

Write a response in which you discuss what specific evidence is needed to evaluate the argument and explain how the evidence would weaken or strengthen the argument.

In this application, the developers request that a jazz music club be built in Monroe. To support their conclusion, they point out that the nearest jazz club is 65 miles away. Moreover, they use a series of evidence to demonstrate the prevalence of jazz music in Monroe. In addition, a nationwide study is cited to prove that there are a great number of typical fans in Monroe who are inclined to spend money on jazz entertainment. Although the new jazz club may finally turn out to be lucrative, close scrutiny reveals that the conclusion lacks critical support and therefore we need more evidence to help evaluate the argument.

First of all, we need evidence to verify that a new jazz club in Monroe will have no difficulty attracting all of the local customers. While the author shows that the nearest jazz club is 65 miles away, no evidence serves to rule out the possibility that customers will continue to go out of town despite the new jazz club in Monroe. Thus, additional evidence gains great significance to determine whether the out-of-town jazz club has other advantages that outweigh the distance disadvantage, for example, a pleasant environment, comfortable service, and most importantly, appealing jazz music. If new evidence shows that the out-of-town jazz club is thus equipped, then it is reasonably safe to claim that people in Monroe will still choose to go there rather than the local jazz club, and therefore the author's recommendation is weakened. However, if new evidence discloses an opposite situation, then the proposal in the argument is lent great support to.

In addition, we need more evidence to ascertain whether jazz music is extremely popular in Monroe. First, although the number of people attended Monroe's annual jazz festival last summer is astonishing at first glance, exact local attendance figures will lend considerable support to the evaluation of the aforementioned statement. If attendance was dominated by non-locals, then the popularity of jazz in Monroe is in great doubt and the developers' conclusion is thereby rendered unconvincing. Second, we need to know the reason why the jazz musicians chose to live in Monroe instead of elsewhere, and whether their residence benefits the vogue of local jazz music. If it turns out that they reside in Monroe simply for the agreeable environment or attractive housing prices, or that they chose Monroe as an ideal place to enjoy life after retirement, which may lead to their constant alienation from jazz, then we are unconvinced of the popularity of the local jazz music. Third, the evaluation of the statement concerning the prevalence of jazz music in Monroe also entails evidence about the competence of 'Jazz Nightly' not only during the weeknights, but also on weekends. If the developers can prove that this radio program has absolute popularity regardless of the time period and its opponents, then we are disposed to believe that jazz is popular in Monroe.

Finally, despite the presence of all the previous evidence, an accurate evaluation of the developers' request requires additional information. Specific evidence is needed to show whether the result of the nationwide study also applies to the local situation in Monroe; that is to say, whether there exist a satisfactory number of typical fans in Monroe who are willing to spend money exclusively on jazz music clubs. If the answer is positive, then the reasoning of the argument is strengthened; however, if people give priority to and spend their money primarily on jazz CDs, concerts or other entertainments than they do to jazz clubs, we are reluctant to believe that the new jazz club will be tremendously profitable.

To sum up, the evidence cited by the developers does not provide enough conclusive information to make their request convincing. As a result, we need additional evidence to better evaluate the argument. (636 words)

中文翻译

在这份申请书中，开发商要求在 Monroe 建一个爵士乐俱乐部。他们指出最近的爵士乐俱乐部也有 65 英里之遥来支持他们的观点。不仅如此，他们还用了一系列的证据来证明在 Monroe 爵士乐很流行。此外，他们援引了一项全国性的研究来证明 Monroe 存在一大批愿意为了爵士乐活动花钱的典型乐迷。尽管新的爵士俱乐部确实可能有利可图，但这一结论缺乏关键的证据来支撑，我们需要更多的证据来判断这一论点的可靠性。

首先，我们需要证据来证明开在 Monroe 的这家新爵士乐俱乐部能够毫不费力地吸引所有的当地客户。虽然作者指出最近的爵士俱乐部也有 65 英里之遥，但没有证据能排除顾客即使有了新的爵士俱乐部也会继续出城的可能性。因此，能证明城外爵士俱乐部是否有能压倒远距离的其他优点的证据是十分重要的，如令人愉悦的环境、让人舒适的服务，更重要的是，引人入胜的爵士乐。如果新的证据表明城外的爵士乐俱乐部装备精良，那么我们或许可以认为 Monroe 的人们仍然会选择去那里而不是新的爵士乐俱乐部，因此作者的建议就不那么靠谱了。然而，如果新的证据表明情况相反，那么文中的建议就会更为可信。

此外，我们还需要更多的证据来确定在 Monroe 爵士乐是否真的相当受欢迎。第一，虽然乍一看去年夏天参加 Monroe 爵士音乐节的人数非常惊人，但我们需要确切的本地出席人数来佐证上述声明。如果大部分参加音乐节的人并不是本地人，那么爵士乐在 Monroe 可能并不那么受欢迎，而开发商的结论也就不那么可信了。第二，我们需要知道为什么爵士音乐家选择在 Monroe 而不是其他地方定居，并且他们住在 Monroe 是否会有益于本地爵士乐的风尚。如果他们住在 Monroe 只是为了宜人的环境或有吸引力的房价，又或者他们把 Monroe 当作退休后享受生活的桃花源，这让他们和爵士乐疏远了，那么我们对当地爵士乐的受欢迎程度是存疑的。第三，在评价 Monroe 地区爵士乐十分流行的主张时也需要考虑能证明"爵士之夜"在工作日晚上之外、在周末的竞争力的证据。如果开发商能证明这一电台节目无论在任何时间段、面对任何竞争对手时都十分受欢迎，那么我们倾向于相信在 Monroe 地区，爵士乐确实很流行。

最后，在上述证据以外，我们还需要额外信息来准确地评价开发商的要求。我们需要具体的证据来表明全国性的调查同样适用于 Monroe 的本地情况；也就是说，Monroe 地区是否存在数量喜人的典型乐迷愿意在爵士乐俱乐部中一掷千金。如果答案是肯定的，那么论点的推理就得到了强化；然而，如果人们首先把钱花在爵士乐 CD、音乐会或其他活动而不是爵士俱乐部上，我们很难相信新的爵士俱乐部能带来巨大的利润。

总之，开发商列出的证据不能提供足够的结论性信息使他们的要求令人信服。因此，我们需要更多证据来更好地评价他们的论点。

📝 文章解析与点评

这道题目在 Argument 的 Direction 的方法论讲解时已经做了详细的阐述，在这里就不再重复对题目的解析了。

值得再次提醒大家的是，逻辑图的使用能够很好地帮助我们梳理清楚原 Argument 的推理过程，进而让我们文章的思路和原 Argument 的推理思路保持一致，从而达到 6 分要求中提到的思路和组织上的"logical"和"cogent"。

另外，从逻辑图可以看出，作者做了四次推论，每一次推论都存在问题，而我们是可以对这四次推论都进行评析的。所以，理论上我们可以写四个中间段。但是大家可以发现，这篇文章只有三个中间段。这是因为考试时间有限，我们不可能也没有必要面面俱到，而只要把最核心的部分比较充分地呈现出来即可。三个中间段是一个比较实际的段落数。

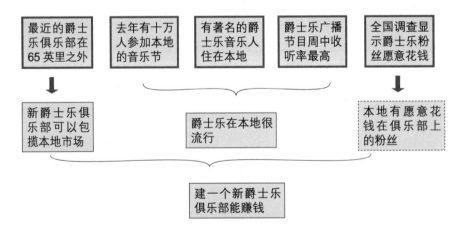

1️⃣ Woven baskets characterized by a particular distinctive pattern have previously been found only in the immediate vicinity of the prehistoric village of Palea and therefore were believed to have been made only by the Palean people. Recently, however, archaeologists discovered such a "Palean" basket in Lithos, an ancient village across the Brim River from Palea. The Brim River is very deep and broad, and so the ancient Paleans could have crossed it only by boat, and no Palean boats have been found. Thus it follows that the so-called Palean baskets were not uniquely Palean.

Write a response in which you discuss what specific evidence is needed to evaluate the argument and explain how the evidence would weaken or strengthen the argument.

The author of this article argues that since a type of basket that is originally thought to be produced solely in the prehistoric village of Palea was found in Lithos, the purportedly "Palean baskets" are not uniquely Palean. To further support this argument, he/she emphasizes that as Palea and Lithos are divided by the broad and deep Brim River, the only means of transportation between them is by boat. Since boats have not been found in Palea thus far, the basket could not have been transported across the river. Although the presence of an alleged Palean basket in Lithos may indeed suggest that Lithos also produced similar baskets, more evidence is needed to help us evaluate the author's conclusion. Close scrutiny reveals several key conclusions in his/her argument that lack critical support.

Firstly, evidence revealing Brim River's geologic past is critically needed to assist the evaluation of the author's assertion that the Brim River has always been deep and broad and could only have been crossed by boat. Thus far, this assertion does not receive any support and could possibly be wrong, since Earth's geologic features could have changed over thousands of years. A long and continuous record of river sediments may help us determine the Brim River's history. If it shows the Brim River was indeed broad and inaccessible when civilizations in Palea and Lithos first developed and thrived, the author's argument will be undoubtedly strengthened. If, however, it turns out that the Brim River was a shallow creek or even did not come to existence at all when humans first settled in this region, then we must reject the assertion that Palean baskets could only have reached Lithos by boat.

Secondly, even if we acknowledge for now that the Brim River has always been broad and deep since the human settlement in Lithos and Palea, more evidence is needed to help us evaluate whether boats were unavailable in the entire region. The author mentions that no boats were found in Palea, but gives no information regarding boats in other villages. If new discoveries indicate that Lithos villagers possessed boats, the transportation of Palean baskets by boat was possible and the Palean basket found in Lithos could indeed have been transported in this way. On the contrary, new evidence revealing an absence of boats in the entire Brim River vicinity during this time would help support the conclusion that the so-called Palean baskets are not unique to Palea.

Finally, granted that no boat was available to cross the Brim River, we must consider the possibility that the baskets could have been transported indirectly on land from Palea to Lithos. Yet, based on current information offered by the author it is challenging to evaluate the likelihood of such a scenario. If additional evidence emerges suggesting that trade was prevalent in this region and that both Lithos and Palea were actively engaged in trade, the author's argument will be weakened, since the baskets could have been merchandise that made its way from Palea to Lithos via a large trade network. On the other hand, if we have evidence such as local chronicles indicates Palea and/or Lithos societies were relatively isolated and had limited interaction with nearby prehistoric villages, then it is unlikely that Palean baskets could have arrived in Lithos. In this case, the author's conclusion is strengthened.

To summarize, the evidence which the author quotes does not provide conclusive information about the origin of the basket found in Lithos. As a consequence, we need additional information to better evaluate of the author's claim. (593 words)

中文翻译

本文的作者认为由于在 Lithos 发现了最初被认为只在史前村庄 Palea 生产的篮子，因此所谓的 "Palea 篮子" 并不是为 Palea 所独有的。为了进一步支持这一论点，他/她强调 Palea 和 Lithos 被一条既广且深的 Brim 河所分隔，它们之间唯一的交通工具是船只。由于目前为止还没有在 Palea 发现船只，篮子不可能被跨河运送。虽然在 Lithos 存在的那个所谓的 Palea 篮子可能确实证明了 Lithos 也生产类似的篮子，但我们需要更多的证据来评价作者的结论。仔细的研究揭示出，作者论点的几个重要结论都缺乏关键证据。

首先，我们极为需要能揭示 Brim 河地质变迁的证据，来帮助评价作者的主张——Brim 河一直以来都既广且深，只能坐船通过。到目前为止，没有任何证据支持这一主张，它可能是错的，因为地球的地貌在数千年的时间中可能已经发生了改变。一份长期而连续的河流沉积的记录可以帮助确定 Brim 河的历史。如果它表明 Brim 河过去也很宽，在 Palea 和 Lithos 的文明首次发展和繁荣时，它并不能轻易通过，那么作者的论点无疑就被强化了。然而，如果事实证明 Brim 河一度是条浅溪，或在人们第一次定居此地时尚不存在，那么我们就不能同意 "Pelea 篮子只能通过船被运到 Lithos" 的主张。

第二，即使我们暂且承认 Brim 河自人们定居 Lithos 和 Palea 以来就既广且深，我们也需要更多的证据来帮助我们评估整个地区是否都没有船只。作者提到 Palea 没有发现船只，但没有提供有关其他村庄的船只信息。如果新的发现表明 Lithos 村民有船，那么用船运输 Palea 篮子是有可能的，而在 Lihos 发现的 Palea 篮子可能正是如此被送过去的。相反，若有新的证据表明整个 Brim 河附近地区在这一时期都没有船，那么作者 "所谓的 Palea 篮子并不是 Palea 独有" 的结论就获得了支持。

最后，即使姑且认为没有船能让人通过 Brim 河，我们也必须考虑篮子可以间接地经陆路从 Palea 运到 Lithos 的可能性。然而，根据作者提供的现有信息，评估这种情况的可能性存在一定挑战。如果有额外的信息表明该地区的贸易十分普遍，且 Lithos 和 Palea 都积极参与贸易，那么作者的论点就被削弱了，因为篮子可能经由一个大型贸易网络从 Palea 被卖到了 Lithos。另一方面，如果我们有如本地编年史这样的证据表明 Palea 和 / 或 Lithos 社会相对孤立，并且与附近的史前村庄互动有限，那么 Palea 篮子就不太可能被卖到 Lithos。在这种情况下，作者的结论就得到了强化。

总而言之，作者援引的证据不能提供关于在 Lithos 发现的篮子的确切起源信息。因此，我们需要更多的信息来更好地评估作者的主张。

⤵ **文章解析与点评**

文章的基本语气客观，并没有强调论证作者一定错了，而是在每一段都反复强调"现有证据不足以支撑作者的观点"，同时举出了作者可能错误的情况。

本文的两个论证要点是：1. 两个村落之间的河流在过去可能不存在，或者并不如现在这样既宽且深，所以人们可以自由渡河；2. 现在没有发现任何船只，不代表过去就没有可以利用的船只。另外，即便人们过去因为河流既宽且深而且没有可以利用的船只，但篮子依然可以通过其他方式从 P 地达到外地。

正文部分的过渡和衔接非常平顺自然，通过让步句（"even if we acknowledge for now that the Brim River has always been broad and deep"和"granted that no boat was available to cross the Brim River"）把各个段落有机地结合了起来。

注意写作指令中提到了"explain how the evidence would weaken or strengthen the argument"，文章对此有很好的照应：在每一段说明需要新证据之后，既分析了什么样的证据能够削弱作者观点，也分析了哪些证据能够增强作者观点。根据我们的经验，很多考生在写作过程中容易忽略增强作者观点的证据。

文章的句式变化、词汇选择都比较得体，这也是拿到 Argument 高分的必要条件。

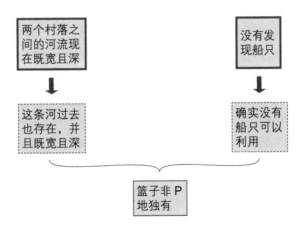

70 The following appeared in a memo from a vice president of a large, highly diversified company.

"Ten years ago our company had two new office buildings constructed as regional headquarters for two regions. The buildings were erected by different construction companies—Alpha and Zeta. Although the two buildings had identical floor plans, the building constructed by Zeta cost 30 percent more to build. However, that building's expenses for maintenance last year were only half those of Alpha's. In addition, the energy consumption of the Zeta building has been lower than that of the Alpha building every year since its construction. Given these data, plus the fact that Zeta has a stable workforce with little employee turnover, we recommend using Zeta rather than Alpha for our new building project, even though Alpha's bid promises lower construction costs."

Write a response in which you discuss what specific evidence is needed to evaluate the argument and explain how the evidence would weaken or strengthen the argument.

In this letter, the vice president of a large company recommends using Zeta instead of Alpha for their newly proposed building project. The vice president insists that Zeta is a better choice despite Alpha's more competitive bid because of buildings Alpha and Zeta constructed ten years previously. Although Zeta's construction costs were higher than Alpha's, its building's maintenance costs and energy consumption have been lower than those of the Alpha-constructed building. Moreover, the vice president cites Zeta's stable workforce and low turnover rate in hopes of proving Zeta's competency. Although this argument may seem quite convincing at first glance, the vice president does not conclusively justify his/her endorsement of Zeta. More evidence is needed in order to fully assess the vice president's recommendation.

To begin with, more information about maintenance costs and energy consumption of the two buildings is needed. This is because the vice president implies that the difference in maintenance costs and energy consumption is due to Zeta and Alpha's work quality. This could be wrong, however, because environmental factors can also affect both maintenance costs and energy consumption. For example, the building Alpha erected may be located in a region with a cold, harsh climate and frequent extreme weather, which would result in higher maintenance costs due to weather damage and more expensive energy bills due to higher heating demands. If the evidence suggests this, the vice president's argument will be considerably weakened. On the other hand, if evidence indicates a close similarity between the two regions in terms of natural conditions, the vice president's comparison is more reasonable.

Even if higher maintenance costs and energy consumption are the direct result of Alpha's construction, it is unclear whether the Alpha-constructed building's total costs are higher than the building erected by Zeta. By the total cost, I refer to the sum of construction costs and subsequent operation costs. The vice president mentions that the Zeta building's construction costs were higher so it is possible that Zeta's building was more expensive in terms of total cost. However, a lack of quantified information prevents detailed evaluation. We certainly need the exact construction costs and operation figures over the past ten years to determine which company actually offers a better economical solution.

What is more, even if the Zeta building's overall cost is lower than the Alpha building's, whether or not Zeta should win the contract remains questionable because cost should not be the only factor considered. Besides cost, factors such as building quality, safety standards and speediness of construction ought to be taken into consideration. If Zeta's building, though cheaper, is very shabby or contains high levels of toxic materials which pose a serious health threat to its inhabitants, it would be dangerous to give Zeta the project. On the contrary, a report from a certified independent quality-control agency endorsing the Zeta building's overall quality would certainly boost the vice president's recommendation.

Additionally, the author mentions that Zeta has low employee turnover and thus has a more stable workforce. However, it is not clear whether a company's workforce stability is equivalent to its service quality. Alpha's allegedly higher turnover rate (though this has not yet been established) could result from strong intra-company competition which results in the dismissal of underperforming employees. In this case, Zeta's superiority over Alpha is hardly proven. Feedback from the two company's previous clients regarding employee performance would allow for a more comprehensive assessment of the true quality of each company's employees.

In conclusion, although the vice president provides some information to support his/her argument, there are still some problems with his/her lines of reasoning. Zeta may indeed be a good candidate, but we cannot logically draw this conclusion based solely on the information provided by the vice president. More evidence is needed to determine whether Alpha or Zeta should be selected as the new project's contractor. (641 words)

🔊 中文翻译

在这份备忘录中，一家大型公司的副总裁提议让 Zeta 而不是 Alpha 来负责他们的新建筑项目。该副总裁坚持认为尽管 Alpha 的出价更具竞争力，但考虑到二者 10 年前所建的楼，Zeta 是一个更好的选择。虽然 Zeta 的建筑成本高于 Alpha，但维护成本和能耗都低于 Alpha 的建筑。不仅如此，副总裁还援引了 Zeta 稳定的员工队伍和低流失率来证明 Zeta 的竞争力。虽然乍一看副总裁的论点很有说服力，但并不能确凿证明他/她对 Zeta 的背书是正确的。我们需要更多的证据以充分评估副总裁的建议。

首先，我们需要更多关于两幢建筑的维护成本和能耗的信息。这是因为副总裁暗示了 Zeta 和 Alpha 的工作质量造成了不同的维护成本和能耗。然而，这可能是错的，因为环境因素也可能会影响维护成本和能耗。例如，Alpha 所建的建筑可能地处寒冷恶劣的地区，时常遭遇极端天气，天气造成的损坏导致了更高的维护成本，而对暖气的更多需求导致了更高昂的电费账单。如果有证据能证明这一点，那么副总裁的论点就会被大大削弱。另一方面，如果证据表明两幢建筑所处地的自然条件非常接近，那么副总裁的比较就显得更为合理了。

即使是 Alpha 的建设直接导致了更高的维护成本和能耗，我们也不清楚 Alpha 所建建筑的总成本是否高于 Zeta 所建的建筑。所谓总成本指的是建筑成本和后续运营成本之和。副总裁提到 Zeta 的建筑成本更高，所以就总成本而言，Zeta 建筑可能更为昂贵。然而，缺乏量化信息让我们无法做出详细评估。无疑，我们需要确切的建筑成本和过去十年的运营数据来决定哪家公司的方案更为经济。

更重要的是，即使 Zeta 建筑的总成本低于 Alpha 公司，由于成本不应当是唯一考虑的因素，我们对是否应该签约 Zeta 公司仍然存疑。在成本之外，诸如建筑质量、安全标准和作业速度之类的因素也应当被考虑在内。虽然 Zeta 的建筑更便宜，但如果它非常破旧或含有高剂量的有毒物质、对其居民构成了严重的健康威胁，那么让 Zeta 负责项目是非常危险的。相反，若有来自经认证的独立质量控制机构的报告为 Zeta 建筑的整体质量背书，那么副总裁的建议就获得了大力支持。

此外，作者提到了 Zeta 的员工流动率更低，因此拥有更稳定的工作队伍。然而，我们并不清楚一家公司工作队伍的稳定性是否等同于它的服务质量。所谓 Alpha 更高的流动率（虽然这还没有被证实）可能是因为激烈的公司内部竞争，那些表现不佳的员工被解雇了。在这种情况下，Zeta 并不一定优于 Alpha。两家公司服务过的客户对员工表现的反馈能让我们对其员工的真实素质作出更全面的评估。

总而言之，虽然副总裁提供了一些信息来支持他/她的论点，其推理思路仍然存在一些问题。Zeta 也许确实是很好的候选者，但我们无法从副总裁给出的区区信息中推理出这一结论。我们需要更多的证据来决定应当选择 Alpha 还是 Zeta 作为新项目的承包商。

文章解析与点评

涉及两个对象作比较的 Argument 题目，如这道题目，在题库中并不少见。很显然，对于两方比较类的题目，最基本的思考切入点在于"究竟现有信息能否判断孰优孰劣"。对本文而言，由于写作指令限定了要从证据出发，因此上述的问题变成"需要什么样的信息才能帮助我们判断 A 和 Z 哪家公司更好"。

本文有一个疑点在最后一句 "Alpha's bid promises lower construction costs." 是否需要讨论。有同学认为这一句也需要分析，但注意，作者自己的结论是支持 Z 而反对 A，因此我们要看的是现有证据能否推导出 Z 比 A 好，如果不能的话，还需要什么证据。对此，A 的成本更低并非支持 Z 的证据，所以我们后续讨论过程中不用围绕这一点展开（但在文章中简单提及一句是可以的）。

与之类似的一句话是 "Although the two buildings had identical floor plans, the building constructed by Zeta cost 30 percent more to build." 这里，因为我们不需要对作者的结论本身发表意见，所以我们没有用这个事实来反驳作者立场。注意：作者不一定对不代表其一定错，我们要用更客观的视角来看待问题（见第三段 "The vice president mentions that the Zeta building's construction costs were higher so it is possible that Zeta's building was more expensive in terms of total cost."）。

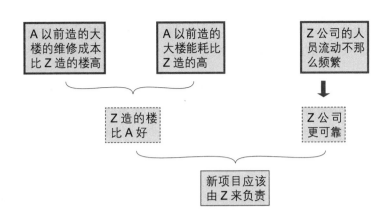

36 The following report appeared in the newsletter of the West Meria Public Health Council.

"An innovative treatment has come to our attention that promises to significantly reduce absenteeism in our schools and workplaces. A study reports that in nearby East Meria, where fish consumption is very high, people visit the doctor only once or twice per year for the treatment of colds. Clearly, eating a substantial amount of fish can prevent colds. Since colds represent the most frequently given reason for absences from school and work, we recommend the daily use of Ichthaid—a nutritional supplement derived from fish oil—as a good way to prevent colds and lower absenteeism."

Write a response in which you discuss what specific evidence is needed to evaluate the argument and explain how the evidence would weaken or strengthen the argument.

In this report, the author alleges the efficiency of Ichthaid—a nutritional supplement derived from fish oil—in preventing colds and further asserts the capability of Ichthaid to lower absenteeism in local schools and workplaces. To buttress his/her recommendation, the author cites a study showing high fish consumption and low doctor-visiting frequency in Meria. We are also informed that colds are the most frequently given reason for absences from local school and work. However, close scrutiny of this argument reveals a great lack of critical evidence and we are therefore unable to evaluate the conclusion. As a result, further information is needed to form a better evaluation of the author's recommendation.

To start with, while the author provides information concerning the high fish consumption and less frequent medical visits for the treatment of colds in Meria, we need more evidence to demonstrate the casual relationship between the former and the latter. For example, we need to know whether high fish consumption in Meria means that people eat a large amount of fish; in addition, detailed proof will be of great significance to determine whether people visit doctors infrequently because of a lower incidence of catching colds as opposed to other reasons, such as excessively high hospital fees. If new evidence shows that people do eat a massive amount of fish and catch colds less often, then fish's efficiency in preventing colds can be confirmed and the author's recommendation is thereby more convincing.

In addition, although the writer claims that the most frequently given reason for absence from local school and work is colds, he/she needs to provide more evidence to validate the assertion. Since absence due to illness is widely accepted in both schools and workplaces, using colds as an excuse not to study or work is naturally a reasonable possibility. Therefore, we need additional evidence indicating whether people asking for absence have lied about the reasons. If new evidence shows that colds do play a crucial role in absenteeism, then we are disposed to believe that the author's conclusion is advisable. On the contrary, if the evidence shows us the contrary, then we remain doubtful of the recommendation given in the argument.

Even if new evidence is provided to demonstrate both fish's efficiency in preventing colds as well as the contribution colds make towards local absenteeism, we need more information to show that Ichthaid is as effective, if not more, as fish in the prevention of colds. Specifically, we need to know whether fish's ability to prevent colds originates in its oil and not in any other parts such as the bones. Moreover, it would be of great help to know whether elements in fish remain functional after a series of artificial processes. In addition, the author would benefit from clarifying the relationship between the usage of Ichthaid and its efficiency in preventing colds. If it is fishbone instead of fish oil that prevents colds, or artificially processed medicine lags in efficiency, or overuse of Ichthaid is found to be counterproductive, then the author's conclusion is weakened and the recommendation should therefore be rejected. Otherwise, it should be encouraged.

To sum up, the current information available in this argument does not sufficiently substantiate that the proposed usage of Ichthaid will preclude colds in schools and workplaces and further lower local absenteeism. As a result, we need more evidence to better evaluate the writer's recommendation.
(565 words)

中文翻译

在这份报告中，作者称源自鱼油的营养补剂 Ichthaid 对预防感冒很有效，他/她进一步断言 Ichthaid 能够减少本地旷课和旷工的情况。作者援引了一份研究来佐证其观点，该研究表明 Meria 地区鱼的消费量很大，看病的频次很低。我们还被告知感冒是当地旷工或旷课时最常被给出的理由。然而，这一论点经不起仔细推敲并缺乏关键证据，我们因此难以判断作者的结论是否可信。我们需要更多的信息来评价作者的建议。

首先，虽然作者告诉我们在 Meria 鱼的消费量很大，人们找医生看感冒的频次较低，我们仍需要更多的证据来证明这二者之间存在因果关系。例如，我们需要知道在 Meria 鱼的消费量更高是否意味着人们吃大量的鱼；此外，我们需要更多具体的细节来证明人们更少看病是因为更少得感冒，而不是出自其他理由，例如过于昂贵的医疗费用。如果新的证据能够证明人们确实吃了大量的鱼并更少得感冒，那么吃鱼对预防感冒有效这一观点可以被确认，作者的建议也因此更有说服力了。

此外，虽然作者声称旷工和旷课时人们最常给出的理由是感冒，他 / 她需要提供更多证据来证实这个主张。因为学校和职场都接受因病请假，用感冒作为缺席的借口是很合乎情理的。因此，我们需要更多证据来说明人们是否会在请假理由上说谎。如果新的证据表明感冒确实引起了大量的旷工和旷课，那么我们倾向于相信作者的建议是可取的。反之，如果证据表明事实恰恰相反，那么我们对这一建议存疑。

即使新的证据证明了鱼能有效预防感冒且感冒导致了大量旷课旷工，我们仍然需要更多的信息来证明 Ichthaid 在预防感冒上比直接吃鱼更有效或至少一样有效。具体而言，我们需要知道是否是鱼油而不是鱼的其他部位，比如鱼骨，在预防感冒上发挥作用。此外，鱼所含有的元素在加工后是否仍然有效也将帮助我们评价该建议。不仅如此，通过解释清楚 Ichthaid 的用法和它对预防感冒的有效性也会帮助作者更好地阐释观点。如果不是鱼油而是鱼骨能预防感冒，加工将会降低该物质的有效性或过度使用 Ichthaid 会适得其反，那么作者的论点就会被削弱，而他 / 她的建议也不应该被采纳。否则，作者的建议应当被采纳。

总之，这篇论证中现有的信息不足以证实使用 Ichthaid 能够降低学校或工作场所的感冒发病率，并进一步减少当地的旷课或旷工行为。因此，我们需要更多的信息来更好地评价作者的建议。

文章解析与点评

这篇文章里有一句极具迷惑性的信息："colds represent the most frequently given reason for absences from school and work（感冒是学生和上班族最常给出的请假理由）"。很多考生会把这句话直接等同于"人们请假的最主要原因是感冒"。但是如果我们稍微留心一下"given reason"这个词组，就可以发现，感冒只是人们给出的请假理由，却并不一定代表人们真的是因为感冒而请假。虽然这两者的区别很微妙，但也就因为这个区别，我们把前者看作事实性信息，而把后者当作作者的主观论断。也因为这两者存在这个区别，大家可以看到本篇文章专门用一整段的篇幅来分析。

此外，题目中提到了作者建议每日使用 Ichthaid 这种从鱼油中提取而出的药物（"we recommend the daily use of Ichthaid—a nutritional supplement derived from fish oil"），就这一句话，其实有很多值得推敲的地方。如：鱼身体里能治感冒的部分真的是鱼油吗？就算鱼油也能治感冒，但经过加工之后的鱼油提取物依然有效吗？就算经过加工的鱼油提取物依然有效，用量对效果有影响吗？如作者所推荐的"每日使用"这样的用量可以吗？这些都是作者推论过程中可能存在问题的地方。而文章也单独用一整段的篇幅来论述这些问题。不过，虽然我们可以这样思考，更加重要的应该是结合 Direction 的要求，从"证据"的角度进行分析。

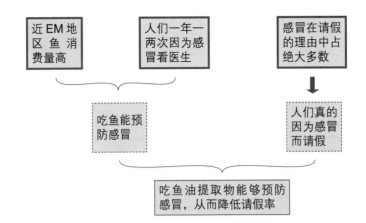

85 In a study of the reading habits of Waymarsh citizens conducted by the University of Waymarsh, most respondents said that they preferred literary classics as reading material. However, a second study conducted by the same researchers found that the type of book most frequently checked out of each of the public libraries in Waymarsh was the mystery novel. Therefore, it can be concluded that the respondents in the first study had misrepresented their reading habits.

Write a response in which you discuss what specific evidence is needed to evaluate the argument and explain how the evidence would weaken or strengthen the argument.

In this argument, the author concludes that there is a discrepancy between two studies concerning the reading habits of Waymarsh citizens. In the first study, respondents exhibited a great interest in literary classics as reading material; however, the second study revealed that mystery novels were most frequently checked out in public libraries. Consequently, the writer attributes the inconsistency to a misrepresentation of reading habits by respondents in the first study. However, I remain doubtful of this conclusion and require more evidence to substantiate it.

First of all, despite the presence of these two studies, we need more evidence to demonstrate their validity. That is to say, additional evidence is required to determine whether such two studies accurately reflect readers' reading habits. For the first study, the author would benefit from ruling out the possibility that the questions were biased and therefore induced the respondents to give answers in ways that did not accurately reveal their true reading habits. More specifically, we need to know what aspects of books they assign most significance to: contents, designs of covers or prices, for example. If new evidence helps to preclude such a probability that the interviewed citizens in the first study were biased, then the author's conclusion is strengthened; otherwise the argument is undermined.

What is more, the author should provide evidence to confirm the validity of the second study. First, the mere fact that mystery novels are most frequently checked out of the public libraries does not necessarily serve as an indicator of people's reading interests. Thus, we need to know whether people borrowed books from public libraries for other reasons, such as assisting with school assignments. If specific evidence shows us that reading interests did not even play a significant, if not unique, role in influencing people's checking out behavior in libraries, then the argument is weakened and the respondents in the first study were truthful. Second, as a matter of fact, people who are fans of a certain book genre do not always need to check out those books but can instead read them in the library. If evidence proves this scenario true, then the argument is seriously questioned; in other circumstances, however, the argument is lent great support to. Third, while the first study focused on Waymarsh citizens, the second study apparently narrowed its focus to those who borrowed books from the public libraries. Therefore, it is likely that people who enjoy literary classics could borrow books from private libraries or buy ones directly from bookstores. If new evidence is provided to exclude such a possibility, then I would be inclined to believe the author's conclusion; otherwise I remain unconvinced of the argument.

Even if the results from the two studies accurately reveal the readers' authentic reading habits and these two results are inconsistent, we need further evidence to demonstrate that this inconsistency is a direct result of respondents deliberately misrepresenting their reading habits. Since we are not informed with the length of time between the two studies, we cannot be sure that people's reading habits did not change during this period. If new evidence shows that literary classics lost their dominance during this period, then the respondents in the first study were actually telling the truth when they stated that they preferred literary classics, which does not contradict the second survey's subsequent results that mystery novels were borrowed from public libraries more than literary classics were.

To draw a conclusion, we need further proof to form a better evaluation of the argument. Only after weighing all of the evidence which serve to weaken the conclusion as well as those supporting the argument, can we come to a decision about the soundness of this argument. (616 words)

中文翻译

本文作者认为关于 Waymarsh 市民阅读习惯的两项调查自相矛盾。在第一项调查中，受访者对阅读文学经典表现出极大的兴趣；然而第二项调查显示公立图书馆中最常被借出的是悬疑小说。作者由此认为第一项调查中的受访者没有如实描述他们的阅读习惯。然而，我对这一结论持怀疑态度，我需要更多证据来证实这一观点。

首先，我们需要更多证据来证明这两项调查的有效性。也就是说，我们需要更多证据来证明这两项调查是否如实反映了读者的阅读习惯。就第一项调查而言，作者没有考虑到调查问题可能存在偏差，因此没能问出受访者真正的阅读习惯。具体而言，我们需要知道问题中他们把图书的哪些方面排在优先级较高的位置，例如内容、封面设计，或是价格。如果新的证据能排除第一项调查存在偏差的可能，那么作者的论断就更为可信；反之，就不那么可信。

此外，作者还需要提供证据来证明第二项调查的有效性。第一，公立图书馆中最常被借出的书是悬疑小说并不一定能表明人们的阅读兴趣所在。我们需要知道人们是否因为其他理由而从图书馆借书，比如用来完成学校作业。如果特定证据表明人们在图书馆借书时，阅读兴趣并不是唯一的理由甚至不是重要的理由，那么作者的推理将不那么可信，第一项调查中的受访者则是可信的。第二，喜欢某类书籍的人们并不一定要借出这些书，而可以在图书馆中阅读。如果这一猜想是正确的，那么作者的论证是十分可疑的；反之，作者的论证则得到了强化。第三，第一项调查聚焦于 Waymarsh 市民，而第二项调查则缩小了范围，只包括从公立图书馆借书的人。因此，那些喜爱文学经典的人可能从私立图书馆借书或直接从书店买书。如果新的证据能够排除这一可能性，那么我倾向于相信作者的结论；反之，我对该结论存疑。

即使这两项调查的结果准确地揭示了读者真实的阅读习惯而双方的结论大相径庭，我们也需要更多的证据来证明这一矛盾是由读者有意歪曲他们的阅读习惯所导致的。由于我们并不知道这两项调查之间的时间间隔，无法确定人们的阅读习惯在这段时间内没有改变。如果新的证据表明在这段时期内文学经典已不再是人们的最爱，那么第一项调查中的受访者表明他们偏爱文学经典时并没有说谎，这和第二项调查中，相比文学经典人们更多借阅悬疑小说的结论并不构成矛盾。

总之，我们需要进一步的证据以更好地评价该论证。只有既考量了那些支持该观点的证据，又考察了那些削弱该观点的证据，我们才能最终决定该论证是否可靠。

⚑ 文章解析与点评

这道题目本身非常清晰，作为事实性信息的证据有两个，即两个关于市民阅读习惯的调查研究，而这两个研究的结果是矛盾的。作者根据这两个研究的结果得出结论：第一个研究的调查对象错误地表达了自己的阅读习惯。

然而，如果只针对作者在题目当中所呈现出的推理过程来组织我们的文章，那么全文只有一个中间段——因为作者只做了一次明显的推理。一个中间段既不能很好地说清楚问题，同时段内的层次可能也比较混乱。因此，我们在用逻辑图还原作者的推理过程时加入了两个作者所暗示的小结论，或说假设，即：这两个研究都能够正确反映被调查者的真正阅读习惯。而正是基于这两个假设，作者得出了最终的结论：第一个研究的调查对象错误地表达了自己的阅读习惯。

按照逻辑图，我们可以有以下的思考：

首先，第一个研究不一定能够正确地反映读者的真实阅读习惯。这可能是因为研究的问题设计具有引导性或者迷惑性。

其次，第二个研究也不一定能够正确反映读者的真实阅读习惯。这可能是因为：人们从图书馆借出某种书籍并不一定能够说明他们的阅读兴趣，而可能是出于其他需求，如完成课业；或者，人们要阅读某种书籍不一定需要从图书馆借出，而只需要在图书馆内阅读即可；另外，第二个研究明显把研究对象放在了公立图书馆的借书情况上，但人们除了从公立图书馆借书，还可以有其他途径读到相关书籍，如从私立图书馆借书，或直接购买相关读物。

最后，即便两个研究能够正确反映各自调查对象的真实阅读习惯，但我们也不能保证两个研究所显示的矛盾的结果就一定说明第一个研究的调查对象错误地表达了自己的阅读习惯。很有可能两个研究先后被发起，而在这期间人们的阅读习惯已经发生了改变。如果从这一角度考虑，那么两个研究的结果都是正确的，但却是不可比的。

以上就是一个比较完整的提纲了，之后大家需要做的就是按照 Direction 的要求组织具体的语言。

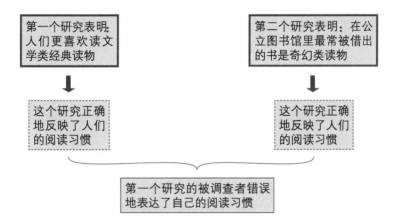

3 "Explanation 类" Direction

Write a response in which you discuss one or more alternative explanations that could rival the proposed explanation and explain how your explanation(s) can plausibly account for the facts presented in the argument.

中文翻译

写一篇文章，在这篇文章中，讨论一个或者更多的解释，这个解释也同样能合理地说明文章中的事实。

讲 解

这种 Direction 所对应的题目非常有限，在 177 道 Argument 题目里只有 11 道。这种题目首先会陈述一个事实或现象，接着会给出作者对这个事实或现象的解释，然而，这种解释可能并非唯一的解释。因此，Direction 要求我们提出其他可能的解释，并具体说明这些解释能够如何说明文章中的事实和现象。

☘ 例题举证

Workers in the small town of Leeville take fewer sick days than workers in the large city of Masonton, 50 miles away. Moreover, relative to population size, the diagnosis of stress-related illness is proportionally much lower in Leeville than in Masonton. According to the Leeville Chamber of Commerce, these facts can be attributed to the health benefits of the relatively relaxed pace of life in Leeville.

Write a response in which you discuss one or more alternative explanations that could rival the proposed explanation and explain how your explanation(s) can plausibly account for the facts presented in the argument.

这道题中，作者列举了两个现象：L 地的人们请假少；L 地诊断出的关于压力的疾病少。作者对这两个现象给出了统一的解释：L 地的生活节奏舒缓。

其实，我们可以进一步细化作者的推理过程：首先，作者暗示，一方面人们请假少是因为人们身体状况好；另一方面由压力引起的疾病的低诊断量可以被归结为人们心理状况好。之后，作者把人们良好的身体和心理状况归功于当地舒缓的生活节奏。然而，作者的解释并不唯一。例如，我们可以把人们请假少归结为人们不愿意请假，或者公司不给假；我们也可以认为压力引起的疾病很难被诊断出来是因为医院的仪器落后，或者医生水平低下；所以，当地人的身体和心理状况不一定好。最后，即便我们承认当地人口的健康状况良好，这也不一定是由于舒缓的生活节奏，完全可能是因为当地的环境好、食品安全，等等。当然，对于题目中的现象，可能还存在其他解释，这些解释都可以出现在我们的写作中，在这里就不一一列举了。

综上，应对 Explanation 类的 Direction，我们只需要找出其他可能的解释，并运用这些解释来说明原 Argument 当中的现象即可。当然，我们也可以通过逻辑图来理清楚原文的论证结构，并以此为据来组织我们的段落。如下图所示：

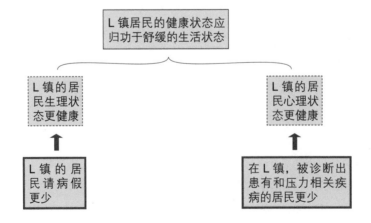

　　希望大家注意的是，我们应对 Explanation 类 Direction 的逻辑图和其他几类 Direction 的逻辑图有所不同。在其他几种 Direction 的逻辑图中，事实性的信息被置于逻辑图最上层，而题目中的最终结论被放在了最下层。这种构图原则是希望反映出：作者以这些事实性信息为基础，得出了关于未来的的预测或者建议。而 Explanation 类题目的思考方向刚好相反，作者是根据现有的事实性信息，追溯过去，探讨可能导致这一事实的原因。可以说，Explanation 类题目的思考过程和其他几类题目相反。

　　如图中所示，作者推导了三次结论，所以我们也可以据此写三个中间段来分别评论这三次推导过程。

　　总结一下对应这种 Direction 的答题步骤：

　　单段写法（每一段中都应包含下面所示的①②，而不是①②各成一段）：
　　①复述作者对题目中现象的解释，指出其解释不唯一。
　　②给出其他解释并详细说明。

　　如何把各个中间段组织起来：
　　根据逻辑图，作者做了几次从现象到原因的推导，就写几个中间段。

题库范文

> **92** Workers in the small town of Leeville take fewer sick days than workers in the large city of Masonton, 50 miles away. Moreover, relative to population size, the diagnosis of stress-related illness is proportionally much lower in Leeville than in Masonton. According to the Leeville Chamber of Commerce, these facts can be attributed to the health benefits of the relatively relaxed pace of life in Leeville.
>
> Write a response in which you discuss one or more alternative explanations that could rival the proposed explanation and explain how your explanation(s) can plausibly account for the facts presented in the argument.

In this argument, we are informed that workers in Leeville take fewer sick days than workers in Masonton, a larger city than Leeville. Also, a smaller proportion of people in Leeville are diagnosed with stress-related illness. The Leeville Chamber of Commerce attributes these two facts to the health benefits of the relatively relaxed pace of life in Leeville. While I concede that such a lifestyle could result in a healthier physical and mental state, I maintain that other plausible explanations can also account for the facts presented in this argument. However, with only the current information, we are unable to decide which explanation is best. Nor is it utterly certain that one factor alone is responsible for the facts presented in the argument.

To begin with, the Chamber of Commerce claims that Leeville workers take fewer sick days due to better health. While I admit that this might be the case, I also argue that fewer sick days taken by the local workers do not necessarily spring from a healthier state. Absence of significant information contributes to the failure to rule out the possibility that workers would still attend work even if they were seriously ill. More specifically, the workers' limited absence from work in Leeville may not lie in their satisfactory health conditions, but could be ascribed to a strict or even harsh working discipline. What is of equal possibility is that Leeville's workers themselves are reluctant to take sick days, which could be explained by their extraordinary passion for jobs. In addition, it will be unfair to keep blind to the possible scenario wherein the comparatively smaller number of sick days taken by workers in Leeville could also derive from Leeville's sparse population of local workers. All of the aforementioned explanations pose a great challenge upon, if not utterly reverse, the proposed one in the argument.

In addition, the author ascribes a lower proportion of diagnoses of stress-related illness in Leeville to the relaxed pace of life. However, the proportion of diagnoses alone does not sufficiently indicate a healthier state of people in Leeville. The lower proportion could also be explained by unsatisfactory medical resources in Leeville, both in terms of the number of hospitals and the capabilities of local doctors. If this is this case, then the relaxed pace of life in Leeville is less responsible, if at all, for local people's excellent health, since Leeville citizens could be suffering from a variety of diseases, which have been neither diagnosed nor treated.

Even if workers in Leeville are indeed healthier than workers in Masonton, it is doubtful that the relaxed pace of life is the only factor responsible. Generally speaking, good physical and mental states stem from a variety of factors: appealing environment, pleasant social relationships, and healthy diets, to name a few. While we cannot assert that these factors are present and lead directly to local people's good health, we are confident that these explanations could rival the one proposed in the argument.

To summarize, although it is reasonable to believe that a relaxed lifestyle contributes to better health in Leeville, there are several alternative explanations that could challenge the author's one and can also plausibly account for the facts presented in the argument. However, it is unreasonable to draw hasty conclusions about which explanation is best until further examination concerning Leeville town is performed. (557 words)

中文翻译

通过本文我们得知 Leeville 的工人相比 Masonton 的工人更少请病假，后者是一个比前者大的城市。此外，更少比例的 Leeville 人被诊断有和压力相关的疾病。Leeville 商会将这两个事实归功于 Leeville 相对轻松的生活节奏所带来的健康益处。虽然我承认这样的生活方式可能会促进身心健康，但我仍然认为还有其他适当的理由能解释文中所提的事实。然而，根据现有信息，我们无法判定什么是最佳解释。我们也无法完全确定文中所列的事实背后是否是单一的原因。

首先，商会宣称 Leeville 的工人因为身体更好所以更少请病假。虽然我承认这可能是事实，但我要指出当地工人请病假更少不一定是因为他们更健康。关键信息的缺失让我们无法排除工人是否会带病上班。更具体而言，Leeville 的工人更少缺勤可能不是因为他们的健康状态更好，而是因为他们的工作纪律十分严格乃至过于严苛。同样有可能的是 Leeville 的工人自身不愿意请病假，比如他们对工作抱有超凡的热情。此外，我们不能对 Leeville 人口更少的可能性视而不见，相对更少的员工可能是更少的病假天数的原因。上述解释即使没有推翻作者的论点，也至少对其提出了巨大的挑战。

此外，作者将 Leeville 更低的压力相关疾病的诊断比例归功于当地轻松的生活节奏。然而，仅靠诊断比例并不能充分说明 Leeville 人生活得更健康。更低的诊断比例可能是由于 Leeville 不尽人意的医疗资源所造成的，包括医院数量和医生水平。如果是这种情况，Leeville 轻松的生活节奏不一定能促进本地人的健康，因为 Leeville 市民可能患有各种疾病，这些疾病既没有被诊断出也没有获得治疗。

即使 Leeville 的工人比 Masonton 的工人更健康，轻松的生活节奏是否是唯一的原因也是存疑的。一般来说，良好的身心健康取决于多种因素——仅举几例，吸引人的环境、愉快的社会关系、健康的饮食。虽然我们无法断言这些因素都存在并直接提高了当地人的健康质量，至少这些理由可以和文中提到的解释一较高下。

总之，虽然有理由相信轻松的生活方式提高了 Leeville 人的健康，还有其他几个解释可以挑战作者的解释，也能说明文中所提到的事实的原因。然而，在没有进一步考察 Leeville 之前，草率判定哪个是最佳解释是不合理的。

📝 文章解析与点评

这道题目也是属于比较简单的 Explanation 类的题目。但本文的组织是值得大家借鉴的。

在题目中，作者对两个事实性的信息给出了统一的解释：L 镇居民更少请病假，这是源于他们舒缓的生活节奏；在 L 镇，被诊断出跟压力有关疾病的案例更少，这也是源于他们舒缓的生活节奏。如果按照这样的思路，我们只需要写两个中间段来分析作者的推理过程，而如果每一段展开不够充分的话，最后文章可能不够饱满。所以，文章采用了以下的组织方式：

1. L 镇居民更少请病假也许不是因为他们的生理状态更好，也许是因为他们即使病了也不愿意请假，或是公司不准假。

2. 在 L 镇，被诊断出跟压力有关疾病的案例更少，这可能不是因为他们心理状态健康，而是因为他们很少去看心理医生，或是看了心理医生也没有被诊断出来。

3. 即便 L 镇居民的心理和生理状态都更健康，但这也不一定能够归功于当地舒缓的生活节奏，而可能源于宜人的生活环境、安全的食品等。

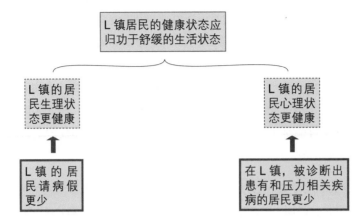

104 The following appeared in a memo from a vice president of a manufacturing company.

"During the past year, workers at our newly opened factory reported 30 percent more on-the-job accidents than workers at nearby Panoply Industries. Panoply produces products very similar to those produced at our factory, but its work shifts are one hour shorter than ours. Experts say that fatigue and sleep deprivation among workers are significant contributing factors in many on-the-job accidents. Panoply's superior safety record can therefore be attributed to its shorter work shifts, which allow its employees to get adequate amounts of rest."

Write a response in which you discuss one or more alternative explanations that could rival the proposed explanation and explain how your explanation(s) can plausibly account for the facts presented in the argument.

In the memo, the vice president describes the coincidence between a higher rate of on-the-job accidents at his/her factory and a shorter work shift at nearby Panoply Industries. The vice president further ascribes the lower number of accidents to the shorter work time. While this might be the case, we cannot easily ignore other explanations which could rival the proposed one endorsed by the vice president.

To begin with, while we could readily attribute the lower rate of on-the-job accidents at Panoply Industries to a higher level of safety, this is not the only explanation. Since we do not know the total number of workers at Panoply, we cannot rule out the possibility that a smaller number of employees at Panoply contribute to its comparatively lower rate of accidents. In addition, we should be cautious of the word "report", which is highly subjective and relies heavily on the kinds of accidents reported. Therefore, the lower rate of accidents at Panoply could have resulted from Panoply concealing accidents or could be due to different accident-reporting standards. Either of these two explanations, once proves true, could easily compete the one proposed by the vice president.

Even if Panoply is safer than the vice president's factory, it is hasty to attribute this safety solely to its shorter work shifts. Generally speaking, a safe working environment originates in a variety of factors: well-experienced employees, advanced and easily operated devices, and scrupulous supervision, any of which could exert a positive influence upon the improvement of safety level of working conditions at Panoply. Without further information, we cannot unhesitatingly preclude the possibility that Panoply's safe environment stems from any of the aforementioned factors, or a combination of these factors. Thereby it is ill-conceived to solely credit Panoply's safe working conditions to shorter shifts.

Granted that no other factors contribute to the safe environment at Panoply, the causal relationship between shorter work shifts and fewer accidents is open to doubt. In this memo, citing the experts' words, the vice president implies that in his/her factory, it is the insufficient sleep, which derives from longer work shifts, that leads to fatigue and sleep deprivation among workers and further gives rise to more accidents. However, even if the experts' words are trustworthy, it is likely that even if the work shifts were shortened, workers at the vice president's factory would spend the time doing other things rather than sleeping. Consequently they will not be energetic and the high rate of accidents will remain unchanged. Likewise, it is of equal possibility that workers at Panoply do not spend their free time sleeping and accordingly suffer fatigue and sleep deprivation as much as workers in the vice president's factory do. That is to say, the larger number of accidents in the vice president's factory could have resulted from workers' off-work activities. I therefore reserve my approval of the vice president's claim which attributes the lower rate of accidents to shorter work shifts.

To summarize, while a shorter work shift may plausibly account for a lower rate of on-the-job accidents, I remain open to different explanations that also help to illustrate the facts presented in this argument. Unless the vice president offers clarification, I remain doubtful that his/her explanation is the only possibility. (541 words)

🖑 中文翻译

在这份备忘录中，副总裁描述了在他/她的工厂中所发生的较高的操作事故率和在附近的 Panoply 工业公司较短的轮岗时间之间存在某种联系。这位副总裁进一步将较低的操作事故数归功于较短的轮岗时间。尽管这种联系可能是存在的，但在副总裁提出的理由之外还存在着其他解释。

首先，尽管我们可以轻易地将 Panoply 工业公司较低的操作事故率归因于他们更高的生产安全性，但这并不是唯一的解释。因为我们并不知道在 Panoply 工作的工人数目，因此无法排除更少的员工导致相对更低的事故率这样的可能性。此外，我们也应谨慎对待"报告"这个词，这是一个非常主观的词，并且很大程度上依赖于哪些事故种类被选择"报告"。因此，Panoply 更低的事故率可能是因为他们隐瞒了事故或采取了不同的标准来决定是否报告事故。若这两种解释中的任何一种为真，那么副总裁所提出的解释便站不住脚了。

即使 Panoply 比副总裁所在的工厂更为安全，我们也不能轻易地认为是更短的轮岗时间提高了生产的安全性。一般而言，工作环境是否安全取决于多种因素：经验丰富的员工、先进且易于操作的设备、严格的监督——其中任何一个都可能提高了 Panoply 的工作环境的安全水平。在没有进一步的信息前，我们不能完全排除 Panoply 安全的生产环境是由上述一个或几个因素促成的。因此单纯把 Panoply 安全的生产环境归功于更短的轮岗时间有欠考虑。

即使我们假定并没有其他因素促成 Panoply 安全的生产环境，更短的轮岗时间和更少的事故数之间的因果关系也是存疑的。在这份备忘录中，副总裁援引了专家的话，认为在他 / 她的工厂中，较长的轮岗时间让工人睡眠不足，由此导致的疲劳和缺乏睡眠引发了更多的事故。然而，即使专家的话是可信的，尽管缩短了轮岗时间，工人们也可能不会花时间睡觉，而是做其他事情。因此他们不会变得精力充沛，而事故率也将居高不下。同样的，Panoply 的工人可能也没有把时间用来睡觉，和该副总裁工厂的工人们一样疲劳且缺乏睡眠。也就是说，该工厂的事故可能是因为工人们下班后的活动所导致的。因此，我对副总裁的看法，即较短的轮岗时间降低事故率，持保留意见。

总而言之，尽管更短的轮岗时间可能会降低操作事故率，我仍乐于接受其他有助于澄清论点所提事实的解释。除非副总裁提供进一步说明，否则我对他的解释的唯一性存在疑问。

文章解析与点评

这道题目的推理思路是这样的："我们"工厂比 P 工厂的事故数量多30%，但这不是因为"我们"工厂生产的产品更具有危险性或者难度更高（因为两个工厂生产的产品是类似的），而是由于"我们"工厂的工作时间更长。在这里，作者似乎只做了一次推理，即将多发的事故归因于更长的工作时间。

但是稍加推敲，其实我们可以采用这样的思考方式：

1. P 工厂的事故量更少，但不一定是因为它的工作环境更加安全，而可能是由于其他原因。如：P 工厂的工人基数更小；或两个工厂对事故的定义以及事故上报的规则不一致。

2. 即使我们承认 P 工厂更加安全，这种安全的工作环境也不一定是来自 P 厂工人更充足的睡眠时间，而有可能是来自 P 厂工人更高的工作素质、P 厂更加先进安全的设备，等等。

3. 即便 P 工厂更加安全，且这是因为他们的工人得到了更充足的睡眠时间，但他们的睡眠时间也不一定来源于更短的工作时间。换言之，即便"我们"工厂缩短了工人的工作时间，他们也可能把这个时间花在其他活动上，因此完全有可能是这些活动导致了"我们"工厂更多的事故量。

对于这样一道题，很多考生容易偏离 Direction 的要求。比如，在表述上面的第 3 点时，很多考生可能会写到："作者主观认为缩短了工厂的工作时间就能避免事故的发生，这是武断的。因为即使人们的工作时间短了，他们也不一定会去休息，而是会把时间花在其他事情上。"这样的思考角度是可以的，但是却没有按照 Direction 的要求来写，即：不是在为题目中的现象找"其他解释（alternative explanation）"。大家可以结合中文提纲和英文段落，仔细揣摩这种 Direction 的应对策略。

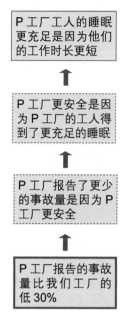

165 Humans arrived in the Kaliko Islands about 7,000 years ago, and within 3,000 years most of the large mammal species that had lived in the forests of the Kaliko Islands were extinct. Previous archaeological findings have suggested that early humans generally relied on both fishing and hunting for food; since archaeologists have discovered numerous sites in the Kaliko Islands where the bones of fish were discarded, it is likely that the humans also hunted the mammals. Furthermore, researchers have uncovered simple tools, such as stone knives, that could be used for hunting. The only clear explanation is that humans caused the extinction of the various mammal species through excessive hunting.

Write a response in which you discuss one or more alternative explanations that could rival the proposed explanation and explain how your explanation(s) can plausibly account for the facts presented in the argument.

In the argument, we are informed that humans arrived in the Kaliko Islands around 7,000 years ago and that these inhabitants witnessed the ensuing extinction of large mammals species in the forests of the Islands within the subsequent 3000 years. Referring to archaeological discoveries, such as fish bones, as well as simple tools like stone knives, the author ascribes the extinction of the various mammal species to excessive human hunting. Reasonable though this explanation might appear, we cannot safely claim that it is the only one that can reasonably account for the facts presented in the argument. Therefore, we must thoroughly consider the following explanations, which rival the proposed one in the argument.

To begin with, the writer attributes the discovery of fish bones to human fishing in the Kaliko Islands. While human fishing might well have resulted in the fish bone remains, the latter could have also sprung from other factors. First of all, it is likely that the unearthed fish bones trace back to a period when human habitation was scarce, or non-existent. If this is the case, then human behaviors had little to do with the fish bone remains and the subsequent mammal extinction. Consequently, the fish bones can be explained as stemming from the fish's natural death and eventual deposit on the sites later discovered. Second, even if human occupancy in the Kaliko Islands does correspond with the fish habitation, the fish bones cannot be exclusively attributed to human fishing. Instead, it is of equal likelihood that other animals also caught and ate fish and thus contributed to the disappearance of various mammals in the Kaliko Islands. Once the assertion that Kaliko people relied on fishing proves unwarranted, the underlying logic would be weakened, namely: if Kaliko relied on fishing, they must also have had a dependence on hunting the mammals.

In addition, the uncovered simple tools, including stone knives, lend great support to the arguer's explanation that the annihilation of mammal species arises from human hunting. However, those tools might not have necessarily been used for the stated purpose, but presumably for other reasons as well. For instance, humans living in the Kaliko Islands could have used those tools to document what they had passed through day in and day out or those tools could have been made for aesthetic purposes. Moreover, people could also have used those tools to protect themselves from animal attacks. Without further examination, we cannot decide which explanation finally led to the discovery of such tools. It is even likely that all the aforementioned factors might have conspired to the finding of those tools.

Finally, even if we admit that the uncovered fish bones and those simple tools were used by humans to hunt mammals on the Kaliko Islands, it is reckless to claim that human hunting has reached such an excessive degree that it directly contributed to the extermination of mammals. Other explanations could readily rival the alleged one in the argument. Considerable climate change, which went beyond mammals' adaptation abilities, the vanishing of food resources on which those mammals relied, or attack by other animals are all possible factors that could have triggered or accelerated the mammal extinction in the the Kaliko Islands.

To draw a conclusion, although human behavior could have exerted negative influence on nature, in the absence of sufficient information, we cannot establish a causal relationship between it and waning of other animal species. The extinction of mammals in the Kaliko Islands is such a case which requires more considerations of alternative explanations that could account for the facts presented in the argument. (598 words)

中文翻译

在此论证中，我们被告知人类约在 7000 年前抵达 Kaliko 岛，这些居民在接下来的 3000 年中目睹了群岛森林中大型哺乳动物的灭绝。根据考古发现的鱼骨以及简单工具如石刀等，作者将各种哺乳动物的灭绝归因于人类的狩猎行为。尽管这一解释乍看很有道理，但根据文中所给出的事实，我们并不能完全认为这是唯一合理的解释。我们必须仔细考虑下列解释，它们和作者提出的解释是同样有道理的。

首先，作者将鱼骨的发现归因于 Kaliko 岛上人类的捕鱼活动。虽然人类的捕鱼活动会残留下鱼骨，但鱼骨的出现也可能出自其他因素。第一，这些地下鱼骨可能上溯到人类还很少或根本还没来的时期。如果是这样的话，那么人类的行为和鱼骨的残骸以及之后哺乳动物的灭绝就是无关的。因此，鱼骨残骸可能是由于鱼群的自然死亡并沉积在之后发现的遗址上所造成的。第二，即使当时已有大量人类在 Kaliko 岛上居住，也不能把鱼骨完全归因于人类的捕鱼活动。相反，其他动物同样有可能捕食鱼类并导致 Kaliko 岛上各种哺乳动物的消失。只要 Kaliko 人依赖捕鱼为生这一论断被证明是站不住脚的，作者得出结论的潜在逻辑也就被削弱了，即：如果 Kaliko 人依赖捕鱼为生，他们也会狩猎哺乳动物。

此外，发现包括石刀在内的简单工具支持了作者的观点——人类的狩猎活动导致哺乳动物的灭绝。然而，这些工具未必如作者声称的那样用于捕猎，而可能有其他用途。例如，居住在 Kaliko 的人类用这些工具来计算时日或作为装饰。此外，人们还可能用这些工具来保护自己免受动物攻击。在没有进一步考察之前，我们无法判定这些工具的用途。甚至，有可能这些工具包含了上述所有的用途。

最后，即使我们承认被发现的鱼骨和简单工具是 Kaliko 人用来狩猎哺乳动物的，我们也不能轻率地声称人类的捕猎肆意到直接导致了哺乳动物的灭绝。除了文中提到的观点，还有其他合理的解释。剧烈的气候变化超出了哺乳动物的适应能力、哺乳动物赖以生存的食物来源的消失、其他动物的攻击，这些都可能导致或加速 Kaliko 岛上哺乳动物的灭绝。

总之，虽然人类活动可能会对自然产生负面影响，但在没有充足信息的情况下，我们不能认为人类活动和其他物种的衰减之间存在因果关系。Kaliko 岛上哺乳动物的灭绝即是一例，我们需要考虑能够解释文中所提到事实的其他原因。

文章解析与点评

在这道题目中，有两个事实性的信息，即鱼骨和简易工具的发现，作者将其都归因于人类的捕杀。很明显，作者在这里做了两次推理（第一次：作者认为鱼骨的发现可以归结为人们捕鱼；第二次：作者认为简易工具的发现可以归结为人类的捕杀），而我们要做的，就是去检查这两次推理是否有问题，并且找出可以匹敌作者解释的其他解释。然而，如果我们只写这两点，文章会略嫌单薄，因此，我们对文章内容做了这样的处理：

1. 鱼骨的发现并不一定代表人们捕鱼。很有可能鱼生活的年代并不存在人类活动，因此鱼可能是自然死亡。

在这里需要注意，作者似乎认为：只要人类捕鱼这一假想被确立，那么人类猎杀哺乳动物的假想也就成立。因此 1 的的说法可以削弱作者的这一推理。

2. 简易工具的发现并不代表人们猎杀动物。人们制作工具很有可能是为了记录或者出于审美需求。

3. 就算人们捕杀哺乳动物，但也不代表他们的捕杀行为足以导致哺乳动物的灭绝。哺乳动物的消失很有可能还存在其他原因，如：自然灾害、食物短缺等。

据此，文章写了三段，每一段的展开和说明也都比较充分。

另外值得一提的是，大家在应对 Explanation 类的 Direction 时，肯定会用到的表达包括“A 导致 B”，或“B 由 A 导致”，这两者形式不同，但表意一致。这篇文章中就有很多这样的表达。下面做了一个总结，大家可以从中挑选几个，在自己写文章时进行同义替换。

A 导致 B：	**B 由 A 导致：**
A lead to B	B result from A
A cause B	B spring from A
A result in B	B stem from A
A trigger B	B rise from A
A contribute to B	B is ascribed to A
A give rise to B	B is attributed/attributable to A

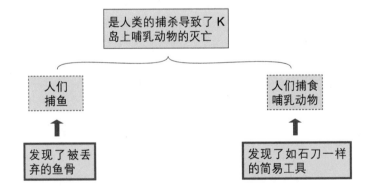

176 The following appeared as part of an article in a Dillton newspaper.

"In an effort to bring new jobs to Dillton and stimulate the city's flagging economy, Dillton's city council voted last year to lower the city's corporate tax rate by 15 percent; at the same time, the city began offering generous relocation grants to any company that would move to Dillton. Since these changes went into effect, two new factories have opened in Dillton. Although the two factories employ more than 1,000 people, the unemployment rate in Dillton remains unchanged. The only clear explanation for this is that the new factories are staffed with out-of-town workers rather than Dillton residents."

Write a response in which you discuss one or more alternative explanations that could rival the proposed explanation and explain how your explanation(s) can plausibly account for the facts presented in the argument.

In this article in a Dillton newspaper, the author concludes that the two new factories, which recently moved to Dillton where the city began offering generous relocation grants, must be staffed with out-of-town workers instead of Dillton residents. He/She arrives at his conclusion from Dillton's unchanged unemployment rate despite the fact that the factories employ more than 1,000 people. While the author's explanation could be the reason for this, there are at least two alternative explanations that could rival the one endorsed by the author. Unfortunately, due to very limited amount of information, it is too early to state with certainty which is the most likely explanation.

To begin with, the proposed explanation is related to the actual number of the unemployed. Although the two factories hire more than 1,000 employees, these newly employed may actually be Dillton residents who already have a job in Dillton. That is to say, the total number of employed and unemployed people in Dillton remains the same. The reason for this migration within the labor force could be that those positions require highly skilled workers, while those who are currently unemployed in Dillton are not qualified. In this scenario, the unemployment rate would not be affected because the addition of more than 1,000 positions are accompanied by the exact same number of job vacancies elsewhere that cannot be fulfilled by the existing labor force.

If we divide the labor force into the employed and unemployed population, the abovementioned scenario indicates internal turnover within the employed population without any impact on either the number of the unemployed or the total work force. With this definition at hand, a second possibility emerges: the 1,000 new jobs were accompanied by a reduction of 1,000 jobs elsewhere, possibly due to fierce market competition brought by the advent of the new factories. Hence there is an exchange between the employed pool and the unemployed population, but the net effect on employment rate is nil.

Finally, another possible explanation originates from the fluctuation of total population, and specifically speaking, the total size of the work force. While in pure theory the new factories could incorporate more than 1,000 new employees from the unemployed population, the change in the total size of work force is capable of offsetting this increase. For argument's sake, let's suppose that the city's unemployment rate is 50% and the total work force increased by more than 2,000, exactly twice as many as newly hired employees in the aforementioned two factories. In this case, the employment rate and thus the unemployment rate, remains unchanged. Multiple reasons for the increase in the size of the work force can be put forward, one of these being immigration from other areas in hopes of seeking better jobs. Another reason could be a large number of people in Dilton turning 20 and being considered as the member in labor force. Regardless of the specific reasons, we can achieve a steady unemployment rate by adjusting both the number of employee and the size of the labor force.

To summarize, the three possibilities discussed above are alternative explanations that can challenge the one proposed by the author. However, due to a lack of critical evidence, we cannot determine which one is best until a more thorough investigation of Dillton's job market is presented. (550 words)

中文翻译

在 Dillton 报纸的这篇文章中，作者认为因 Dillton 开始提供丰厚的搬迁补助金而迁徙到本地的两家工厂，一定聘用了外地员工而不是 Dillton 本地人。他/她从"尽管两家工厂雇佣了超过 1000 人，但 Dillton 失业率没有变化"得出这一结论。尽管作者的这一解释可能是造成该事实的原因，然而还有至少两种解释可以同作者认可的解释一争高下。不过受限于信息，现在宣称哪种解释最有可能仍为时尚早。

首先，作者提出的解释和失业人员的实际人数有关。虽然两家公司雇佣了 1000 多名员工，但这些新近雇佣的员工可能是已有工作的 Dillton 人。也就是说，Dillton 就业和失业人口总数保持不变。这些劳动力换了工作可能是因为那些岗位需要技术高超的工人，而当前的失业人口不能胜任。在这种情况下，失业率不会受到影响，因为新增的 1000 多个岗位意味着其他地方空出了同样多的岗位，而现有的劳动力无法填补这些空位。

如果我们将劳动力分为就业和失业人口，上述情况表明了就业人口的内部流动，对失业人口或总劳动力没有影响。根据这一定义，第二种可能性出现了：这 1000 个新岗位意味着其他地方减少了 1000 个岗位，这可能是因为新工厂的到来引发了激烈的市场竞争。因此，就业人口和失业人口中存在交换（译者注：即，有的就业人口失业了，有的失业人口就业了），但对就业率的净效应为零。

最后，另一种可能的解释源自总人口的波动，具体而言，是劳动力的总规模。虽然在纯理论层面，新工厂可以吸纳来自失业人口的 1000 多名新员工，但劳动力总体规模的变化可能会抵消这一增长。为了方便讨论，我们假设城市的失业率是 50%，总的劳动力增加了 2000 多人，正是上述两家公司新雇佣员工的两倍。在这种情况下，就业率和失业率保持不变。我们可以举出许多造成劳动力规模上升的原因，其中之一就是来自其他地区的、希望找到更好工作的人迁移到了此地。另一个原因可能是 Dilton 有大量的将满 20 岁的人口，他们也被当作了劳动力。无论具体原因如何，通过调整雇员人数和劳动力规模，我们可以获得稳定的失业率。

总而言之，上面讨论的三种可能性都是可以同作者提出的解释一争高下的替代解释。然而，由于缺乏关键信息，在对 Dillton 的就业市场进行更彻底的调查之前，我们无法判断哪一个是最佳解释。

文章解析与点评

文章严格按照写作指令的要求，没有花太多篇幅去讨论作者的论证哪里存在问题。本文一个易错点在于过度讨论背景信息，从正文的第一句到 "two new factories have opened in Dillton" 都属于背景信息，和原文的论证没有太多关系。但我们发现有不少学生花了很大篇幅去论证这些信息是错误的，这就偏离了题目的要求。

根据逻辑图可以看出，原文的推理结构相当简单。但如何为题目的现象找到其他解释则是难点。另外，值得注意的是，这里并没有强调原文给出的解释是错的，也没有强调我们给出的他因就比原解释更合理，全文更多是在探索可能性。

本题的突破点在于对失业率的理解，文章从"失业率 = 失业人数 / 适业人数"这一定义出发，分别分析了"失业人数不变"和"就业人数变化但比例不变"的情况。即，造成失业率不变的可能性包括：1. 新工厂的确新招了 1000 人，但同时在其他地方又有相同的人数失业；2. 新工厂新招的 1000 人是来自被其他地方解雇的工人。

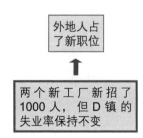

84（微臣线下 325 班讲解文章）The following is a letter to the editor of an environmental magazine.

"Two studies of amphibians in Xanadu National Park confirm a significant decline in the numbers of amphibians. In 1975 there were seven species of amphibians in the park, and there were abundant numbers of each species. However, in 2002 only four species of amphibians were observed in the park, and the numbers of each species were drastically reduced. One proposed explanation is that the decline was caused by the introduction of trout into the park's waters, which began in 1975. (Trout are known to eat amphibian eggs.)"

Write a response in which you discuss one or more alternative explanations that could rival the proposed explanation and explain how your explanation(s) can plausibly account for the facts presented in the argument.

The author of this letter attributes the decline in the number of amphibians in Xanadu National Park between 1975 and 2002 to the introduction of trout into the park's waters beginning in 1975. While trout could be the reason behind the decline, since they are known to eat amphibian eggs, the information currently available is not conclusive to qualify the proposed explanation the only one capable of elucidating the fact in the argument. Several alternative possibilities could also account for the decrease in both the number and species of amphibians.

Before considering the cause of the reduced amphibian population, we must consider the possibility that the studies confirming the decline are inaccurate. The alleged decline both in species and population could be the result of an underestimate in the 2002 investigation. For example, researchers may have only surveyed a specific area of the park where the amphibian population was particularly low and subsequently extrapolated this regional observation to the entire park. Such a methodology would lead to an ostensible decline in numbers despite the accurate numbers of each species actually remaining constant or even rising.

Even if we acknowledge that the amphibian population and number of species had dropped in the 27-year period, there are at least two explanations apart from the introduction of trout that can account for the change. The first is anthropogenic factors. For example, environmental pollution resulting from economic development in the nearby region could have adversely affected the amphibian species' survival. Amphibians spend the first stage of their life in natural water bodies and may be very sensitive to water quality. If pollution, such as waste discharge containing toxic elements, enters the amphibian habitats, the amphibian population might decrease consequently. Another possible anthropogenic factor which may have impacted the amphibian population is hunting. Amphibians may be hunted for their medical values. If demand for amphibian-derived medicine increased between 1975 and 2002, amphibian hunting in Xanadu National Park could have intensified.

Other than human causes, natural factors may also play a role in wiping out amphibians. Drastic environmental changes, other than the presence of trout, could have occurred in the park. Climate change is a likely candidate, which would have a huge impact on amphibians because they cannot regulate their body temperature. Reduced precipitation is capable of worsening the quality of amphibian habitat as well. In these scenarios, amphibians would migrate from the park because it had become inhabitable for them.

In a nutshell, there are multiple possible explanations that can account for the decline in the amphibian population and number of species in Xanadu National Park, if the decline is accurate in the first place. However, given the limited information at hand, it is difficult, if not impossible, to determine the real cause(s). Additional information on changes in the park, both manmade and natural, during this timeframe would be helpful. (475 words)

中文翻译

这封信的作者将 1975~2002 年间 Xanadu 国家公园两栖动物数量的下降归咎于 1975 年鲑鱼被引入了公园的水域。尽管以两栖动物的蛋为食的鲑鱼可能是两栖动物数量下降的罪魁祸首，但现有的信息并不足以证明作者提出的解释是唯一可以阐明事实的解释。其他几种可能性也可以解释两栖动物数量和物种的减少。

在考虑两栖动物群体减少的原因前，我们必须考虑这样一种可能性——那份证实数量下降的研究是不准确的。所谓的物种和数量的减少可能是因为 2002 年的研究低估了物种和数量。例如，研究者可能只调查了公园里两栖动物数量特别低的特定区域，随后又将对该区域的观察结果推广到了整个公园。尽管每个物种的确切数量实际上保持不变甚至有所上升，但这种方法得到的结果会显示数量的明显下降。

即使我们承认 27 年间，两栖动物的物种和数量都有所下降，在引入鲑鱼之外，还有至少两种原因能解释这一变化。首先是人为因素。例如，附近地区经济发展所造成的环境污染可能会对两栖动物的生存造成不利影响。两栖动物在水中度过生命的第一阶段，它们可能对水质非常敏感。如果像含有毒元素的废物这样的污染物进入了两栖动物的栖息地，它们的数量可能会因此下降。另一个可能影响两栖动物数量的人为因素是狩猎。人们可能会因为两栖动物的药用价值而猎杀它们。如果对以两栖动物为来源的药物的需求在 1975-2002 年有所增加，那么在 Xanadu 国家公园的两栖动物的狩猎可能会加剧。

在人为因素之外，自然因素也可能造成两栖动物的减少。除了鲑鱼之外，公园里可能发生了剧烈的环境变化。气候变化很有可能对两栖动物产生了巨大的影响，因为两栖动物不能调节自己的体温。降水的减少可能加剧了两栖动物栖息地的恶化。在这些情况下，两栖动物可能从公园中迁徙出走，因为那里已变得不再宜居。

总而言之，如果 Xanadu 国家公园的两栖动物的物种和数量确实减少了，那么有多种原因可以解释为何下降。然而，鉴于信息有限，我们不能或很难确定真正的原因。这段时间内发生在公园里的变化——人为的和自然的，与此相关的信息都是有用的。

文章解析与点评

文章开头简明扼要地分析了原作者的逻辑，这一方面是体现考生对于原文意思的理解，另一方面也是为自己后文的写作定下一个提纲，使之不至于跑偏。但需要注意，开头段大家需要同义改写题目，而不是照抄题目。

第二段在分析原因之前先对数据的合理性进行分析——很明显，如果数据本身不能让人信服，对于数据的分析也失去了意义。这不仅是 Argument 作文可以用到的技巧，也可以运用到现实的学术写作中。并且，这种分析也同样贴合了 Direction 的要求。即：被观测到的 amphibian 数量的减少并非源于其真实数量的减少，而是源于错误的观测方法。

在假设数据本身没有问题时，本文考虑了如何对数据进行不一样的解读，即寻找两栖类动物数量减少的他因。之后两段的分析分别从人类活动（包括污染和捕杀）以及自然环境改变两方面进行了讨论。

需要注意的是，有的同学花了很多笔墨来论证"引入 trout"和"两栖动物数量减少"之间不存在因果关系是不对的。第一，我们不能确定它们真的没有因果关系；第二，题目写作指令考查的不是作者自己的逻辑问题。因此要像本文开头所说的："While trout could be the reason behind the decline, since they are known to eat amphibian eggs, the information currently available is not conclusive."

是鲑吃掉了两栖动物的蛋，导致其数量减少

↑

两栖动物数量减少，公园引入了鲑

④ "Question 类" Direction

Write a response in which you discuss what questions would need to be answered in order to decide whether the recommendation is likely to have the predicted result. Be sure to explain how the answers to these questions would help to evaluate the recommendation.

中文翻译

写一篇文章，在这篇文章中，讨论需要问什么问题来判断题目中的建议是否会取得预想的结果。解释这些问题的答案会如何帮助你评价题目中的建议。

讲　解

这一种 Direction 在本质上和其他几种 Direction 并没有区别，都是引导我们评价作者的论证过程。只不过，评价的方式变成了"问问题"。

还是拿最初的那道题举例。要评价"新爵士乐俱乐部在本地没有竞争对手"这一论断是否正确，除了"旧爵士乐俱乐部在 65 英里外"这一信息，我们还需要问一些问题，诸如："本地人是否有车？"，"旧爵士乐俱乐部的服务质量、音乐品质和消费水平如何？"，等等。如果本地人有车，或者旧爵士乐俱乐部的服务好、音乐品质高、消费低，那么人们可能就不会去新开的爵士乐俱乐部，这样一来，即便开新的爵士乐俱乐部，也可能不会取得作者预期的结果。反之，则新爵士乐俱乐部可能会赢利。

这道题的剩余部分，以及诸段落之间的组织，可以参照第一种 Direction 的讲解。唯一的不同是，在 Question 类 Direction 的要求下，我们需要遵循以下的破题步骤：

如何写单段（每一段中都应包含下面所示的①②③，而不是①②③各成一段）：

① 指出我们现在还无法评价原 Argument 中的某一论断。

② 说明为了更好地评价这一建议，我们还需要问什么样的问题。

③ 给出问题的答案并用答案来评价题目中的建议（既可以正面评价，也可以负面评价）。

如何把各个中间段组织起来：

根据逻辑图，作者做了几次结论的推导，就写几个中间段。

除了到此为止介绍的四类 Direction 之外，Argument 还有其他四个 Direction，但是这四个 Direction 都可以归并到 "Question 类" Direction 中，应对方法也一致。在这里就不再赘述，只给出这些 Direction 及其中文释义。

Write a response in which you discuss what questions would need to be answered in order to decide whether the recommendation and the argument on which it is based are reasonable. Be sure to explain how the answers to these questions would help to evaluate the recommendation.

中文翻译

写一篇文章，在这篇文章中，讨论需要问什么问题来判断题目中的建议和论证是否合理。解释这些问题的答案会如何帮助你评价题目中的建议。

Write a response in which you discuss what questions would need to be answered in order to decide whether the prediction and the argument on which it is based are reasonable. Be sure to explain how the answers to these questions would help to evaluate the prediction.

中文翻译

写一篇文章，在这篇文章中，讨论需要问什么问题来判断题目中的预测和论证是否合理。解释这些问题的答案会如何帮助你评价题目中的预测。

Write a response in which you discuss what questions would need to be answered in order to decide whether the advice and the argument on which it is based are reasonable. Be sure to explain how the answers to these questions would help to evaluate the advice.

中文翻译

写一篇文章，在这篇文章中，讨论需要问什么问题来判断题目中的建议和论证是否合理。解释这些问题的答案会如何帮助你评价题目中的建议。

Write a response in which you discuss what questions would need to be addressed in order to decide whether the conclusion and the argument on which it is based are reasonable. Be sure to explain how the answers to the questions would help to evaluate the conclusion.

中文翻译

写一篇文章，在这篇文章中，讨论需要问什么问题来判断题目中的结论和论证是否合理。解释这些问题的答案会如何帮助你评价题目中的结论。

题库范文

35 （微臣线下 325 班讲解文章）The following appeared in a letter from the owner of the Sunnyside Towers apartment complex to its manager.

"One month ago, all the showerheads in the first three buildings of the Sunnyside Towers complex were modified to restrict maximum water flow to one-third of what it used to be. Although actual readings of water usage before and after the adjustment are not yet available, the change will obviously result in a considerable savings for Sunnyside Corporation, since the corporation must pay for water each month. Except for a few complaints about low water pressure, no problems with showers have been reported since the adjustment. I predict that modifying showerheads to restrict water flow throughout all twelve buildings in the Sunnyside Towers complex will increase our profits even more dramatically."

Write a response in which you discuss what questions would need to be answered in order to decide whether the prediction and the argument on which it is based are reasonable. Be sure to explain how the answers to these questions would help to evaluate the prediction.

In the letter, the owner of the Sunnyside Towers apartment complex predicts a dramatic profit increase for Sunnyside Corporation. His/her prediction relies heavily on the seemingly pleasing results from showerhead modifications in the first three buildings of the Sunnyside Towers complex. In those buildings, the maximum water flow has been restricted to one-third of what it used to be. While reducing the amount of shower water might be desirable both environmentally and financially, whether the author's prediction is reasonable hinges on the answers to the following questions.

The first series of questions I am going to put forward revolve around the actual consequences brought about by modifying the maximum water flow. More specifically, I need to ask what the exact water usage readings are before and after the adjustment. Will people take longer showers now that the water flower is restricted? If the answer to this question is positive, then a decrease in water usage is not safely guaranteed and therefore the writer's final prediction is open to doubt. On the contrary, if it turns out to be the other way around, then the prediction is strengthened instead. In addition, while the arguer claims that few problems with showers have been reported since the adjustment, it is still a question whether one-month period of time is too short for all problems to have emerged; have any problems or complaints been concealed or even suppressed? If the answer to either of these two questions is yes, then the argument's prediction is undermined; otherwise it is shored up.

Witnessing the seemingly positive result of the showerhead adaptation, the author further recommends a wider application of the adaptation to all the twelve buildings in the Sunnyside Towers complex. However, before reaching that conclusion, we need to know whether such a generalization is hasty. The current few complaints might derive from the possibility that people who were not satisfied with the adaptation in the first three buildings went elsewhere for shower. Therefore, we need to ask whether it is possible that once we implement the author's proposal and modify all the showerheads throughout all twelve buildings in the Sunnyside Towers complex, is the corporation going to lose the customers? If it will unfortunately suffer from a great loss of customers, then the prediction in the argument is unreasonable; in other circumstances it is not.

Even if people accept the showerhead modifications, whether such modification surely leads to a growth in profits remains an unanswered question. While we are informed that the corporation pays for water each month and therefore the water fee may decline due to the showerhead adjustments, we have no information concerning the modification expenses. Simply speaking, how do the savings resulting from the adjustments compare to the expense of adjusting them? If the savings are slight, then we cannot expect profits to rise and the author's recommendation should therefore be rejected; but if the savings are significant, then the proposal should be encouraged.

While I sympathize with the author's intention to reduce costs, whether we should resort to showerhead modification in all the buildings is subject to more consideration. We especially need to know how people react to the modifications, the adjustment expenses, and the potential savings as a result of the modifications. (542 words)

在这封信中，向阳塔公寓大楼的业主预测向阳公司的利润将会大幅增加。他/她的预测很大程度上取决于向阳公寓大楼前三幢楼的淋浴头改造似乎取得了喜人的成果。在这几幢楼中，最大水流量被限制为从前的 1/3。尽管减少洗澡耗费的水量是环保且有经济效益的，但作者的预测是否合理还取决于如下问题的答案。

首先我要对改造最大水流量的实际成果提问。更具体而言，我需要知道调整前和调整后的确切的用水量读数。现在水流变小了，人们会花更长的时间来洗澡吗？如果回答是肯定的，那么我们并不能保证用水量会减少，而作者的最终预测也会受到质疑。相反，如果答案是否定的，那么作者的预测就显得更可信了。此外，尽管作者声称在改造后只收到了个别投诉，但一个月的时间还不足以暴露出所有问题；住客的投诉是否被隐瞒或压制了呢？如果这两个问题的答案有一个是肯定的话，那么作者的预测就会被推翻；反之，他/她的预测就更可信了。

在看到淋浴头改造看似喜人的成果后，作者进一步建议对向阳塔的 12 座公寓大楼都进行改造。然而，在得出这一结论之前，我们需要知道这样的推而广之是否是草率的。有可能前三幢楼里的人去了其他楼里洗澡所以公寓方才没有收到太多的投诉。因此，我们需要问，一旦采纳了作者的建议在 12 幢楼里都改造了淋浴头，公司会不会损失他们的客户？如果公司会因为大量失去客户而蒙受损失，那么作者的建议是不合理的；在其他情况下，则可能是合理的。

即使人们接受改造淋浴头，我们仍然不知道改造计划是否会带来利润的增长。我们知道公司每月付水费，因此改造淋浴头后水费会降低，但我们不知道公司为改造淋浴头要花多少钱。简单来说，改造所节省的水费和改造本身的费用孰多孰少？如果节省的费用是很少的，那么我们不能指望利润将会上升，而作者的建议也不会被采纳；但如果能节省的水费是十分可观的，那么作者的建议应该被采纳。

尽管我同意作者想要降低成本的意图，但决定在所有楼中改造淋浴头前，我们还需要思考更多方面。我们尤其需要知道人们对改造的反应、改造费用和改造后可能节省的钱的多少。

这道题目的论证架构也很清楚。根据逻辑图，我们可以得出，作者进行了三次推论，这三次推论都存在问题。一个可供参考的提纲如下：

首先，既然水龙头的水量调整前后的读数还未知，那么我们就无法判断该调整能否帮 S 公司节约钱。人们可能因为水量变小而延长洗澡时间，最终导致总的用水量不减反增。同时，虽然此时并没有太多抱怨之声，但我们并不知道以后抱怨会不会增加，或者即便是现在，抱怨之声也可能只是被压制了而已。

其次，即便前三栋建筑物的水龙头水量改造取得了不错的效果，我们也不能草率地推导出所有建筑物的水龙头的水量都可以进行相似的调整这一结论。很有可能届时人们会怨声载道，S 公司也可能因此失去自己的顾客。

最后，即便水龙头水量的改造能帮 S 公司削减相当数量的支出，但我们不知道改造水龙头的费用为多少。如果改造水龙头需要支付高昂的费用，那最终 S 公司可能入不敷出，增加利润也就成了镜花水月。

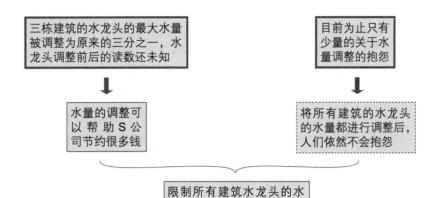

74 The president of Grove College has recommended that the college abandon its century-old tradition of all-female education and begin admitting men. Pointing to other all-female colleges that experienced an increase in applications after adopting coeducation, the president argues that coeducation would lead to a significant increase in applications and enrollment. However, the director of the alumnae association opposes the plan. Arguing that all-female education is essential to the very identity of the college, the director cites annual surveys of incoming students in which these students say that the school's all-female status was the primary reason they selected Grove. The director also points to a survey of Grove alumnae in which a majority of respondents strongly favored keeping the college all female.

Write a response in which you discuss what questions would need to be answered in order to decide whether the recommendation and the argument on which it is based are reasonable. Be sure to explain how the answers to these questions would help to evaluate the recommendation.

In this argument, a debate is presented between the president of Grove College and the director of alumnae association regarding abandonment of the college's century-old tradition of all-female education. Supporting this recommendation, the president cites other all-female colleges that adopted a similar education system and witnessed a subsequent increase in applications. On the opposite end of the spectrum is the director of the alumnae association who opposes the plan. Citing opinions of Grove's incoming students and alumnae, both of whom endorse preserving the all-female tradition, the director argues that such a tradition is an essential college identity. Plausible as both sides of this debate may appear, in order to decide which recommendation is more reasonable, we need to ask more questions and the answers to these questions might help us settle on the ultimate decision.

To begin with, we need to raise a series of questions and the answers to these questions might contribute to confirming the causal relationship between the coeducation system and the increase in applications. Firstly, even though we are informed that adoption of the coeducation system was followed by an increase in applications in some all-female colleges, we may still wonder whether such an increase could occur in this case. Normally, an application increase might spring from various factors, such as excellent faculty with strong academic backgrounds, an appealing campus, for example, and in most cases those factors conspire to influence whether students decide to apply. Therefore, unless the president gives a positive answer showing that adoption of the coeducation system is the only reason responsible for the application increase, we remain unconvinced of such a system's efficiency in attracting students. Secondly, even if the aforementioned causal relationship is confirmed, we need to question whether Grove College will experience a similar application increase by adopting the coeducation system. This question further behooves us to inquire the extent to which Grove College is analogical to other all-female colleges mentioned in the argument. If the president provides answers to demonstrate sufficient similarities between those colleges and Grove College, then we are inclined to accept his/her recommendation. Otherwise we reserve our approval.

Similarly, we should also carefully ponder the director's assertion. Although the director shows us the incoming students' ardor for Grovel College's all-female status, we need to know how other students view such a status, since they may contribute to future application increase. If these potential students exhibit great interest in studying at Grovel even without the all-female status, then we should reconsider the director's claim and maybe initiate the coeducational system. Likewise, what we also need to know is whether the respondents of the alumnae survey stand representative. Since the survey may have been biased in terms of its design, we need to ask whether only those who favor the all-female education responded to the survey. A positive answer to this question renders the director's claim less convincing and a negative one lends it more credibility.

Finally, even if the president's and the director's assertions are sufficiently supported by authentic facts, in order to make a reasonable recommendation concerning the admission system of Grovel College, it is of great significance to take into consideration aspects other than application rate and college identity. If extra factors, such as college reputation, matters as much as or more than the aforementioned two factors, then we should give second thought to the two speakers' recommendation.

To sum up, despite the passionate proposals put forward by the president and director, as well as the respective reasons they give, we should defer our conclusion about which is superior until the questions discussed above are carefully examined. (603 words)

中文翻译

在文中，Grove 学院的校长和校友会主任就该校是否应该放弃女子教育的百年传统进行了辩论。校长以采取相似教育制度的其他女校为例，认为开放男女同校可以提高申请人数。而另一方面，校友会主任反对这一计划。她引用了 Grove 新生和校友都认为应当保存全女子教育的传统的观点，认为这一传统是该大学的核心认同感所在。尽管辩论双方的观点看似都很可信，在决定哪一方的建议更合理前，我们需要提出更多的问题，而这些问题的回答能帮助我们做出最终决定。

首先，我们需要提出几个问题，这几个问题的答案能帮助我们确认男女同校的教育制度和申请数增长之间是否存在因果关系。第一，即使我们被告知在男女同校后，一些女子学校的申请数获得了增长，我们仍然需要知道这样的增长是否也会发生在 Grove。通常而言，许多因素可能导致申请数的增长，比如有较强学术背景的优秀教师、引人入胜的校园；在大多数情况下，这些因素会共同作用，影响学生是否决定申请。因此，除非校长能够给出肯定的回答，表明采用男女同校是导致申请增长的唯一原因，我们对男女同校能有效吸引学生这一观点只能存疑。第二，即使我们确认了上述因果关系，我们还需要质疑 Grove 学院采取男女同校后收到的申请是否会有相似的增长。该问题进一步要求我们就 Grove 学院和文中提到的其他女校的相似程度提出疑问。如果校长能证明 Grove 和其他学校之间足够相似，那么我们倾向于接受他 / 她的建议。否则我们将持保留意见。

同样的，我们也需要仔细考虑校友会主任的观点。虽然主任表明了新生喜爱 Grove 的全女子教育，我们需要知道其他学生如何看待这一情况，因为这些人可能有助于在未来提高申请数。如果这些潜在的学生在全女子教育之外也对 Grove 表现出极大的热情，那么我们就需要再次斟酌主任的言论、并可能会开始实行男女同校。同样的，我们还需要知道校友会调查的受访者是否有代表性。由于调查可能在设计方面存在偏差，我们需要质疑是否只有那些喜欢全女子教育的人回复了调查。如果答案是肯定的，主任的主张就不那么可信；而如果答案是否定的，主任的主张就更为可信。

最后，即使事实充分支持了校长和主任的主张，为了对 Grove 的录取制度提出合理的意见，考虑申请率和大学认同感之外的方面也是十分重要的。如果其余因素，例如学校声誉，和上述两个因素同样重要或更为重要，我们就需要再次考虑两位发言者的建议了。

总之，尽管校长和主任热情洋溢地提出了建议并各自给出了理由，在我们提出的上述问题获得解答前，我们不应该对二者孰优孰劣下结论。

文章解析与点评

这道题目算是 Argument 题目中比较独特的一道。绝大多数 Argument 题目中只有"一个声音"，即只有一个结论及支持这个结论的论据。而这道题目中有"两个声音"：校长和校友会主任各执一词，校长认为应该废弃女校传统，转而采纳合招制度；校友会主任认为应该继续传承女校传统，因为这是学校的标志。

　　为了支持各自的观点，校长和校友会主任分别举出了各自的论据。校长说到：有一些女校也采用了合招制度，继而新生的报名率和入学率上涨了；而校友会主任对此回应道：根据年度的入学新生和校友的调查显示，他们都青睐女校的传统。那么问题是，面对这两种声音，我们应该如何抉择呢？

　　答案是：我们不需要作抉择，也不应该作抉择。Argument 题目对我们的要求是：评析题目当中的论证过程。既然这道题目中校长和主任都有各自的结论，也有各自的论据和论证过程，那么我们就需要对他们二人的论证过程分别进行评论。事实上，他们二人的论证过程也都存在各自的问题，这在文章的第二和第三段分别有详细的阐述。

　　另外，要决定一个大学的招生政策，我们真的只需要考虑校长提到的报名率，以及主任所强调的招生传统吗？我们还需要考虑其他因素吗？这也是可以考虑的问题。如果其他需要考虑的因素更加重要，那么很有可能校长和主任的提议都不是最佳方案，那么我们就要对他们的建议谨慎对待了。这一层面的分析在文章的倒数第二段有简短扼要的论述。

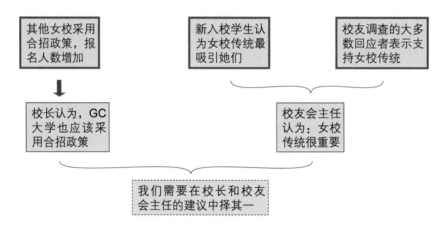

76 The following appeared in a newsletter offering advice to investors.

"Over 80 percent of the respondents to a recent survey indicated a desire to reduce their intake of foods containing fats and cholesterol, and today low-fat products abound in many food stores. Since many of the food products currently marketed by Old Dairy Industries are high in fat and cholesterol, the company's sales are likely to diminish greatly and company profits will no doubt decrease. We therefore advise Old Dairy stockholders to sell their shares, and other investors not to purchase stock in this company."

Write a response in which you discuss what questions would need to be answered in order to decide whether the advice and the argument on which it is based are reasonable. Be sure to explain how the answers to these questions would help to evaluate the advice.

In this newsletter, the author advises Old Dairy stockholders to sell their shares and other investors not to purchase stock in this company. To strengthen his/her recommendation, the author cites a recent survey, which indicated more than 80 percent of the respondents' desire to abstain from foods containing fats and cholesterol. In addition, the abundance of current low-fat products in many food stores, as well as the great number of Old Dairy's high-fat and high-cholesterol products, are also given to support the predicted diminished sales and decreased profits of the company. However, before we reach a final decision about whether or not this advice is reasonable, we first need to raise several questions, and the answers to these questions would help us assess this proposal.

First of all, despite the survey indicating most respondents' desire to refrain from foods containing fats and cholesterol, we need to know whether this desire would directly lead to a decrease in the products of Old Dairy Industries. Specifically, we need to ask: are the respondents swayed by other factors when selecting foods, such as flavor or price? Also, are the respondents able to distinguish the foods containing fats and cholesterol from those that do not? If flavor and price do influence the respondents' purchase behavior more than nutritional elements do; or if the respondents cannot tell the difference between high-fact and high-cholesterol foods and other foods, a definite decline in high-fat and high-cholesterol foods of Old Dairy would not be guaranteed, and the author's suggestion is undermined. Otherwise, the conclusion of the argument may be verified and the advice is reasonable.

Secondly, even though the author informs us that many food products currently marketed by Old Dairy Industries are high in fat and cholesterol, he/she would benefit from clarifying the question: what fraction do these products comprise of all foods produced by Old Dairy Industries? Or, more specifically, does Old Dairy Industries also produce low-fat and low-cholesterol foods? If the answer is yes, then even if the foods containing high fats and cholesterol might suffer from a decline in sales, this decline could probably be offset by an increase in sales of the company's low-fat and low-cholesterol products. As a result, the company's overall sales would not witness a decrease and neither would their profits. However, if Old Dairy Industries relies heavily on sales of high-fat and high-cholesterol food, then the company is subject to a significant decrease in both sales and profits.

Finally, granted that low-fat and low-cholesterol foods may come to dominate the food market and Old Dairy Industries mainly produces foods with high fats and high cholesterol, before deciding whether Old Dairy Industries is worth investing in, we need to know the company's intent. That is to say, we need to ask: will the company change its strategy and main products in the future? If Old Dairy is flexible in its strategy and can therefore efficiently exchange its products in order to appeal to those favoring low-fat and low-cholesterol foods, we may advise stockholders against selling shares and persuade others to invest. If the opposite is true, then we may encourage Old Dairy stockholders to sell their shares, and at the same time deter other investors from purchasing stock in this company.

To sum up, although the financial market fluctuates greatly, we should not make hasty decisions in response to every erratic market change. In order to decide whether the recommendation in the argument is reasonable, we need to ask the aforementioned questions and the answers to the questions would contribute to a better evaluation of the proposal. (597 words)

中文翻译

在这篇通讯中，作者建议 Old Dairy（以下简称 OD）的股东出售股票，其他投资者不要再购买该公司的股票。为使他/她的建议更可信，作者援引了近期一项调查，该调查表明逾 80% 的受访者表示希望戒除含脂肪和胆固醇的食品。此外，作者还以许多食品店中出售种类繁多的低脂产品和 OD 公司拥有数量庞大的高脂和高胆固醇产品来佐证他/她的预测：OD 公司的销量和利润将会下降。然而，在我们最终判定这项建议是否合理之前，我们首先需要提出几个问题，而这几个问题的答案将帮助我们评估作者的建议。

首先，尽管调查显示大多数受访者希望避免摄入含脂肪和胆固醇的食物，我们需要知道这种想法是否真的会减少 OD 产品的销售额。具体而言，我们需要问：受访者在挑选食物时是否还会受到其他因素如口味或价格的影响？此外，受访者们是否能够甄别不含脂肪和胆固醇的食物？如果口味和价格比营养元素对受访者的影响更大，或受访者无法甄别高脂、高胆固醇的食物，那么我们不能保证 OD 高脂、高胆固醇产品的销量将会显著降低，而作者的建议也就不那么合理了。若答案是肯定的，那么作者的结论将被证实，而他/她的建议也是合理的。

其次，尽管作者告诉我们 OD 目前销售的许多产品都是高脂、高胆固醇的，阐明这一问题对他/她的论点不无裨益：这些食品在 OD 生产的所有食品中占多少比例？更具体而言，OD 是否也生产低脂、低胆固醇的食品？如果回答是肯定的，那么即使高脂、高胆固醇食品的销量会下降，这部分损失也可以被增长的低脂、低胆固醇食品的销量抵消。因此，公司的整体销售额和利润未必会减少。然而，如果 OD 极为依赖于销售高脂、高胆固醇食品，那么公司的销售额和利润就会大幅下降。

最后，即使我们姑且认可低脂、低胆固醇食品将会主导食品市场且 OD 主要生产高脂、高胆固醇食品，在决定 OD 是否值得投资前，我们还需要知道公司的打算。也就是说，公司将来会改变它的战略和主打产品吗？如果 OD 采用灵活的战略，能有效改变它的产品以吸引喜欢低脂、低胆固醇食品的顾客，我们也不会建议股东出售股票并建议其他人进行投资。如果事实恰恰相反，那么我们可能会建议 OD 的股东出售股票，同时让其他投资人打消购买 OD 股票的想法。

总之，虽然金融市场波动很大，但我们不应该草率应对市场的每一次无常变化。为了判定作者的建议是否合理，我们需要提出上述问题并获得回答来更好地评价他/她的建议。

文章解析与点评

这道题目相对来说比较简单。不过我们依然要借助逻辑图来组织文章。

从逻辑图可以看出，题目一共给出了三条事实性信息：

1. 绝大部分调查对象表示自己愿意减少脂肪和胆固醇的摄入；
2. 市面上存在很多低脂肪和低胆固醇的产品；
3. OD 的很多产品都是高脂肪和高胆固醇的。

根据这三条事实性信息，我们可以找出作者明确说明或者暗示的一些推论。例如：根据事实信息 1 和 2，作者得出推论：调查对象会真的选择市场上那些低脂肪和低胆固醇的产品。然而，很有可能调查对象并没有甄别低脂肪、低胆固醇产品的能力；或者，相比于营养价值，可能他们最终还是更看重口味和价格，所以依然会选择 OD 的产品。

另外，值得一提的是"respondent（回应者，即调查对象）"这个词，虽然有 80% 的调查对象都表示自己愿意减少脂肪和胆固醇的摄入，但很有可能只有那些有这样意愿的人才回应了调查，而更多人依然会选择高脂肪和高胆固醇的产品。这一点大家也可以考虑。

另一方面，虽然 OD 的很多产品都是高脂肪和高胆固醇的，但是我们并不知道 OD 是否也生产同样多或者更多的低脂肪和低胆固醇的产品。如果有，那么 OD 的产品总销量可能还是不会降低。

最后，即使现在 OD 的产品销量可能会降低，我们也不知道它是否会根据市场调整自己的营销和生产策略。如果调整得当，OD 之后的盈利可能会再上升。

以上就是作者推理过程中的漏洞，在梳理出这些漏洞之后，我们就需要根据 Direction 的要求进行语言上的组织和整理了。

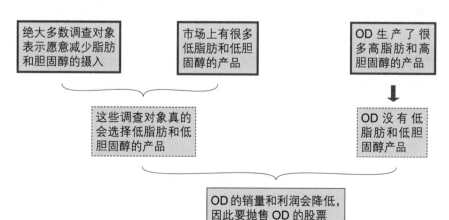

94 The vice president of human resources at Climpson Industries sent the following recommendation to the company's president.

"A recent national survey found that the majority of workers with access to the Internet at work had used company computers for personal or recreational activities, such as banking or playing games. In an effort to improve our employees' productivity, we should implement electronic monitoring of employees' Internet use from their workstations. Using electronic monitoring software is the best way to reduce the number of hours Climpson employees spend on personal or recreational activities. We predict that installing software to monitor employees' Internet use will allow us to prevent employees from wasting time, thereby increasing productivity and improving overall profits."

Write a response in which you discuss what questions would need to be answered in order to decide whether the prediction and the argument on which it is based are reasonable. Be sure to explain how the answers to these questions would help to evaluate the prediction.

In this recommendation, the vice president proposes the usage of electronic monitoring software at Climpson Industries. He/she further predicts that such software would help preclude the employees from wasting time and thereby increase their productivity, in turn contributing to an overall increase in profits. While I sympathize with the vice president's intention to enhance the staff's working efficiency, I highly doubt that this recommendation is reasonable. To better assess the vice president's proposal, I need answers to several questions, which concern, but may go beyond, the necessity and effectiveness of this policy.

Firstly, I need to know whether there is sufficient need to initiate the electronic monitoring software at Climpson Industries. While the vice presidents refers to a recent national survey which shows the tendency of most workers to spend work time on personal or recreational activities, I question whether this also occurs at Climpson. If the employees at Climpson are highly self-disciplined and will in all circumstances refrain from participating in distracting activities, then the vice president's recommendation is deprived of a significant premise and is thereby unreasonable. Even if some employees at Climpson do spend some time engaging in personal or recreational activities, we still need to question whether such behavior has reached a point that has impaired their working efficiency and therefore jeopardized the overall profits of Climpson. If the answer turns out to be yes, then I agree with the vice president and wholly support the application of the electronic monitoring software; otherwise, the suggestion might need further consideration.

Granted there are a significant number of employees at Climpson who are distracted by non-working activities, which supports adoption of the electronic monitoring software, the efficiency of this software in preventing people from wasting time is open to doubt. On the one hand, even if the software is implemented, will the employees try various means to avoid detection? In all likelihood, they would. If the employees manage to elude the monitoring software, then the effort to prevent them from wasting time on personal or recreational activities will have been in vain. On the other hand, even if this software impedes employees from becoming distracted by online activities, will they choose to waste their time in other ways instead? These may include snoozing or chatting. We cannot know the answer to this. Employees who are by nature sluggish will always be reluctant to work without distraction and any policy against their sloth will likely be futile.

Even if the usage of the electronic monitoring software generates a subsequent conspicuous decrease of employee distraction, the question remains unanswered whether this software will further contribute to increased productivity and overall profits. Specifically we need to ask if the usage of this software will provoke discontent or resent from the employees? Will this later lead to a subsequent decline in the staff's productivity? In addition, is the cost of installing this software prohibitively high? Will software maintenance require additional cost? If the answer to any of these questions is yes, then the predicted result of this recommendation are not guaranteed, and we may need to abandon the proposal.

To summarize, while I fully understand the vice president's desire to boost the company's overall productivity and profits, I withhold my approval of the recommendation until he/she can provide clear answers to the aforementioned questions. (551 words)

中文翻译

在文中，副总裁提议在 Climpson 工业使用电子监控软件。他/她进一步预测，这样的软件可以让员工不再浪费时间，从而提高他们的生产力。虽然我同意副总裁打算提高员工工作效率的意图，但我高度怀疑这一建议是否可行。为了更好地评价副总裁的建议，我需要如下几个问题的答案，这些问题涉及但不限于这一政策的必要性和有效性。

首先，我需要知道是否真的有必要在 Climpson 安装电子监控软件。虽然副总裁提到，近期一份全国性调查表明，大多数员工强倾向于把时间用于私事或娱乐活动，我怀疑这一情况是否也发生在 Climpson。如果 Climpson 的雇员高度自律并在任何情况下都不会开小差，那么副总裁的建议的前提就不存在了，他/她的提议也因此是不合理的。即使 Climpson 的一些雇员确实会花时间做私事或娱乐，我们仍然需要质疑这样的行为是否真的达到了有损他们工作效率、并因此危及 Climpson 整体利润的程度。如果答案是肯定的，那么我同意副总裁的意见并完全支持使用电子监控软件；反之，对他/她的建议我们仍要三思。

姑且认为 Climspon 一大批员工分心于非工作活动，因此需要使用电子监控软件，但这些软件到底能否有效防止人们浪费时间仍然是存疑的。一方面，即使装上了软件，雇员们是不是会尝试多种方法防止被检测到在浪费时间? 他们十有八九会这么做。如果雇员成功规避了监控软件, 那么公司在防止他们在私事和娱乐上浪费时间所做的努力也不过是竹篮打水。另一方面, 即使这些软件能防止员工在电脑前分心, 员工们会不会选择用其他方式开小差? 比如说, 打盹和聊天。我们无法知道这个问题的答案。生性懒散的员工即使没有开小差, 也不情愿好好工作; 任何防止他们偷懒的政策都可能是白费力气。

即使使用电子监控软件显著减少了员工开小差, 我们仍然不知道该软件是否有助于提高生产力和整体利润。具体而言, 我们需要提问, 使用这一软件是否会引发员工的不满乃至招致愤懑。这会不会有损员工的生产力? 此外, 安装软件的费用是否过高? 如果上述任何一个问题的答案是肯定的, 那么该建议所预期的良好结果就得不到保证了, 而我们可能需要放弃该建议。

总而言之, 虽然我完全理解副总裁想要提高公司的整体生产力和利润, 在他/她明确回答上述问题前, 我对他/她的建议持保留意见。

文章解析与点评

这道题目的推理过程十分清晰。全文只有一个事实性的信息, 即全国性调查所显示的结果。根据这个调查, 作者得出结论: 在 C 公司安装网络监视软件可以防止员工浪费时间, 从而提高工作效率和公司利润。

如何从这样一个简单的推理过程中挖掘出可写的点是我们需要思考的内容。我们为这篇文章列的逻辑图为大家提供了一个很好的范例。

逻辑图呈单线状, 我们在题目的事实性信息和结论之间又构建出了两个作者暗示的小推论。根据此图, 可以得出: 作者做了三次推论。而针对每一次推论, 都可以写出一个段落分析其问题。

那么, 全文就应该呈现出一种让步式的推理过程。如下:

首先, C 公司不一定有安装网络监视软件的必要性。这是因为: C 公司的员工不一定如全国调查所示那般, 将时间花在无用的网络活动中; 而就算 C 公司的员工存在这种行为, 我们也不知道这种行为是否严重到足够影响他们的效率和公司的利润。如果员工的这种行为只是一种劳逸结合, 那 C 公司可能没有必要劳师动众地安装这样一个软件。

就算 C 公司的员工的确把大量时间花在网络活动中, 且这种行为也的确影响到了他们的效率和公司利润, 我们也无法保证安装了网络监视软件之后他们就不再浪费时间。一方面, 员工可能有办法规避软件的探查; 另一方面, 即使他们无法规避探查, 不再把时间浪费在网络上, 他们也可能有其他浪费时间的方式, 如打瞌睡、聊天等。

最后, 就算软件的安装能够杜绝一切浪费时间的行为, 我们也无法保证员工的工作效率和公司利润能提升。因为软件的安装很可能会引起员工的不满情绪, 进而有碍于工作效率的提升;

而软件本身的安装成本和后续的保养费用还是未知的，因此现在就断定公司利润一定能提升未免言之过早。

综上，全文按照这种让步的方式展开。这种展开方式特别适用于线性推理的 Argument 题目。

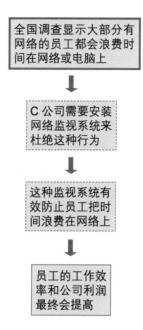

150 The following appeared in a letter from a firm providing investment advice to a client.

"Homes in the northeastern United States, where winters are typically cold, have traditionally used oil as their major fuel for heating. Last year that region experienced 90 days with below-average temperatures, and climate forecasters at Waymarsh University predict that this weather pattern will continue for several more years. Furthermore, many new homes have been built in this region during the past year. Because these developments will certainly result in an increased demand for heating oil, we recommend investment in Consolidated Industries, one of whose major business operations is the retail sale of home heating oil."

Write a response in which you discuss what questions would need to be answered in order to decide whether the recommendation and the argument on which it is based are reasonable. Be sure to explain how the answers to these questions would help to evaluate the recommendation.

In this letter to potential investors, the author recommends investment in Consolidated Industries, one of whose major business operations is residential heating oil, because of the anticipated greater demand for heating oil. To support his/her claim, the author quotes the climate forecast indicating continuing harsh winter weather as well as the increasing number of houses being built in this region. Quite convincing though his/her argument may seem at first glance, there are a number of questions regarding his/her lines of reasoning that requires further analysis. The argument could end up being pretty convincing or invalid in the end, depending on the answers to those questions.

To begin with, the author's reasoning relies heavily on the accuracy of the climate forecaster, a question that is not answered. It is possible that the predictions about future climate are completely wrong, because the Earth's climate system is highly complex and can change rather unpredictably. Without additional information to evaluate future climate and winter weather conditions, it is possible that the northeastern United States could actually experience warmer winters. This scenario would seriously challenge the predicted increase in oil demand, and render the author's recommendation much less advisable. On the other hand, any valid proof that the forecast is well founded will strengthen the author's argument.

Granted that future climate will be extremely cold and given the fact that new houses are being built in this region, whether or not oil demand will increase in response to colder winters and increasing population needs a second look. Behind the author's argument lie two critical implied assertions. The first one is that people will spend their winter in this very region, which could be wrong. The possibility that people would migrate to warmer areas, such as the southeastern United States, during the winter to escape from the bitter cold must be considered and addressed. Yet, if the author can provide information to unequivocally demonstrate that a substantial number of people live in the northeast during the winter, his/her conclusion will have weight.

Furthermore, the second assertion is that oil will remain the major fuel for heating in the future. Although in the past people have traditionally used oil for residential heating, the possibility that new heating methods may emerge cannot be excluded. For example, residential heating powered by nuclear or solar energy may enter the market and begin to compete with traditional fossil fuels. We have no clue if the dominance of oil in energy market will still persist. If no, the demand for oil is unlikely to increase despite the fact that there is indeed a huge demand for residential heating. On the other hand, increased oil demand can be expected from a continued heavy reliance on oil, creating favorable market conditions for Consolidated.

Finally, even if we acknowledge for a moment that oil demand does rise in response to harsh weather and population growth, it remains to be seen whether Consolidated Industries can capitalize on this as the author assumes. Other factors, such as management efficiency and local competition, could potentially affect Consolidated's financial performance. If, for instance, Consolidated is poorly managed and there is widespread corruption within the corporation, it is doubtful that Consolidated will be hugely profitable and worth investment.

To sum up, although a cold, harsh climate and a rising population have the potential to elevate the demand for heating oil, this is not a conclusion that can be derived from the information available in this argument. Furthermore, even if oil demand does rise, the investment recommendation is built upon a shaky assertion, which is still open to different possibilities. Only after those questions are adequately addressed can we effectively evaluate the author's argument and reach a logically sound conclusion. (619 words)

中文翻译

在给潜在投资者的这封信中，作者建议投资 Consolidated 工业公司，因为他/她预期住宅取暖用油的需求会上升，而该公司的主要业务之一是住宅取暖用油。为了支持其主张，作者援引天气预报表明严冬仍将继续，并表示在该地建造的房屋数量不断增加。尽管这个论点乍一看很有说服力，但其推理思路存在一些问题，需要进一步分析。对下列问题的回答决定了该论点最终是令人信服抑或是一无是处。

首先，作者的推理在很大程度上依赖于气候预报的准确性，但我们并不知道这个问题的答案。对于未来天气的预测很有可能是完全错误的，因为地球的气候系统高度复杂，且变幻莫测。我们没有额外信息来评估未来的天气和冬季气候条件，有可能美国东北部正在经历暖冬。这种情况将严重挑战对石油需求增长的预测，并使得作者的建议不那么可取。另一方面，任何有效的、能证明预测是有根据的证据则会加强作者的论点。

姑且认为未来气候将极端寒冷并鉴于该地区正在建造新房屋，我们需要再次考察更寒冷的天气和增长的人口是否会导致石油需求的增长。作者的论点背后暗含着两个重要的主张。第一，人们会在此地度过冬天。这可能是错的。我们必须考虑到并指出人们可能会在冬天迁徙到更温暖的地方，诸如美国东南部，来躲避严寒。然而，如果作者能够提供信息，明确证明相当数量的居民在冬天仍会住在东北部，那么我们应当重视作者的结论。

此外，第二个主张是石油仍然会是未来供暖的主要燃料。虽然在过去，人们传统上将石油用于住宅供暖，但我们不能排除出现新的取暖方法。例如，由核能或太阳能供电的宅用暖气可能会进入市场并同传统的化石燃料展开竞争。我们不知道石油是否能继续在能源市场上占据统治地位。如果不是这样的话，尽管对住宅供暖有大量的需求，但该地对石油的需求未必会增加。另一方面，如果人们依然严重依赖石油，那么对石油的需求的增长是可预期的，这为 Consolidated 公司创造了有利的市场条件。

最后，即使我们暂且承认严酷的天气和增长的人口会带来石油需求的增长，我们仍然需要考察 Consolidated 公司是否能如作者所言借此获利。诸如管理效率、本地竞争等其他因素可能会潜在影响 Consolidated 的财务表现。例如，如果 Consolidated 管理不善，内部腐败丛生，那么 Consolidated 是否会获得巨大利润、是否值得投资，都是存疑的。

总而言之，尽管严寒的气候和增长的人口可能会提高对供暖用油的需求，但这并不是一个可以根据文中所给的信息就能得出的结论。此外，即使石油需求确实增加了，投资建议的根基并不可靠，它存在不同的可能性。只有在上述问题都得到充分的解决后，我们才能有效评估作者的论点，并得出符合逻辑的、可靠的结论。

文章解析与点评

本题的逻辑关系比较复杂（见原文逻辑图），进行的推论和演绎也比较多，这要求在写作前对题目当中的逻辑框架有足够认识，否则可能分析不到重点。

本文覆盖了原文论证当中比较重要的几个问题，并且层层推进，最后引出了"是否盈利"的关键点。因为题目当中最后给出的建议是投资，因此全文最为关键的问题是"要不要投资"。曾经有同学全文都在纠结当地气温会不会下降以及下降之后石油需求会否走高两个问题而忽略了投资这个中心问题。

本文论证的整体节奏很快，这是因为原题的逻辑问题太多，需要在文中把重要的问题全部涵盖，所以为了保证规定时间内完成写作，段落的结构十分紧凑。这种精练的表达大家可以效仿。

由于题目的写作指令是讨论还要回答什么问题才能判断作者的论证和结论，因此形式上自由度比较大，不像其他几类写作指令针对论证的特定环节（假设、其他可能解释、新证据）提出要求。这一点从本文比较多变的语言表达中可窥一二。

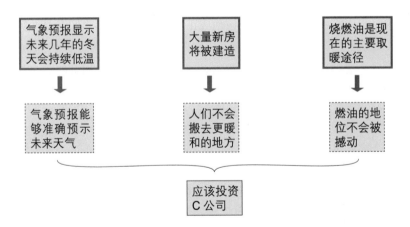

下面来把前面的题目的全篇分别以 Question、Evidence、Assumption 的方式来写一下，方便同学看出三种 Direction 本质上的相通。

Question：

In this letter, the writer states that in the northeastern regions of the United States, oil has been traditionally used for heating in winter months, and, due to decreasing temperatures and an increasing population rate, the writer forecasts an increased demand for heating oil and, therefore, recommends investment in Consolidating Industries, a major retailer of home heating oil. That being said, before any action is taken in regards to the writer's recommendation, there are several questions that need to be taken into account.

Question:

To begin with, before any money is allocated for investments, we must deliberate whether the tradition of using heating oil in homes to fend of the cold will continue in the future. It can be said that the tradition of using heating oil in homes is the fulcrum upon which the writer's recommendation rests, for if the aforementioned tradition didn't exist, there wouldn't be any talk of investment in Consolidating Industries. If, in the future, the tradition of using home heating oil in the winter begins to peter out, the client would, undoubtedly, lose a portion of the money invested in the company. On a more serious note, if said tradition is abolished and ceases entirely, the client may lose a great sum of money and could potentially reprimand the investment firm for poor advice and judgement, thus marring the name of the firm. Therefore, making a hasty decision without giving further consideration to possible fluctuations in heating materials may end up negatively affecting the company, the consulting firm may, in turn, lose credibility, and clients may lose money, which would all invalidate the writer's claim.

Evidence:

Second, in addition to answering the above questions, before the consulting firm advises the client to invest in Consolidating Industries, they need to provide more evidence in regard to the decreasing climate in northeastern America. As we know, weather conditions are volatile and quite susceptible to erratic changes. Without being certain that weather conditions will not fluctuate drastically in the years to come, the consulting firm should not encourage an investment with such ease. If the climate begins to gradually increase over the next couple of years, the need for heating oil would, consequentially, likely be met with a gradual decrease in sales, and the writer's claim will be negatively influenced; however, if evidence proves that weather conditions will remain consistent or gradually decrease, the writer's claim will be fortified.

Assumption:

Furthermore, there is an assumption the writer makes in the above letter. The writer seems to assume that more homes in the region are directly associated to an increased population rate in these regions and a higher demand for home oil. While this could be true, it is only one of myriad possibilities. Some of the homes bought in this region may only be used as summer homes, and the owners may visit only in warmer months of the year, thus they would have little need for home heating oil. Additionally, there may be better, more efficient ways of heating homes in the future, for example, using new construction materials to improve insulation of homes, which could severely diminish or completely eliminate the need for heating oil. Therefore, if the client follows along with the writer's shaky assumption, they could end up losing money, and the author's original claim would be weakened.

Assumption：

Lastly, even if the tradition of using heating oil remains consistent, the climate proceeds to decrease, and the increase in homes and population does stimulate an increase in heating oil sales, there still remains one assumption that needs to be addressed. In the final words of the letter, the writer recommends that the client invest in Consolidating Industries due to their prominence in the home heating oil sales market. However, there is no guarantee that Consolidating Industries's success will persist in the future; perhaps other companies will outnumber Consolidating Industries in sales and flourish in years to come. If this were to be the case, then the client would end up losing the money initially invested in Consolidating Industries. Therefore, the consulting firm should first carry out risk assessment measures, then advise their client on the foundation of their findings. If evidence shows that other companies are predicted to surpass Consolidating Industries in the future, or possess the potential to do so, then the writer's original recommendation would lose force.

Assumption：

To conclude, in order to decide whether or not the client should accept and implement the writer's recommendation depends on the validity of certain assumptions within the writer's letter. If there is little or no foundation and evidence to support the writer's assumptions, then alternative options should be considered in order to address the decreasing climate and home heating issue in the northeastern region of the United States.

中文翻译

Question：

在这封信中，作者指出，在美国的东北部地区，燃油历来用于冬季取暖。由于温度的降低和人口增长率，作者预测，燃油需求会增加。因此，建议投资 Consolidating Industries，一家大型燃油零售商。尽管如此，在对作者的建议采取任何行动之前，有几个问题需要加以考虑。

Question：

首先，在分配资金用于投资之前，我们必须考虑一下在家里使用燃油来抵御感冒的传统是否会继续下去。在家里使用燃油的传统是作者建议所依赖的内容，因为如果上述传统不存在，就不会有投资 Consolidating Industries 的讨论。如果将来在冬天使用家用燃油的传统开始消失，客户无疑会损失投资于公司的一部分钱。更严重的问题是，如果上述传统被完全废除，客户可能损失一大笔钱，可能会谴责投资公司错误的建议和判断，从而影响公司名声。因此，如果不进一步考虑加热材料可能发生的波动，草率作出决定，最终会对公司产生负面影响，咨询公司可能反过来失去信誉，客户可能会赔钱，这将使作者的观点无效。

Evidence：

其次，除了回答上述问题之外，在咨询公司建议客户投资 Consolidating Industries 之前，他们需要提供更多关于美国东北部气候下降的证据。正如我们所知，天气状况是不稳定的，而且很容易受到不稳定变化的影响。如果不确定未来几年天气状况是否会发生剧烈波动，咨询公司就不应如此轻易地鼓励投资。如果气候在未来几年内开始逐渐增加，对采暖油的需求将会导致销售量的逐渐减少，而作者的主张将受到负面影响；然而，如果证据证明天气状况将保持一致或逐渐减少，作者的主张将得到加强。

Assumption：

此外，作者在上面的信中有一个假设。作者似乎认为，该地区更多的住房与这些地区人口增长有直接联系，并且导致家庭对于燃油有更高需求。虽然这可能是真的，但它只是无数可能性中的一种。在这个地区购买的一些房屋有可能只是作为避暑别墅使用，而且业主可能只在较暖和的月份访问，这样他们就不需要家庭燃油了。此外，在未来可能会有更好、更有效的供暖方式，例如，使用新的建筑材料来改善房屋的隔热，这将严重减少或完全消除燃油的需要。因此，如果客户听从了作者的不可靠的假设，他们最终可能会损失金钱，而作者一开始的观点将被削弱。

Assumption：

最后，即使使用燃油的传统保持一致，气候继续减少，家庭和人口的增加确实刺激；燃油的销售，仍然有一个需要解决的假设。在信的最后几句中，作者建议客户投资于巩固行业，因为他们在家庭取暖石油销售市场上占有重要地位。然而，并不能保证 Consolidating Industries 的成功将会持续下去；也许其他公司在未来几年将会超过 Consolidating Industries 的销售和繁荣。如果是这样的话，那么客户最终将失去最初投资于 Consolidating Industries 的资金。因此，咨询公司应该首先进行风险评估，然后根据他们的发现给客户提供建议。如果有证据表明，其他公司预计在未来超过合并行业，或有潜力这样做，那么作者最初的建议将会被削弱。

Assumption：

总之，为了决定客户是否应该接受和执行作者的建议，取决于作者信中某些假设的有效性。如果没有足够的基础和证据来支持作者的假设，那么就应该考虑其他选择，以解决美国东北地区日益减少的气候和家庭供暖问题。

附 录 所有 Argument 3s 版本及专业词汇

题号	Direction	专有名词	3s 版本	类似题目
1	Evidence	Palea Lithos Brim	篮子并非 Palea 地方独有	
2	Explanation	cortisol	生育顺序影响个体应激水平	
3	Question	Plaza Monroe	应禁止在中央广场玩滑板	171 Question，175 Question
4	Assumption	Adam Fitch Realty	Adam Realty 能让房子卖得又快又好	
5	Question	Balmer Gazette Seaville Torseau	Balmer 应限制 moped 的出租数量	159 Question，173 Assumption
6	Evidence	Arctic	北极鹿数量下降是因为无法按迁移习惯穿越结冰海面	
7	Question	Monarch Collegeville	Monarch 书店应该用咖啡馆取代儿童图书区	98 Assumption，99 Evidence
8	Evidence	Buckingham	Buckingham 应建新宿舍	
9	Assumption	Plainsville	Nature's Way 健康食品店的新分店会成功	88 Evidence，90 Assumption
10	Question	Tertia Karp	为获得关于 Tertia 儿童抚养方式的精确信息，应采用对话的研究方式	21 Evidence，23 Assumption
11	Question	Maple Chestnut Pine	如果议案通过，Maple County 房价将大幅上涨	
12	Evidence	Omega Alpha	Omega 应停止学生对教授的评价	
13	Evidence	Prunty Butler	Prunty 应实施和 Butler 一样的道路改善计划	
14	Assumption	Mentian	企业要想成功，应只雇睡眠时间少于 6 小时的员工	118 Question
15	Explanation	margarine Pancake	Pancake 应该用人造黄油代替天然黄油	51 Question，130 Assumption，131 Question，133 Evidence
16	Assumption	Manson	Manson 市政府应增加用于河边休闲设施的预算	
17	Evidence		应该将电台的摇滚乐节目改为新闻和访谈的节目	93 Question，109 Assumption，110 Question

题号	Direction	专有名词	3s 版本	类似题目
18	Assumption		应在所有新闻节目中增加天气和地方新闻的播报	20 Evidence
19	Question	Rockville Medway	KICK 应播放更多的电话咨询节目	
22	Question	Groveton	所有大学应采用诚信制度	119 Explanation, 120 Question, 138 Evidence
24	Question	Mentia salicylate aspirin	食品添加水杨酸可以减少 Mentia 地区居民的头痛情况	26 Evidence, 28 Assumption
25	Evidence	Monroe	在 Monroe 新建爵士俱乐部能赚钱	100 Assumption, 102 Question, 164 Question
27	Evidence		Blue Highway 应修一条自行车道	29 Question
30	Evidence	Calatrava	Calatrava 市会有更充足的资金用于主要供成年人使用的城市设施	
31	Evidence	Trillura Parson	Parson 居民比 Blue 市的更关注为公立学校提供良好教育	
32	Assumption	Panobly Quiot Butler Alta	Panoply 工厂报告的事故少是因为员工睡眠更充足	104 Explanation, 105 Evidence, 106 Question, 167 Question
33	Assumption		电力公司认为无需建造新的发电厂	
34	Assumption	Climpson	给 Climpson 公司安装监视系统会提高员工的工作效率和公司利润	58 Evidence, 94 Question
35	Question	Sunnyside Towers	Sunnyside Towers 限制所有建筑的水龙头最大出水量会增加利润	52 Question, 128 Evidence, 129 Assumption
36	Evidence	Meria Ichthaid	吃鱼油提取物可以预防感冒，从而降低请假率	163 Question, 166 Question
37	Evidence	Transopolis	应将 Transopolis 市另一侧的居住区住房改造为工业用途	
38	Evidence	Sartorian alpaca	Sartorian 厂应重新开始生产高档羊毛外套	95 Assumption, 96 Question
39	Evidence	Captain	Captain Seafood 会受欢迎并获利	174 Question
40	Evidence	calcium osteoporosis	富含奶制品的饮食会增加患骨质疏松症的风险	
41	Assumption		想减少事故，应加强骑车安全教育，而非强调戴头盔	123 Question, 125 Evidence
42	Evidence	Tria Batia	应该对使用 Tria 海滩的人收费	

题号	Direction	专有名词	3s 版本	类似题目
43	Evidence		West Egg 镇的垃圾填埋地的使用时间会很长	
44	Assumption	Crust Copper Fredonia	如果 CCC 公司不放弃采矿，消费者只要停止购买 CCC 的产品，依然可以减少灾害	
45	Question	Humana Omni	开设在线教学项目有助于增加 Humana 的报名人数并解决预算问题	49 Assumption
46	Assumption	Corpora	专家关于长时间使用电脑导致健康状况下降的观点是错误的	
47	Evidence	Galore Marston	Movies Galore 在其他分店实施和 Martson 店类似的方法 (减少营业时间和库存) 可以增加利润	111 Assumption,112 Question
48	Evidence	Clearview	人们应选择 Clearview 作为退休地	
50	Evidence	insomnia lavender	薰衣草花香可以治疗失眠	
53	Evidence	Forsythe Kiran Cholesterol Sulia Benton	Forsythe 居民选择了更健康的生活方式	144 Assumption,151 Question
54	Assumption	Kaliko	人类的捕杀导致了 Kaliko 岛上哺乳动物的灭亡	165 Explanation
55	Assumption	Whirlwind	Whirlwind 公司的游戏销量在未来几个月会猛增	
56	Assumption	Dura Endure	可以通过停止 Endure 工艺来增加利润	57 Evidence,82 Question
59	Assumption	Bower Domus	Bower Builders 公司在所建的住宅中增加家庭娱乐室的面积，并将先进厨房作为标配可以增加利润	
60	Assumption	Waymarsh Consolidated	应该投资 Consolidated 公司	145 Question,146 Evidence,150 Question,154 Question,155 Evidence
61	Question	Grandview Beacon Symphony Orchestra	Grandview 市在下一年的预算中停止对交响乐团的资助	139 Question,141 Evidence,143 Assumption,162 Question
62	Assumption	UltraClean	为了防止严重的感染，应使用 UltraClean	121 Assumption,122 Explanation,124 Evidence

题号	Direction	专有名词	3s 版本	类似题目
63	Assumption	Parkville	Parkville 应停止组织 9 岁以下儿童的体育比赛	
64	Question	Kalinese	Kali 岛的古代等身黏土人物雕塑会贬值，而微缩雕像会升值	
65	Assumption	Stanley Carlton	Stanley 公园增加长凳，会变得受欢迎	
66	Question	Wisconsin Cheddar	增加奶酪店利润的最好方式是停止储备过多进口奶酪、集中储备国产的	107 Assumption，108 Evidence
67	Question	Rialto Apex Arcade	Rialto 必须模仿 Apex 才能保持电影市场份额	
68	Assumption	Sherwood	Sherwood 医院应和动物收容站合作建立一个"收养狗"的项目	
69	Question	Alpha Zeta	新项目应由 Zeta 公司来负责	70 Evidence，115 Assumption
71	Evidence	Waymarsh Garville	Waymarsh 应向拼车通勤的人发放免费的汽油券作为奖励	
72	Evidence	Elthyria	"大多因裁员失业的有能力的工人在找到合适的工作前常连续几年面临严重的经济困难"的观点不对	
73	Assumption	Mozart	Mozart 音乐学校是想把孩子送去学音乐的家长的首选	
74	Question	Grove Alumnae	需要在男女合招政策和保留女校传统中选一个方案	147 Evidence，148 Assumption，149 Question，156 Question
75	Question	Batavia Excello	Batavia 政府应限制奶价来为消费者保证公平的价格	
76	Question	Cholesterol	Old Dairy 公司的销量和利润会降低，所以要抛售此公司的股票	
77	Assumption	Hopewell Brindleburg Vista	改善 Hopewell 经济的最好方式就是建和 Ocean View 类似的高尔夫球场和度假旅店	169 Question
78	Evidence	Palm Buzzoff Wintervale	节省花费的最好方式就是重新使用 Buzzoff 公司提供的灭害虫服务	114 Question，116 Explanation，117 Assumption
79	Question	Newsbeat	Newsbeat 杂志是否采取减少对政治、而增加对经济和个人理财的关注	
80	Question	Super Screen	电影公司应把下一年预算的更大份额用于广告以提升公众辨识度	

题号	Direction	专有名词	3s 版本	类似题目
81	Question	Promofoods tuna nausea	金枪鱼罐头不会产生健康威胁	
83	Evidence	Xanadu trout	引进 trout 导致两栖动物数量减少	84 Explanation
85	Evidence	Waymarsh	Waymarsh 的第一项研究的受访者错误地表达了自己的阅读习惯	87 Assumption
86	Evidence	Delany Personnel Walsh	"用收费较少的 Walsh 人事公司代替 Delany" 是个错误	89 Assumption
91	Evidence	Palean Gazelle	西 Palean 瞪羚绝迹是由东部保护区的大量食肉动物导致的	
92	Explanation	Leeville Masonton	Leeville 居民的健康状态归功于舒缓的生活节奏	101 Assumption, 103 Explanation
97	Question	Shakespeare Bardville Avon Repertory	如果开展 "公园莎士比亚" 活动, 剧场的利润会增加	
113	Question	Acme Spruce	为提高生产率, 所有 Acme 员工应参加 Easy Road 课程	126 Evidence, 127 Question, 161 Assumption
132	Assumption	Centerville	由高中赞助的强制性的驾驶课程是唯一的交通问题解决方案	134 Evidence, 136 Question
135	Evidence	Attra Sanlee Marlee	本校老师布置作业的频次不能超过一周两次	137 Assumption, 140 Question
142	Assumption		通过购买高质量保护装置和反光设备, 溜冰者将能极大地降低他们在事故中受到严重伤害的风险	
152	Question	Bargain Cereal	Bargain Brand 应尽快扩展业务, 开始推出其他廉价食品	153 Assumption
157	Assumption	Emporium Exotic Gulf	在 Exotic Pets Monthly 上刊登广告能使商店重新盈利	158 Evidence
160	Question	Amburg Chamber Belleville	如果安装高照度灯, Amburg 的犯罪率会显著降低	172 Evidence
168	Question	Oak Gazette	没有外地人干扰的情况下, 委员会有能力使 Oak 城成为更美好的适于生活、工作的地方	
170	Question	Route Appian	建议雇佣 Appian 公司为新商业街修通道	
176	Explanation	Dillton	因为外地人占了新岗位, 所以 Dillton 镇失业率保持不变	
177	Question	Ventures Grilldon	应在西南 Grilldon 建新的兴趣店	

题号	Direction	专有名词	3s 版本	类似题目
	独立题目数量：86 道			
	Question：64 道　3 5 7 10 11 19 22 24 29 35 45 51 52 61 64 66 67 69 74 75 76 79 80 81 82 93 94 96 97 102 106 110 112 113 114 118 120 123 127 131 136 139 140 145 149 150 151 152 154 156 159 160 162 163 164 166 167 168 169 170 171 174 175 177			
	Evidence：52 道　1 6 8 12 13 17 20 21 25 26 27 30 31 36 37 38 39 40 42 43 47 48 50 53 57 58 70 71 72 78 83 85 86 88 91 99 105 108 124 125 126 128 133 134 135 138 141 146 147 155 158 172			
	Assumption：50 道　4 9 14 16 18 23 28 32 33 34 41 44 46 49 54 55 56 59 60 62 63 65 68 73 77 87 89 90 95 98 100 101 107 109 111 115 117 121 129 130 132 137 142 143 144 148 153 157 161 173			
	Explanation：11 道　2 15 84 92 103 104 116 119 122 165 176